Super-Flexibility
for Knowledge Enterprises

Homa Bahrami · Stuart Evans

Super-Flexibility
for Knowledge Enterprises

With 20 Figures and 6 Tables

 Springer

Professor Homa Bahrami
University of California
Haas School of Business
Berkeley, CA 94720
USA
bahrami@haas.berkeley.edu
homa@pdgy.com

Dr. Stuart Evans
University of Cambridge
Judge Institute of Management
Trumpington Street
Cambridge CB2 1AG
United Kingdom
s.evans@jims.cam.ac.uk
stuart@pdgy.com

Cataloging-in-Publication Data
Library of Congress Control Number: 2004111937

ISBN 3-540-20576-4 Springer Berlin Heidelberg New York

Springer is a part of Springer Science+Business Media

springeronline.com

© Springer Berlin · Heidelberg 2005
Printed in Germany

Hardcover-Design: Erich Kirchner, Heidelberg

SPIN 10973066   42/3130-5 4 3 2 1 0 – Printed on acid-free paper

For James

Preface

The origin of the ideas presented in this book can be traced back to 1982 when we first came to Silicon Valley. After studying several European multinationals as part of our doctoral field research, the contrast with Silicon Valley was somewhat startling. At the time, the Valley was going through its formative years. The first IBM PC and the Apple Macintosh had yet to be introduced. Many of today's technology giants were fledgling start-ups; some, like Cisco, had yet to be founded. We were fortunate to have "ringside" seats, the opportunity to witness the meteoric rise and growth of entrepreneurial companies and emerging industries.

During the first few years, our research interests, while complementary, were pursued along separate tracks. Homa's focus was on organizational design: how entrepreneurial companies were architected to address the combined challenges of innovation, speed, and growth in turbulent domains. Stuart's focus was on flexibility, especially as it related to developing product and business strategies. These parallel tracks gradually converged as we realized the close inter-linkages between the two fields, especially in practice.

For the past twenty years, we have observed Silicon Valley during several evolutionary phases. Our path has taken us to many technology companies during various stages of growth, ranging from emerging start-ups, to mid-sized adolescents, and global giants. Our journey has taken us to different technology domains, including semiconductors (packaging, equipment, processors and devices), e-business and enterprise software (databases, helpdesk, multimedia, financial industry specialists), disk drives, controllers and peripherals manufacturers, networking and storage archiving products, telecommunications equipment, and life sciences. We have talked to hundreds of entrepreneurs, executives, and knowledge workers, and served on several advisory boards over the years, giving us "unfiltered", first-hand perspectives on critical realities and business challenges. We have immersed ourselves in the phenomenon by conducting field research, observing events close up, participating in various projects, and interacting with venture capitalists, lawyers, accountants and other professionals associated with technology ventures and corporations.

Collectively our observations and experiences lead us to conclude that Silicon Valley and its technology enterprises have experimented with novel approaches to "management", "organization" and "strategy". These experiments cannot be solely attributed to a "quirky Californian mentality", or the need to be just different and unique, although these factors have been clearly influential. We suggest that pioneering entrepreneurs and executive teams of the new generation companies are continually developing novel recipes because they face unique and unprecedented challenges.

This book is a synthesis of our collective learnings and field observations in Silicon Valley. We have set out to distill the most salient themes that have practical implications, and that would be of interest to entrepreneurs, executives, and investors. Our approach is unconventional in several ways. We do not confine ourselves to traditional disciplinary boundaries in that we propose frameworks for developing strategy as well as organizational design and leadership practices. We examine the dynamics of the broad ecosystem as well as the recipes used by individual firms. Our approach is partly descriptive, partly interpretive, and partly prescriptive, drawing on detailed case studies, cross-sectional field research, and action-based reflections. We draw as much on pathological cases of failure as well as the experiences of successful entities.

Our overarching goal is to synthesize our combined research, teaching, and practical experiences of Silicon Valley and its enterprises, as they relate to the challenge of super-flexibility, and to propose conceptual frameworks that underpin pragmatic action steps. We do not pretend to have all the answers to these complex questions. Rather, our hope is that the proposed action principles provide conceptual "coat hangers", helping executives and entrepreneurs examine their current assumptions, reflect on their unique challenges, and devise their own action recipes, using our frameworks as "food for thought". We think the time is ripe for reflection and introspection, as our business entities are clearly experiencing novel and unprecedented challenges worldwide.

Our learning journey would not have been possible without the critical insights and thoughtful contributions of many entrepreneurs, executives, and knowledge workers who have shared their experiences with us during the past twenty years. We have also had the opportunity to discuss many of the frameworks presented in this book with our MBA students at Berkeley and Cambridge, with multi-cultural knowledge workers in executive programs and business seminars around the world, and with business and government leaders visiting Silicon Valley during the past ten years. Their critical insights and constructive feedback have influenced our thinking, helped us refine the ideas, and prompted us to relate them to the practical challenges facing front-line executives. We are truly grateful for all their insights and contributions. Naturally, we are solely responsible for any errors or misinterpretations.

While there are too many people to thank individually, we are especially indebted to several entrepreneurs, investors, and executives who have been willing to share their experiences over time and to provide us with candid, longitudinal perspectives. Among entrepreneurial founders and venture capitalists, we are particularly grateful to Larry Boucher, Ken Coleman, Eric Dunn, Larry Garlick, John Glynn, Till Guldimann, Jim Guzy, Tim Hayley, Trip Hawkins, John Hendrickson, Mark Hoffman, Nigel Keen, Igor Khandros, Roger Lang, Giacomo Marini, Bob Maxfield, Doug Merritt, Bob Metcalfe, Tom Mitchell, Ken Oshman, Will Pape, Jim Patterson, Jon Peters, Carol Sands and George Sollman. A number of senior executives and board members have been generous in sharing their perspectives and experiences. They include Faruq Ahmad, Mark Allen, Deborah Barber, Bob Baxter, Janet Beach, Chris Carlton, Caretha Coleman, Keith Cotterill, Debra Engel, Steve Engle, Mats Engstrand, David Foster, Charlotte Gubler, Jim Illich, Barry Karlin, Barbara Kerr, Tracy Koon, Meghan Leader, Dennis Paboojian, Lynn Phillips, Pete Peterson, Dennis Rohan, Rosemary Remacle, Clent Richardson, Kevin Sullivan and Phil Wilson.

In addition, several academic colleagues have influenced our thinking, and given us critical feedback over the years. We owe special thanks to John Child, Hal Leavitt, Robert Burgelman, Glenn Carroll, Sandra Dawson, John Freeman, Stig Hagstrom, Ralph Keeney, Martin Kenney, Gianni Lorenzoni, Barry Staw, and the late Gunnar Hedlund. We'd also like to express our warm gratitude and sincere thanks to Ulrike Baumoel for her expert advice and professional guidance.

Special thanks are due to our international associates who have encouraged us to relate the experiences of Silicon Valley to broader challenges facing global companies in different industries. They include Tony Andersson, Jacinta Calverley, Ake Ekblad, Hamish Fordwood, Christian Jenny, Reinhard Jung, Guiliana Lavendel, Nils Mehr, Ken Miki, Christophe Soutter, Markus Stricker, Beat Umbricht, and Hubert Weber. We would also like to extend our sincere thanks to Dr. Werner Mueller and the team at Springer-Verlag, who have been patiently supportive throughout the publication process, and to Claire Dolan for her creative artwork. Last but not least, we truly appreciate the inspiration, support and encouragement of our parents, families and friends.

Menlo Park, California   Homa Bahrami
June 2004   Stuart Evans

Contents

Figures

Tables

1 The Need for Super-Flexibility

Business enterprises are radically overhauling their core practices in the post-digital era. The emerging landscape poses new challenges. A key imperative is to become super-flexible, in order to thrive, or at least survive, in dynamic contexts. Some of the recent triggers that highlight the importance of super-flexibility include the dramatic rise and fall of the "Internet bubble", the drastic ups and downs of the stock market, the changing definition of "e-business", the fluctuating fortunes of major corporations, and a sudden re-definition of world alliances in the aftermath of the tragedy of September 11th.

Superimposed on these geopolitical and market shocks, technology is transforming work, communication flows, and - with the advent of electronic commerce - the very nature of administering business. Effective application of knowledge is becoming the core competitive differentiator. An interconnected world economy is bringing about complex geo-political triggers of change. Collectively, these events have eroded the core assumption of stability and predictability and point to a different picture of the business game. Today there is widespread recognition amongst business leaders, academic scholars and management consultants that the business game is changing, and that novel frameworks, recipes and tools are needed to address the new challenges. At its core, the emerging game is about creating, growing, and re-inventing enterprises in environments that, at best, can only be partially predicted. A critical challenge facing business leaders, we suggest, is the need to create "super-flexible" enterprises.

Super-flexibility is a complex construct that does not fit our traditional binary perspectives. On the one hand, it refers to the capacity to "switch on and off" at short notice, to rapidly change course, and to be quickly repositioned as new realities unfold. On the other hand, it is about creating a few stable anchors that can provide the capability to ride out stormy conditions, and to develop a spirit of cohesion and community. While this goal may be unattainable in its purest form, there are examples of dynamic settings where survival depends on the ability to do both; surfing successive waves of market turbulence and technological innovation, without losing a sense of cohesion, identity and partial stability. The term "super-flexibility" is used in this book to describe an enterprise's ability to address both sides of the spectrum; the capability to be agile and versatile, much like an entrepreneurial company, coupled with the capacity to remain robust and resilient, attributes historically associated with established corporations. The challenge is to create super-flexible enterprises that can capitalize on uncertainty and move swiftly by managing for the moment, while providing bedrock anchors of stability.

1.1   Knowledge Enterprises and Super-Flexibility

Business leaders are searching for novel recipes to address the challenge of super-flexibility. This task is easier said than done, especially since our existing frameworks were developed at a different time, when the business scene was relatively more stable and predictable. Major breakthroughs took some time to unfold and could be anticipated and planned for in advance. Examples include the commercial development of the semiconductor, deregulation of airlines, banks, and telecommunications, and the end of the "Cold War". Indeed, this assumption of stability and predictability has been the cornerstone of much of our strategic, organizational and managerial thought and practice during the last few decades.

Business practices are evolving to address the dynamic nature of the business game. Worldwide trends that further underscore the need for flexibility, include extensive reliance on partnering, collaborative arrangements, offshoring, and outsourcing, variable use of contractors and contingent workers, deployment of cross-functional teams and geo-dispersed virtual groups, dissemination of knowledge management systems and e-business tools, transparent governance procedures, and the re-engineering of core business processes.

While many established entities are deploying more flexible practices, these are typically superimposed on their traditional foundations. In order to understand what it takes to become "super-flexible", we need to look beyond established firms setting out to re-model themselves. It is also important to study organizations and environments that not only have to cope with extreme forms of uncertainty, but that are also not constrained by tradition, history, and inertia.

Silicon Valley and its critical mass of entrepreneurial companies provide an ideal research laboratory for studying super-flexibility. Super-flexibility is the critical capability, not just an incremental benefit, in this setting. The pace of change is rapid, frenzied, and intense. Products, markets, distribution channels and competitive boundaries are in a state of continuous flux. The environment has a high propensity for "kaleidoscopic" change. A firm can be seriously impaired by the departure of a key executive, the unexpected loss of a critical account, personality clashes amongst the core team, as well as general challenges related to product performance and market positioning in pioneering domains. Indeed, the nature of change in this arena can be best described as a "Kuhnian inversion"; long periods of frenzied change, punctuated briefly by stable interludes.[1]

Silicon Valley is intensely competitive, continuously innovative, and lives with uncertainties about which there can be limited or no prior knowledge. Typically, there is insufficient lead-time to develop managerial responses to deal with novelty, *ab initio*. Capricious transformations occur frequently and rapidly. In order to compete effectively, technology firms need to continually evolve their trajectories real-time, and re-refocus resources on successive decisive points, often with different rules of engagement.

Many Silicon Valley entrepreneurs intuitively value super-flexibility. The challenge is further underscored when one considers the complex set of challenges facing high-technology companies during various stages of growth:

- Raising successive rounds of funding to ramp-up a fledgling venture.
- Competing, yet co-operating selectively, with competitors.
- Migrating the business trajectory from end-of-life products and services to innovative new products/ solutions and emerging market segments.
- Remaining disciplined, focused, and frugal, while innovating, experimenting and learning.
- Generating consensus amongst expert and opinionated knowledge workers, yet ensuring fast and timely decisions.
- Connecting a globally-dispersed organization through the hard wire of IT while ensuring the development of a community-based culture that provides emotional connectivity for expectant knowledge workers
- Developing simple and standard templates, metrics, and formats for systematic knowledge sharing, whilst ensuring the capability for customized approaches that cater for unique, one-off, situations
- Balancing the need for local accountability and responsiveness, in the context of a well-coordinated global approach
- Re-organizing to address emerging realities, in the context of a few stable anchors that don't change as frequently

---

[1] In his seminal work, Kuhn (1962) emphasized that scientific revolutions follow a similar pattern; long periods of relative stability are periodically ruptured by a major discontinuity. Our view is that the business environment in Silicon Valley can be best depicted in terms of a "Kuhnian inversion", long periods of frenzied change, followed by brief, stable interludes.

The challenge of harnessing uncertainty is aptly captured in the following comment:

"High technology obeys the iron law of revolution, ... the more you change, the more you have to change....., you have to be willing to accept the fact that in this game the rules keep changing."[2]

Many firms create, or quickly enter, pioneering markets with innovative products without the benefit of role models and blueprints for success. They are founded by entrepreneurial teams, populated by cosmopolitan "knowledge workers" with a multitude of career options and complex expectations of self-actualization. In this Darwinian ecosystem, the challenge is to grasp fleeting opportunities, innovate continuously, and compete globally from the outset. As such, Silicon Valley and its innovative, entrepreneurial firms have provided a fertile research laboratory for understanding the core principles and practices of super-flexibility.

Swift action, mobility, and ephemeral entities are critical features of the Silicon Valley business dynamics. Organizational structures and business models undergo frequent adjustments and constant realignments "Today's" successful models may only endure for a short time. Incumbent firms must find new business propositions and reinvent themselves, before they become obsolete.[3] Pioneering products quickly become commodities, and today's premium pricing strategy, with high gross margins, hits the bottom of the waterfall abruptly. Successful start-ups may unexpectedly turn into failed black holes. In such a turbulent setting, super-flexibility is highly valued.

Our central thesis is that Silicon Valley and many of its entrepreneurial enterprises strive for super- flexibility; that their business strategies and organizational structures deal with fleeting opportunities and novel tasks, rather than the development and delivery of routine transactions and standard products and services. Even long-standing Valley enterprises strive to be "forever adolescent", constantly re-assessing market opportunities, pre-emptively killing their own products, and introducing new products and services in rapid succession. Most of a firm's revenues derive from products and services that are typically less than 18 months old. The key imperative is to be super-flexible since conditions are rarely stable enough to enable "perfect adaptation".

The challenge is to organize, strategize and manage for the moment, and keep options open for the long haul. There is no "buffering", no slack, no

---

[2]   Speech given by Bill Joy (co-founder of SUN Microsystems) at the Churchill Club, Palo Alto, California, 1990.

[3]   The "Valley" is resplendent with such recalibrations. Famous examples in recent years include Apple Computer, HP, Oracle, and Intel Corporation.

cushion, to shield ventures, corporations and entrepreneurs from market realities. What counts is *de facto* market acceptance, rather than *de jure* credibility. Does my product have major benefits valued by a target group of potential customers, or is it just a cool technology? Is someone willing to pay for this benefit? Can I continue to deliver value or is this just a quick one-off? No amount of spin, inspirational story, good press, prestigious venture funding, or a distinguished board is likely to sustain the firm in the long run. It may merely sustain it as a "living dead", supported by an artificial life support system. Given the constant turbulence, Silicon Valley is an ideal research laboratory to understand the game of super-flexibility and the rules by which it is played.

1.2 The Concept of Super-Flexibility

Super-flexibility is a complex construct. It means being "agile", able to move rapidly, change course to take advantage of an opportunity or to sidestep a threat. It is also about being versatile, able to do things differently and to deploy various capabilities depending on the needs of a particular situation. The concept also means being robust to withstand shocks, and being resilient to spring back from the brink of disaster.

We subsume all these diverse attributes under the conceptual umbrella term of "super-flexibility" and suggest that its practical deployment requires a broad range of differentiated principles, capabilities, and attributes. For example, having the liquidity to exploit an unexpected opportunity is qualitatively different from possessing a resilient disposition to deal with the negative impact of an accident or a mistake. Similarly, reliance on "redundant" mechanisms, such as insurance, buffers or slack, to protect against potentially damaging situations, is different from the dexterity needed in being agile or versatile. Yet clearly, these notions are in some way related. When we refer broadly to "super-flexibility", it denotes all these different senses. Super-flexibility is about both ends of the spectrum[4]; the ability to move quickly and adopt variable postures, while building-in the capability to withstand shocks and to become resilient. A truly super-flexible enterprise deploys the most appropriate capability, depending on the needs of the moment and the situational context.

---

[4] The two sides of super-flexibility are also reflected in Collins and Porras' (2000) depiction of lasting companies that have stable core beliefs but a *modus operandi* that emphasizes continuous exploration.

1.3   The Organization of the Book

What are the underlying principles and the core practices that can help explain how super-flexibility can be implemented in dynamic business contexts? How do the innovative firms of Silicon Valley vector their business trajectories when, at best, they can only predict a few weeks ahead? How do they organize for rapid growth on the one hand, and sudden downturns on the other? How do they give their knowledge workers anchors of stability and yet retain the flexibility to switch "on and off" at short notice? How do they embark on, and commit to, major initiatives when they have imperfect information and limited resources?

This book is about the strategic, organizational and managerial principles that have shaped Silicon Valley as the innovation engine of the digital age; where the game is partly about super-flexibility, thriving on perpetual uncertainty; where the rules of the game are about harnessing and surfing dynamic waves of change. Our main objective in this book is to propose conceptual frameworks, illustrative examples, and practical lessons for functioning in environments characterized by innovation, speed, and dynamism. Our focus is on business practices that can proactively harness, not just retroactively respond to, uncertainty.

The core principles and practices of super-flexibility are described in the following eight chapters. Chapter 2 focuses on the notion of flexibility, its historical antecedents, and its treatment in various disciplines. We explore the various senses of flexibility; from agility, liquidity, and versatility, to adaptability, robustness and resilience. We synthesize the different senses and present the "arc of super-flexibility" as a conceptual construct, in an effort to pull together its various meanings. A super-flexible firm, we suggest, is agile and versatile, and robust and resilient, all at the same time.

Chapter 3 focuses on our research laboratory, the knowledge ecosystem of Silicon Valley. We describe the core building blocks and the evolution of Silicon Valley during the past 20 years. In this Darwinian setting, the name of the game is kaleidoscopic change, focusing on innovation, changing the rules, and re-inventing the future, while pruning excess to survive, consolidate, and compete. Apart from market and technological dynamics, technology companies also have to guide and motivate expectant knowledge workers, whose preferences and core skills continuously evolve.

Chapters 4 through 8 are about the action principles of super-flexibility: how this capability can be put into practice everyday; how it relates to strategy, structure, and effective approaches for guiding and engaging knowledge workers. As depicted in Figure 1 five inter-locking principles describe the *modus operandi* of super-flexible firms. These are:

1. Recycling know-how, talent, and assets in a multi-polar ecosystem.
2. Maneuvering the fluid business trajectory real-time,
3. Recalibrating assumptions and initiatives as new realities unfold,
4. Orgitechting the workplace to create a versatile yet resilient organization.
5. Aligning multi-cultural knowledge workers by deploying peer-to-peer leadership practices.

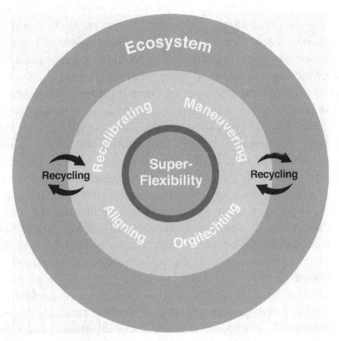

Figure 1. Overview of the book

Chapter 4, on "recycling", is about how the ecosystem turns setbacks into opportunities. It is about learning from failure and putting that learning to effective use. Recycling is one approach for harnessing "failures". The recycling process helps nurture innovation, foster entrepreneurship, and cross-pollinate know-how. It provides the impetus for creating new ventures, blending in "failed" initiatives, and combining elements of old and new. In essence, recycling stimulates life after death; the people, know-how, and capabilities of failed ventures and unsuccessful initiatives are recycled in the broader ecosystem, giving rise to new enterprises, new innovations, and new combinations of talent. Failure is viewed as a temporary "setback", to learn from, not to be punished for. It also provides the foundation for future innovations.

The principle of "maneuvering" is discussed in chapter 5. Maneuvering is about how technology companies develop their business trajectories and try to be super-flexible by not putting "all eggs in one basket". It describes the dynamic process of continually re-focusing a firm's know-how on shifting centers of gravity over time. The maneuvering framework proposes the parallel deployment of offensive and defensive moves before, or after, critical triggers, a continuous search for new opportunities, and constant correction of mistakes. It provides a conceptual "coat hanger" around which intentions, capabilities, and resources can be aligned and re-aligned to focus on successive "decisive points". Four types of maneuver, pre-emptive, protective, opportunistic, and corrective, are proposed to describe the real-time strategic postures of super-flexible entities.

Chapter 6 presents the principle of "recalibrating". Recalibrating refers to real-time adjustments that have to be made as circumstances unfold when implementing new initiatives. It describes the process of learning by experimenting, prototyping, failing, succeeding, and trying again. Analogous to the scientific model of discovery, it describes the inter-linked stages of experimentation, escalation, and integration. Effective recalibration is about changing tack by leveraging fact-based feedback, rapid prototyping, and targeted testing in unchartered fields. In the recalibration model, the processes of strategy formation and implementation are linked together in an iterative process. In unpredictable settings, it is difficult to iron out all the uncertainties and "de-risk" strategies through detailed planning and elaborate analyses. Relevant information is scant and changes frequently. It may be difficult to establish the technical feasibility of a new technology, or the market viability of a pioneering product, through "theoretical" planning. By engaging in action, new information can be brought to light, and unforeseen limitations, and new possibilities, identified.

The organizational configuration of super-flexible enterprises is described in chapter 7. We use the term "orgitechting" to depict the anatomy and the personality of super-flexible entities. Orgitechting is a hybrid term that reflects the three critical dimensions of "organization", "technology" and "architecture". It refers to an enterprise's ability to maintain some degree of cohesion as it morphs and re-organizes over time, by leveraging the clustering, the connective and the cohesive building blocks of organizational design.

The clustering dimension comprises distributed, modular nodes that have complex interdependencies. The connective dimension is a blend of codified processes and spontaneous linkages that tie together the various nodes. The cohesive dimension is about an enterprise's identity and its personality. It is a mixture of "hard" and "soft" glue that binds together the distributed nodes. These three building blocks are blended together to create organizational architectures that are stable yet dynamic, uniform yet differentiated, modular yet interdependent.

The critical challenge is to balance what may seem to be mutually exclusive tensions and to think in terms of "shades of grey". On the one hand, the organization needs to be disciplined, lean, and focused, with minimal duplication of effort, stringent accountability, and guided direction. On the other hand, it is important to minimize complex co-ordination, provide room for entrepreneurial initiatives, and develop the capability for rapid and variable response to front-line realities. Modularity, innovation, and speed, have to be balanced with stability, focus and control. The imperative is to strike a dynamic balance between apparent opposites and to continuously think about the critical "trade-offs" that have to be made.

Chapter 8, on the principle of "aligning" refers to leadership approaches, practices, and tools intended to motivate, engage, and create an environment that enables knowledge workers to pool together their collective talents in realizing common goals. Getting everyone on the same page is easier said than done. It requires thinking about the "softer" themes of emotional engagement, as well as the "harder" elements of project management and collaborative teamwork in multi-cultural, distributed contexts. Effective leadership practices address the importance of guided direction as well as the need for personal initiative. They recognize the significance of financial rewards, and the critical value of intellectual and emotional motivators. In the spirit of peer-to-peer, rather than the traditional parent-child, leadership practices, the aligning framework revolves around four sets of daily practices: "Bridging" or interactive communication of "context"; "binding", or ensuring person-organization "fit"; "blending" complementary skills in collaborative projects; and "balancing" guided control and personal initiative by setting clear expectations and work boundaries. Collectively, these five action principles are the operational means of striving for super-flexibility: being resilient and robust but also agile and versatile; "managing for the moment", while keeping the long-term destination in mind; continuously re-inventing, in the context fundamental core beliefs and value propositions. A super-flexible entity can shift its priorities and trajectory. It can maneuver real-time in harnessing new opportunities and avoiding potential threats. It can recalibrate its approach when faced with new realities. It can recycle people, assets and technologies; and it can re-align its knowledge workers as it morphs and evolves. The generals are aligned with the troops, picking up signals from the front-liners who provide the expertise and the momentum to drive forward. In short, a super-flexible entity is dynamic and mobile, designed to enact change, not just react to change.

Just as scientists learn from controlled experiments in a laboratory, established firms can also benefit from the experience of Silicon Valley and its high tech entities. In chapter 9, we reflect on a few lessons that traditional enterprises can take away from this entrepreneurial ecosystem. At the "meta" level, we suggest that established entities should evolve from traditional "dukedoms" and strive to become super-flexible "ecosystems". An ecosystem has a shared climate for all its citizens and stakeholders, but also encourages differentiation and diversity; it provides equality of opportunity and access, but also thrives on meritocratic norms and fact-based performance feedback. It encourages the formation of autonomous, modular entities that multiply through cross-pollination, but that also have a shared identity and a sense of community. This chapter puts forward a few practical suggestions on how established companies can re-invent themselves for the new game of super-flexibility in the post-digital era.

One target audience for this book include entrepreneurial teams who intend to start their own ventures and want to learn from the lessons of Silicon Valley, as well as business leaders and knowledge workers whose enterprises are experiencing "schizophrenia". They have one foot entrenched in the old camp of tradition, inertia, and recipes born of historic success during the industrial age. Yet, they have another foot firmly placed in the emerging world of technology, globalization and knowledge-based economies. The essence of this book is not just about how business enterprises can learn from Silicon Valley's successes and setbacks in order to adapt to new realities; but how they can reinvent themselves in order to harness new opportunities unfolding in today's turbulent age. As Tom Watson, IBM's leader, observed long ago:

"Technological change demands an even greater measure of adaptability and versatility on the part of the management of a large organization. Unless management remains alert, it can be stricken with complacency-one of the most insidious dangers we face in business. In most cases it's hard to tell that you have caught the disease until its almost too late. It is frequently most infectious among companies that have already reached the top. They get to believing in the infallibility of their own judgment." (Watson 1963, p. 63)

2 Conceptual Foundations of Super-Flexibility

The concept of flexibility has been the focus of research in various disciplines ranging from economics and decision analysis to military strategy and organizational design. This intuitively appealing idea is often invoked as a means of handling "difficulties" in addressing evolving, fluid, or dynamic situations. These "difficulties" may arise partly because of entrenched positions that are inconsistent with the needs of the moment, or when situations do not turn out as expected. The problem is particularly acute in knowledge-based entities due to the confluence of various triggers that can rapidly transform business landscapes. This chapter examines the conceptual foundations of flexibility, describes the multi-disciplinary research contributions on the subject, and concludes with a synthesis of the major themes that impact its implementation in business settings.

2.1 Multi-Disciplinary Contributions

At first glance, previous research on the notion of flexibility in any one discipline may reveal a paucity of contributions. Closer inspection, however, uncovers a substantive body of research, albeit spread across a wide range of disciplines. Some of the earliest interest in the subject can be found in the field of military strategy. The initial contributions were reflected in the practical approaches of the French Generals, Bourcet and Guibert who pioneered the use of the "divisional structure" and faster marching speeds. The objective was to improve the troops' flexibility and effectiveness. Decades later, Clausewitz, the grandfather of modern strategy, emphasized flexibility in three overarching areas: the importance of the moral factors, the ability to concentrate on the decisive point, and the value of a standing reserve (von Guyczy *et al.* 2003, Hahlway 1966).

Flexibility is also reflected in General Sherman's (1875) approach during the American Civil War. His famous march to Atlanta was aided by the use of scouts, not only to forage for food, but also to provide an early warning system. The British historian, Liddell-Hart (1929, 1954), later pioneered the strategy of the "indirect approach", and argued that, to achieve policy goals, plans and dispositions have to be "adaptable to circumstances". Military strategists have continued their interest in the subject, considering it as an essential principle of their craft (Eccles 1959, Taylor 1959). In recent times the concept has taken on a broader significance as a result of the technological intensity and logistical complexity of contemporary warfare.

From an academic perspective, economists have made some of the earliest contributions by examining the impact of oscillations in the business cycle on entrepreneurial firms (Hart 1937a, 1937b, Kindleberger 1937, Knight 1921, Lange 1944, McKinsey1932, Stigler 1939, Tinbergen 1932). Their focus was on the creation of new firms during the Depression of the 1930s. Another group of economists considered flexibility as a potential response of farmers to agricultural price fluctuations (Backman 1940, Mason 1938, Nicholls 1940, Timoshenko 1930). Several studies have examined how to respond flexibly by considering crop selection and rotation, or by switching between milk and cheese production. This agricultural context provided the basis for some of the later research on the subject (Carley and Cryer 1964, Collins 1956, Cowden and Trelogan 1948, French *et al.* 1956, Kerchner 1966).

Decades later, the Oil Crisis of 1973 triggered renewed interest in the topic, particularly as it impacts corporate strategy (Ansoff 1975, Eppink 1978a, 1978b). Management researchers view strategic flexibility as a generic response to the unforeseen (D'Aveni 1994, Evans 1982a, 1982b, Harrigan 1980, 1985, Krijnen 1979, Volberda 1998). A related stream of research has discussed the importance of organizational flexibility in rapidly changing environments (Ackoff 1977, Bahrami 1992, Bahrami and Evans 1987, 1989b, Galbraith 1994, Hatum and Pettigrew 2003, Perrow 1970, Raynor and Bower 2001, Thompson 1967, Tomlinson 1976).

Decision theorists have formalized the impact of evolving preferences on multi-period choices (Day 1969, Koopmans 1964, Kreps 1979) developed probabilistic measures of flexibility (Heimann and Lusk 1976, Klein and Meckling 1958, Mandelbaum 1978, Marschak and Nelson 1962, Merkhofer 1975) and examined the "robustness" of decisions to withstand future changes (Pye 1978, Rosenhead 1980, Rosenhead *et al.* 1972, Rosenhead *et al.* 1986). Theoretical progress has also been made in developing the notion of flexibility as a criterion for optimal decision-making. The idea has been applied to business decision-making as well as to the design of complex systems in aerospace and information technology (Chen and Lewis 1999, Hamblin 2002, Saleh *et al.* 2001). Research in finance has focused on the relationship between flexibility and liquidity as related to options and portfolio theory (Frazer 1985, Goldman 1978, Jones and Ostroy 1976, 1984, Mason, 1986). More recently, a body of literature has developed around "real-options" theory (Ekstrom and Bjornsson 2003, Raynor 2001, Triantis and Hodder 1990, Trigeorgis 1996, Trigeorgis and Schwartz 2001).

Discipline	Focus
Military strategy	Adapting operations in the "fog" of battle; Graduated response
Economics	New firm creation, modelling uncertainty
Agricultural economics	Price fluctuations, crop rotation, technological capabilities
Manufacturing systems & operations management	Ordering of activities, sequencing of job shops, range and volume of product
	Modular manufacturing, product mix
	Supply chain agility, E-business
Strategic management	Meta-flexibility; managing the "unforeseen"
Decision theory	Future options, expected value of information
Child Psychology	Children and teenagers rebounding from adversity
Information systems	Agile IT infrastructure
Organizational science	Structural flexibility
Finance	Liquid asset deployment, exchange rates, "futures' and options
Systems analysis & environmental research	Damaged ecosystems

Table 1. Disciplinary contributions to understanding flexibility

The concept has also been used by systems analysts to describe an ecosystem's ability to recover from a traumatic shock, such as a dam rupturing or the unintended consequences of disposing hazardous wastes (Collingridge 1983, Fiering 1982, Hashimoto *et al.* 1982a, 1982b, Holling 1973, Keeney 1983). This work has been extended to consider the sustainability of both, natural and socio-technical ecosystems (Gunderson 1999). Furthermore, tactical issues have led to the development of algorithms for evaluating flexibility in relation to energy generation and distribution systems (Draaisma and Mol 1977, Friedman and Reklaitis 1975, Fuss 1977, Guerico 1981, Schroeder *et al.* 1981, Van der Vet 1977), and flexible manufacturing systems (Adler 1988, Buzacott 1982, De Meyer *et al.* 1989, Gerwin 1982, Hutchinson 1973, Iravani *et al.* 2003, Mandelbaum and Brill 1989, Spur *et al.* 1976, Tilak 1978). These studies have largely focused on flexible responses to product mix and volume uncertainty.

More recently, a substantial body of literature has emerged, focusing on supply chain agility in the production and delivery of high technology products. Several attempts have been made to integrate the various senses of flexibility and to model them into operations management. A further attempt was made in this field to introduce the term "flexagility" as the conjunction of the two (Wadhwa and Rao 2003a, 2003b). With the advent of "autonomic" or self-adaptive computing, the significance of this stream of research will be further highlighted, especially in the context of its impact on the evolution of e-business (Shi and Daniels 2003).

While there have been many research contributions on the subject of flexibility, their focus has been somewhat varied, reflecting disciplinary priorities as well as the needs of the time. Moreover, various terms have been used to describe the research. In some cases, such as machine tool scheduling, addressing fluctuations in product type, mix and demand, it has been termed "operational" flexibility, concentrating on logistics. In other cases, the term "strategic" flexibility has been applied to military strategy or to the business portfolio mix, as it relates to the long-term trajectory of a company. More recently, strategic resilience has been used to describe a firm's ability to bounce back from downturns and to sustain its innovative capability (Hamel and Valikangas 2003), a concept previously reflected in studies that focus on the regeneration of natural ecosystems (Holling 1973), such as Florida's everglades (Carpenter et al. 2001). In the post Internet bubble era, organizational agility is put forward as a way to restore the effectiveness of IT systems (Del Prete et al. 2003).

Research findings highlight the vague and intangible nature of the concept, yet there is universal agreement that "flexibility", however defined, is a desired capability that can help harness uncertainty. The design, development, and deployment of this capability, however, is more complex than simply installing something extra at the margin to address incremental oscillations. The value of flexibility is seldom precise but rarely in doubt; it is how to get it and deploy it that causes consternation.

2.2 Flexibility: Related Concepts

Throughout this extensive body of multi-disciplinary research, several terms are used to denote various aspects of flexibility. The terms most frequently used are, agility, adaptability, versatility, resilience, and robustness. Other related concepts include elasticity, liquidity, malleability, modularity, and mobility. These terms are often used in an inter-related and transposable fashion, although they reflect different dimensions of the

concept of flexibility (Evans 1982a). In order to figure out how to operationalize the concept, we need to understand the meanings and the nuances
associated with related terms. Table 2 lists concepts that are related to
flexibility and describes their meaning.

Concepts	Definitions
Adaptability	Accommodating a transformed environment
Agility	Moving nimbly into and out of different domains
Elasticity	Stretching & shrinking to meet different perturbations or pressures
Hedging	Mitigating against the losses associated with the "down-side" potential
Liquidity	Transforming from one form to another without substantial switching costs
Malleability	Molding into unorthodox conditions. Pliable or able to bend in order to meet unusual circumstances
Mobility	Re-deployable assets and capabilities
Modularity	Re-configurable blocks or units allowing up-gradeability when something new comes along, or extensibility when demand is high
Robustness	Taking hits with minimal damage to functional capability
Resilience	Bouncing back from the brink after sustaining damage, or degrading gracefully before termination
Versatility	Functioning with dexterity in different settings

Table 2. Concepts related to flexibility

The similarities are evident, as are the differences. For example, having the
liquidity to exploit an unexpected opportunity is different from possessing
a resilient disposition to bounce back from an accident or to recover from
some from of trauma. Similarly, reliance on "redundant" mechanisms,
such as insurance, buffers or slack, to protect against potentially damaging
situations, is different from the dexterity and the suppleness required to be
agile when entering new markets or versatile when deploying novel technology. The next section explores concepts that are most closely related to
the notion of flexibility.

2.1.1 Adaptability

The term "adaptability" is defined as "adjusting to the conditions of a changed environment". It is a term most frequently used as synonymous with flexibility. Stigler (1939) was the first to make the distinction between the two terms. He suggested that adaptability implies an optimal adjustment to a newly transformed environment, whereas flexibility enables successive, but temporary, approximations to a "best case" state. The term has been used in the strategic management literature (Eppink 1978a) to describe an enterprise's ability to respond to foreseen changes; for example, when a projected scenario, such as deregulation of a major industry, becomes reality. In a business context, it may refer to planned reorganizations, or to downsizing, in response to declining market demand.

2.1.2 Agility

The term "agility" describes the extent to which an entity can move nimbly backwards, forwards, and sideways with dexterity. In business settings, it can refer to moving out of the way of an impending disaster, or leaping into an unknown area of opportunity. The term has been used in the literature to characterize a firm's organizational structure (Hatum and Pettigrew 2003) and its IT infrastructure (Del Prete *et al.* 2003). Recently, there has been increasing interest in agile supply chains. In this body of research, flexibility requirements are addressed in terms of the variety of products produced, the volume and the logistics of shipping semi or finished goods. Agility is perceived as either a combination of speed and flexibility, or as an extension of flexibility. The term "flexagility" was proposed to capture the overlapping meaning of the terms (Wadhwa and Rao 2003a).

2.1.3 Versatility

The term "versatility" is defined as "turning readily from one subject or occupation to another", as well as "capable of dealing with many subjects". The term has been used in military operations research to conceptualize how various systems could be deployed in different theaters of operations, or utilized to achieve various objectives within a given theater of operations. It is argued that versatility is achieved by installing the capability to respond to a wide range of scenarios ahead of time, or by rapidly modifying an approach, once a change has occurred (Bonder 1976).

In a business context, versatility is about being able to seamlessly switch between different modes and priorities; for example, from prototyping to production, or from R&D to sales. It is also an essential characteristic of effective entrepreneurial teams, where the need to constantly shift gear and direction is at a premium. It can also be useful when assessing a knowledge worker's capacity to multi-task and deal with different priorities, reporting relationships, and stakeholders in complex matrix organizations.

2.1.4 Resilience

The term "resilience" refers to the tendency to rebound or recoil, showing buoyancy or recuperative power, and the capability to withstand shocks without permanent damage or rupture. Systems analysts have used the term to denote a natural ecosystem's ability to regenerate itself after a catastrophic event or a radical change (Fiering 1982, Grümm and Breitenecker 1981, Hashimoto et al. 1982a, Holling 1973). For example, the construction of a hydroelectric dam changes the surrounding habitat by diverting or stopping the flow of water. Resilience in this setting refers to the ability of the natural species living in the habitat to recover to their former population levels.

In a business context, the term refers to an entity's ability to recover from shocks and setbacks. Knowledge enterprises inevitably experience setbacks and have to deal with the challenge of recovery. Some setbacks result in damage. Whatever the cause of the damage, an enterprise must bounce back by having the ability to rapidly regenerate itself, or by degrading gracefully. In a similar vein, educational psychologists use the term to refer to individuals who have become stronger as a result of overcoming major problems in their lives (Carver 1998, Masten et al. 1990). There are clear parallels with knowledge enterprises in Silicon Valley, where entrepreneurs and technologies often become successful after they have overcome major obstacles or learned from earlier setbacks.

2.1.5 Robustness

The term "robust" is defined as "not slender or delicate or weakly". The concept has been used in operations research to examine large-scale systems, such as the U.K.'s National Health Service, and their ability to endure shocks and perturbations (Rosenhead et al. 1972, Rosenhead 1980). The term refers to a system's ability to gain the highest proportion of good, or the lowest proportion of undesirable consequences, within a given "action space".

An enterprise's robustness is a measure of how much it can withstand shocks when "hitting" obstacles in high-risk arenas. From a practical point of view, it is analogous to having a "forcefield" around the enterprise, an "air-bag" to absorb a blow, "Teflon" coating to deflect the impact, or shock absorbers placed in areas of maximum impact. Simply put, robustness refers to the ability to go through turbulence, and remain unscathed.

2.3   Discussion of Related Concepts

In addition to the concepts discussed above, several other terms are also used to denote different facets of flexibility. For example, "malleability" refers to the ability to be easily molded into shape and remolded when necessary. In a business context, malleability allows an entity to spontaneously stretch organizational boundaries to accommodate new circumstances, for example in seeking partnerships or in forging collaborative relationships.

Economists use the concept of liquidity to highlight its role in producing financial flexibility (Frazer 1985, Goldman 1974, 1978, Jones and Ostroy 1976, 1984). An asset is liquid if it can be easily converted into some alternative form of wealth with little or no conversion costs or associated penalties. Similarly, installing "slack" is also viewed as a means of achieving flexibility. Cyert and March (1963) refer to "organizational slack" as a buffer between the organization and external discontinuities. Having slack is similar to "hedging", a concept related to the maxim of "not putting all eggs in one basket" (Ansoff 1965). However, "hedging" only mitigates the losses associated with the downside potential, at the expense of foregoing the full benefits of any upside potential (Merkhofer and Saade 1978).

This brief conceptual analysis of related terms reflects the many different senses of flexibility. It also highlights the complex and multi-faceted nature of the concept (Meffert 1969). In some contexts, as is the case with resilience, malleability or elasticity, the term is used to denote a degree of pliability. The object in question can be bent, bowed or twisted without breaking, implying that whatever is being manipulated will yield to pressure. In other cases, such as liquidity or adaptability, it means that the object is susceptible to modification; for example, liquid assets can be converted to another form without incurring any switching costs. Yet other terms, such as agility and versatility, denote an object's capacity to redefine itself in the light of novel imperatives, or in a proactive sense, to precipitate a new state of affairs.

2.4   Super-Flexibility: A Constructivist Definition

Our analysis of related terms leads us to conclude that flexibility is a polymorphous concept. Those attributes and capabilities that provide flexibility in one situation, need not be the same as, transferable to, or appropriate for, the provision of flexibility in other situations. Yet to be truly flexible, an entity needs to possess the capacity to embrace all the different attributes of the concept simultaneously. On the one hand, it needs to be agile and versatile, capable of harnessing novel situations with speed and efficiency. On the other hand, it has to be robust and resilient, able to absorb shocks, withstand pressure and bounce back from the brink of disaster. The former requires suppleness and malleability, coupled with versatility in functioning. The latter requires the ruggedness to withstand, and the elasticity to rebound from, shocks.

We use the term "super-flexibility" to denote the multi-faceted meaning of the concept, from agility, versatility, and adaptability, to resilience, robustness and malleability.[5] As depicted in Figure 2, the "arc of super-flexibility" provides a visual construct that incorporates the various aspects of the concept. A super-flexible enterprise needs the capacity to enact and use its different dimensions, depending on the situation. At times, it may need to be robust and resilient; at other times, it may have to be agile and versatile. Oftentimes, it may have to deploy all the senses simultaneously. The objective is to remove potential points of friction, when deviating from its current trajectory so that it can do things differently when circumstances change.

Fundamentally super-flexibility is about having several approaches and diverse capabilities for harnessing uncertainty. As indicated from our review of related concepts, there are different ways of being flexible. As depicted in Figure 2, various capabilities are required in different proportions. These have to be uniquely configured according to the needs of the situation, the capabilities of those executing the change, and the overall "disposition" of the enterprise. There is no "silver bullet" solution that can solve the "universal" challenge of flexibility. What may be appropriate one day in a particular set of circumstances may be totally inappropriate in similar circumstances on another day. One size does not fit all.

---

[5] The term "super-flexibility" has been used with regard to workforce adaptation. (Cofield 1999).

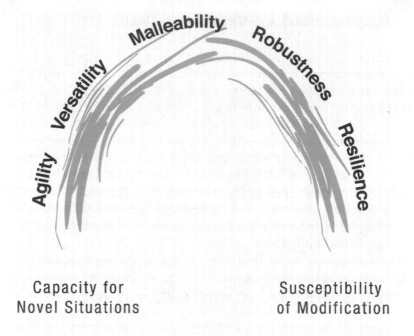

Capacity for
Novel Situations

Susceptibility
of Modification

Yielding To Pressure

Figure 2. The arc of super-flexibility

2.4.1 Super-Flexibility as Yielding to Pressure

Knowledge intensive firms are a mixture of the "soft" or organic components, such as people and their socio-technical interactions, and a "hard" or physical component, such as legal patents, infrastructure resources, and capital assets. These elements fuse imperfectly together to create an engine that can generate wealth on an ongoing basis.

However, it is clear that few firms achieve a "steady-state" for extended periods without interventions. Performance varies over time in dynamic domains. Even when performing well, just like any other engine, lubrication is required to improve performance. Lubrication reduces the friction between the various parts of an enterprise, especially when pressure builds up during acceleration or deceleration. When braking hard and changing direction, the friction between the parts can result in an even greater build up of pressure.

In the multi-disciplinary literature on flexibility, there is a core assumption that flexibility is an attribute or a quality of a decision, asset, structure or an entity. Our view is that super-flexibility can also provide the necessary lubrication to relieve the pressure that builds up in parts of the enterprise experiencing friction, especially when spontaneously deviating from a prior course of action. Being super-flexible, we suggest, is not just about having the right combination of capabilities or assets. It is also about having various types of lubricants that may be required from time to time to relieve the friction as pressure builds up.

The conceptual frameworks presented in the next few chapters address practical approaches for developing super-flexible capabilities. They also reflect on the necessary "lubrication" that may be needed from time to time.

2.4.2 Super-Flexibility as Capacity for Novel Situations

Several successful entrepreneurs we have talked to, refer to "determining moments" in their companies' trajectories. With hindsight, these are referred to as "knot-holes". Knot-holes may be about facing the sudden end of life of a blockbuster product, or the extensive exposure experienced in becoming a public company, or just going through pivotal episodes in the sheer struggle for survival. Successful companies seem to endure several of these episodes and, in so doing, develop the capacity to manage novel situations spontaneously. The process, when successfully addressed, typically crystallizes an enterprise's "purpose" to a highly clarified level of granularity. It is precisely in these circumstances where super-flexibility is vital. Paradoxically, it is these situations that are also least likely to be forecasted or imagined ahead of time. This process can also result in a firm "shedding its old skin" as if emerging from a chrysalis.

While it is possible to put in place adaptation mechanisms, such as contingency plans based on envisioned scenarios, ahead of time; it is precisely these "knot-hole" situations that test the adaptive capability of an enterprise to the limit. Improvisation (Bastien 1988, Brown and Eisenhardt 1998), and the ability to deal with novel situations spontaneously, are critical for achieving super-flexibility in the fast-moving world of knowledge enterprises.

2.4.3 Super-Flexibility as Susceptibility to Modification

The object of becoming super-flexible is to be able to either intentionally precipitate a transformation, or to make modifications in response to changing situations. Adaptation occurs either during the course of, or after, an unfolding change episode, and may simply be random in that one may be just at the right place at the right time. The assumption that super-flexibility can be acquired before it is needed is an ideal to hope for but unrealistic to expect, because having super-flexibility and not using it is, at best, an expensive indulgence.

Real-time adaptation is demonstrably difficult. It takes ingenuity to face a novel situation and true leadership to improvise on the spot. This is why simplicity is critical for effective, real-time adaptation. After extensive research on machine tool scheduling, Iravani *et al.* (2003) conclude that simple machines, at the end of the day, were much easier to modify for novel outputs than those optimized for dealing with "imagined" contingencies. The latter require complex modifications and were ineffective when they had to adjust to unanticipated oscillations in demand or product mix. As Stigler (1939) postulated, flexibility is more like approximations to the "optimal" adaptive response. Our experience in Silicon Valley bears this out. Simpler things are easier to change, especially when complex "real time" modifications are needed.

2.5 Conclusion

This chapter described the multi-disciplinary contributions to the subject of flexibility, and explored several related concepts with a "family" resemblance. We proposed using the umbrella term "super-flexibility" in order to cluster and synthesize its various dimensions and nuances. We suggested that the effective application of super-flexibility depends on an entity's ability to act spontaneously, to be configured for simplicity, and to provide lubrication in order to minimize friction.

Keeping these core themes in mind, the following chapters describe how super-flexibility can be achieved in business settings. However, since most business situations are unique, we do not intend to propose "best practices" or generic approaches. Instead, we propose five action principles as "conceptual coat-hangers". These are derived from our observations, field research and practical experience in Silicon Valley during the past twenty years. We hope these principles enable our readers to reflect on their own personal and enterprise experiences and to address how they can strive for super-flexibility, using our frameworks as "food for thought".

There are no easy answers to follow and no perfect role models to emulate. No single perspective can grasp the complexities of running a dynamic, knowledge enterprise, let alone generate standard approaches for enhancing or instilling super-flexibility. We put forward various approaches and actions that present entrepreneurs, executives, and knowledge workers with a menu of options to consider. Taken collectively, we hope the action principles, presented in the following chapters, provide an alternative optic for reflecting on the ongoing challenges of perpetual adaptation in knowledge enterprises.

Concepts	Implications for Knowledge Enterprises
Adaptability	Willingness to do things differently based on empirical pragmatism. Is related to enterprise strategy and values, especially the attitude and role modeling impact of its leaders.
Agility	Taking adroit action in a nimble manner as danger approaches and/or opportunities unfold.
Elasticity	Allowing units to expand or contract as business demands change; impacts enterprise architecture, especially in forming and dissolving collaborative partnerships.
Liquidity	Moving people and assets around without friction or penalty costs; impacts staffing methods and resource allocation processes.
Malleability	Bending and stretching the boundaries of organizational units, budgets and processes in response to pressure and friction..
Mobility	Re-deploying talent, assets and capabilities around the enterprise and the relevant ecosystem.
Modularity	Setting up scalable, plug and play, work units with compatible interconnects to other units; impacts organizational architecture and process linkages.
Robustness	Creating a solid core to fall back on; impacts core values, encoded competencies, and financial reserves..
Resilience	Regenerating damaged parts of an enterprise or unit. Or degrading gracefully when damaged
Versatility	Recruiting and developing people with the ability to do different assignments; customizing the "skin" around a common platform for different market segments; evolving a single product into a family of different products; impacts HR policies, product development approaches, marketing strategies and diversification options.

Table 3. Dimensions of super-flexibility and their impact on a knowledge enterprise

3 The Research Laboratory:
Silicon Valley's Knowledge Ecosystem

Silicon Valley is an ideal research laboratory for studying super-flexibility. Living on the cutting edge of uncertainty, nothing stays stable for long. Emerging technologies transform competitive landscapes almost overnight. New start-ups keep the incumbents on their toes. Multi-cultural entrepreneurs bring in diverse recipes from all over the world. Knowledge workers change roles and move between assignments. New players enter arenas from unexpected directions; and today's successful "quasars" become tomorrow's "black holes".

Although Silicon Valley has endured several economic downturns during the past 20 years, it continues to be a global center for high tech innovation and entrepreneurship. It is the epicenter for global venture capital and attracts entrepreneurial talent from different parts of the world. Although time will tell whether this trend will continue in the future, Silicon Valley has shown considerable resilience in the face of skepticism about its continued viability. This chapter examines the special features of Silicon Valley, its historical antecedents, its core building blocks, and its relevance as a research laboratory for studying super-flexibility.

There are a number of precedents for studying flexibility in circumscribed settings, bounded by time frames, industries, or societal conditions. As discussed in Chapter 2, the Great Depression of the 1930s unleashed a number of pioneering studies on the notion of flexibility (Hart 1937a, 1937b, McKinsey 1932, Stigler 1939) with a focus on creating new businesses, and how farmers could respond to oscillations in the price of agricultural produce (Backman 1940, Mason 1938, Nicholls 1940). Later "strategic-flexibility" was studied from the vantage point of corporate responses to the immediate aftermath of the 1973 Oil crisis (Eppink 1978a, 1978b). The notion of "resilience" was examined by studying natural ecosystems and the impact of human expansion (Holling 1973).

Silicon Valley has been at the forefront of many contemporary trends in business. For example, the practice of "offshoring", the focus of much recent debate in technology circles, was initiated by the area's disk drive and semiconductor industries during the 1980's. Firms in the Valley are early adopters of new technologies developed by local firms, serving as beta-test sites for other companies' latest products. We believe Silicon Valley can provide practical insights on how to operationalize super-flexibility in the age of technological discontinuity and global entrepreneurship.

We characterize Silicon Valley as a "Darwinian", dynamic, knowledge ecosystem. The term "ecosystem" is defined here as a "community of independent players, that operate inter-dependently, that feed off, compete and collaborate with one another, and that operate within a common climate". Its core, modular, building blocks include:

- The "knowledge originators": comprising universities and corporate and government research laboratories, nurturing talent, ideas, and emerging technologies.
- The "knowledge hatcheries", the critical mass of seasoned entrepreneurs, "angel" investors, and venture capital firms, providing risk funding to seed start-ups and fuel their growth.
- The "knowledge generators": the critical mass of emerging start-ups, mid-sized adolescents, and established giants that produce innovative products and services. They also provide the entrepreneurial talent pools from which many recombinant spin-offs are drawn.
- The "knowledge lubricants", the groupings of specialized lawyers, accountants, executive search specialists, consultants, and other service providers that coalesce into a complementary support infrastructure.

Enterprises in Silicon Valley are embedded in symbiotic and interdependent relationships with the broader ecosystem. Buyers become suppliers; customers turn into competitors; partners become vendors. The close physical proximity between firms, and the incessant movement of people, ideas and information create a setting that is analogous to a biological ecosystem. The walls between the "enterprise" and its ecosystem are not solid but opaque and decidedly permeable. The destiny of an enterprise is as much contingent on the ecosystem within which it is embedded and on the ability of the ecosystem to promote or inhibit super-flexibility.

3.1 Conceptual Underpinnings

The ecosystem concept is not new or limited to Silicon Valley. Indeed, clusters of firms in related industries have historically coalesced around a critical mass of business activity (Porter 1990). During the 19th century, for example, many firms in Birmingham, UK, clustered around the critical mass of expertise in, what is known in the vernacular as, "metal bashing". Subsequently, during this century, the automobile sector amassed around Birmingham (U.K.), as it did in Detroit (U.S.A.), and Stuttgart (Germany). In the City of London, financial industries have evolved around the famous "Square Mile". Similarly, Italy's textile industry has coalesced around the city of Prato. High technology industries of the information era also appear to conform to this tendency.

Several regional technology clusters have sprouted around the U.S. in recent decades - including Boston's "Route 128", Austin's "Silicon Hills", Seattle's "Technology Corridor", Illinois' "Silicon Prairie", New Jersey's "Princeton Corridor", San Diego's "Golden Triangle", and Utah's "Software Valley". Scotland's "Silicon Glen" and Cambridge's "Silicon Fen" have also attracted many technology-based companies. During the 1980s and early 90s, Singapore, and later Bangkok, became centers for disk drive and computer sub-systems manufacturing. India's Bangalore region, today the hotbed of entrepreneurial companies, built its reputation in Unix programming during the 1980s. Additionally, a number of government-sponsored science park initiatives, such as France's Sofia Antipolis, and Taiwan's Hsinchu, have also induced a critical mass of technology companies during the past decade. By far, the best known and the largest cluster of high technology firms is located in California's Silicon Valley.

According to the "2003 Index of Joint Venture Silicon Valley", the region covers an area of 1500 square miles in the San Francisco Bay Area, has a population of 2.3 million, and is home to 393 public companies and more than 22,000 high tech establishments. Its economy has evolved spectacularly during the past 30 years, triggered by the periodic emergence of major innovations. Initially boosted by defense spending during the 1960s, the epicenter of innovation shifted to semiconductors and integrated circuits in the 1970s, evolved to personal computers, disk drives and peripherals during the 1980s, and became dominated by software and networked Internet products and disk archiving services in the 1990s. The next emerging growth sector is projected to be in the biomedical and life sciences arena.

3.2 The Antecedents

There was no singular event or grand plan which led to the meteoric rise of "Silicon Valley".[6] Instead, a series of independent events, coupled with fortuitous timing, transformed a regional agricultural community into a global engine for technological innovation and entrepreneurship. The region evolved organically over time, when several complementary forces gelled together and resulted in the formation of a critical mass of high technology firms.

---

[6] Addressing a meeting of the Churchill Club in Palo Alto (October 1992), Bill Hewlett suggested that the origins of Silicon Valley, in his opinion, almost date back to the development of ship-to-shore radio and the early days of television, before RCA moved its R&D labs to the East coast.

From a technological perspective, the parallel development of two major innovations forged the foundational building blocks that underpinned the rapid growth of Silicon Valley during the 1960's and 1970's. The first, and the best known of these, was the commercial development of the transistor at AT&T's Bell Labs in 1947. The second was the development of disk drives or information storage technology using magnetic recording techniques. Using tape in 1953 and magnetic disks by 1957, the technology was developed at IBM's Santa Theresa Research Laboratory (Harker *et al.* 1981).

William Shockley co-invented the transistor at Bell Laboratories in New Jersey in 1947. He moved to Palo Alto in 1954 and set up Shockley Semiconductor Laboratories. His core tem of eight scientists became the founding nucleus for the growing West Coast semiconductor industry. They left Shockley Lab in 1957 and founded Fairchild Semiconductor. Further advances in semiconductor technology and the emergence of a major market in the defense industry helped launch many spin-offs, largely out of Fairchild, during the 1960's; among them National Semiconductor, AMI, Advanced Micro Devices and Intel.

During the same period, IBM set up its "skunk works" in Los Gatos with the aim of producing technical breakthroughs and innovative products. The development of Winchester disk drive technology[7] later led to the formation of a multi-billion dollar industry in Silicon Valley (Mulvany *et al.* 1975, Stevens 1981). Several members of the IBM team were later responsible for the founding of Memorex, Shugart, Seagate, Conner Peripherals, Adaptec, Auspex, Maxtor, and Quantum. The disk drive industry has been a major source of innovation and international dominance for US companies.[8] Chapter 4 reflects on the early evolution of this defining sector in Silicon Valley.

Stanford University's Dean of Engineering, Frederick Terman, played a crucial role during the early years by forging a close working relationship between the engineering school and the local technical firms. The formation of the Stanford Industrial Park in 1951 was an additional catalyst. It provided a mechanism for transferring technology from the university to

---

[7] The team included L.D. Stevens and Ken Houghten, who later became the Dean of Engineering at Santa Clara University (It was he who coined the term "Winchester" as a code name for the drive).

[8] The US disk drive industry is dominant in merchant production, although much of its manufacturing is conducted offshore, or with Japanese partners. The industry remains vibrant, as attested by the sustained growth rates and the pace of new product development (see McKendrick *et al.* 2000).

the nearby firms.[9] During the 1960's, the Park became an attractive location for the growing electronics companies. Their number expanded steadily, from 32 in 1960, to almost 70 by 1970 (Rogers and Larsen 1984).

Boosted by California's unique pioneering spirit, these critical building blocks formed the foundation of Silicon Valley's entrepreneurial setting. Since the days of the Gold Rush in the 1850s, and later the "Dust Bowl" migration during the 1930s, California, the frontier land, had attracted the innovative and the ambitious (Kotkin and Grabowicz 1982). It is hardly surprising that many entrepreneurs, who felt the need to challenge the *status quo* and to break with tradition, found a conducive home in Northern California. By the mid 1960's, a critical mass of technology companies had been established in the South San Francisco Bay Area. Santa Clara Valley was transformed from prune yards and orchards into a large Petri dish for creating entrepreneurial ventures and knowledge-based enterprises.

Sector	Number of Employees	Number of Establishments
Software	114,639	4,505
Semiconductor	103,443	816
Computers/ Communications	150,974	1,127
Innovation Services	112,150	6,257
Professional Services	103,856	11,897
Defense/Aerospace	27,567	94
Environmental	8,342	244
Bioscience	51,854	847

Table 4. 2001 Silicon Valley employment by sector (Source: Zhang 2003, p. 97)

During the past 20 years, Silicon Valley has nurtured the growth of many global technology companies. Well-known examples include Intel, Apple, Seagate, Quantum, Cisco, Oracle, Siebel, eBay, Intuit, National Semiconductors, Electronic Arts, and SUN Microsystems. In addition, Silicon Valley is home to several thousand start-ups and mid-sized technology enterprises. From 1990-2000, 29, 247 high tech start-ups were founded in

---

[9]   The first tenant was Varian Associates, a spin-off from the University Physics department. HP followed in 1954. David Packard and Bill Hewlett, Terman's former students, had co-founded HP in 1939.

Silicon Valley, with 70% engaged in "professional or innovation services" (Zhang 2003, p. 13). As indicated in Table 4, dominant industry clusters include semiconductors and semiconductor equipment, computer and communications hardware, electronic components, biomedical and life sciences, and software and related services.

3.3   The Building Blocks

Several specialized components, each playing different yet complementary roles, have turned Silicon Valley into an inter-dependent knowledge ecosystem. There are several major groupings, ranging from universities and research labs, to venture capital, support services, and the core enterprises. Based on their unique contribution to the ecosystem, we characterize these as "knowledge originators", "knowledge hatcheries", "knowledge generators", and "knowledge lubricants". This classification is somewhat rudimentary and is not intended to form a comprehensive taxonomy of the various "species" in the ecosystem. Without extending the parallels with the biological analogy too far, the remainder of this chapter describes the core building blocks and the "climate" of this ecosystem. We conclude by reflecting on why Silicon Valley has been an effective learning laboratory for studying super-flexibility.

3.3.1 The Knowledge Originators

A knowledge ecosystem nurtures new ideas and their practical development into new products and services. In Silicon Valley's case, product innovations are, almost exclusively, based on technological breakthroughs. In this context, universities and research institutes are the ecosystem's most visible building block. They are a critical source of early stage technologies. Additionally, they train the scientists and the engineers who eventually become the entrepreneurs and the knowledge worker talent pools. It may even be argued that they are the knowledge "originators" of the ecosystem.

Nurturing and training the knowledge worker talent pool is a critical contribution of the universities. This role is especially significant given the global nature of technology enterprises. Silicon Valley has been a magnet for multi-cultural knowledge workers from different parts of the world. Many come to attend the region's universities and remain in the area; others are recruited to work for Valley-based companies overseas and may transfer back to the home base. Since high technology firms are global from their inception, multi-cultural talent pools facilitate rapid development of global operations. Based on 2003 data from the non-profit organization, Joint Venture Silicon Valley, 34% of Silicon Valley's population was born outside the US.

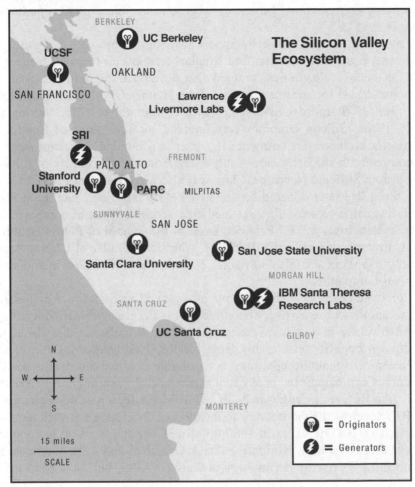

Figure 3. The knowledge originators

Universities are also catalysts for networking and relationship building. These links play a crucial role during the process of enterprise formation. For example, two IT professionals from the Stanford Business School and the Computer Science Department co-founded Cisco Systems in the mid-1980s. SUN Microsystem's co-founders included two Stanford MBA students, a graduate student from the Stanford Engineering School, and a PhD student from Berkeley's Computer Science Department. All four founders of ROLM were graduate students at the Stanford Engineering School, as were Yahoo's co-founders, Jerry Yang and David Filo. "Google" was founded by student friends Sergey Brin and Larry Page, who according to the official history of the firm *"were not terribly fond of each other when they first met at Stanford University as graduate students in Computer Science in 1995"*.[10]

From time to time, faculty members also start companies. For example, Bill New, a professor at Stanford Medical School, co-founded Nellcor in 1981, a medical electronics company that developed the oximeter as an indispensable aid for anesthesiologists. John Hennesy, who later became the President of Stanford University, was a co-founder of MIPS during the early 1980s. Silicon Graphics was founded by Jim Clark of Stanford's Computer Science Department. He later co-founded Netscape with a young research student, Marc Andreessen, from the University of Illinois. Apart from SGI and Netscape, Clark was also a co-founder of MyCFO and Healtheon. He later donated the funds to set up the Bio-X facility at Stanford. Its goal is to cross-fertilize medicine and biology with computer science and engineering. Ed Penhoet, Dean of the School of Public Health at the University of California, Berkeley, was a co-founder of Chiron. Many faculty members are also advisors, consultants, and board members of growing companies.

Corporate research institutes have also played a crucial role in generating technological expertise. Sometimes, as is the case with IBM's storage research center in San Jose, the pioneer of the Winchester disk drive, the parent can benefit considerably from the R&D innovations. Other times, the technical breakthroughs may not generate commercial profits for the parent but can benefit the ecosystem as a whole. A case in point is Xerox's Palo Alto Research Center or PARC. Bob Metcalfe, a research scientist at PARC, developed Ethernet, the foundation of local area network technology (LAN). He left Xerox in 1980 to form 3Com and went on to commercialize the technology. Similarly, Chuck Greschke and John Warnock developed the Postscript technology at Xerox PARC, but later spun-off to form Adobe Systems during the 1980s.

Local research institutes have also been responsible for several pioneering technologies. Optical disk drives, the mouse pointing device, and the magnetic ink character system for bank checks, for example, were all initially developed at the Stanford Research Institute (SRI International); Funding from public institutions, such as DARPA and NSF, or from pri-

---

[10] Source: www.google.com/corporate/history.html.

vate foundations, have also been critical in promoting fundamental re-search and facilitating its targeted application.[11]

A distinguishing feature of local universities is their openness towards information exchange, and the opportunities they provide for cross-fertilization between business and academia. Collaboration may take the form of joint research projects, exchange of staff, or hosting of conferences and networking forums. During the early 1990s, for example, UC Berke-ley's Haas School of Business started the first entrepreneurial incubator. The initial intention was to provide facilities for recent graduates who wanted to start their own ventures. It also offers its wide network of con-tacts in the legal, accounting and venture communities to help kick-start new ventures. Both Stanford and Berkeley leverage a broad range of ad-junct faculty in their medical, business, computer science, and engineering schools. These experienced entrepreneurs and professionals bring consid-erable experience, expertise and connections into the classroom.

The inter-linked processes of cross-fertilization, collaboration, network-ing, and information exchange are critical in the formation of new entre-preneurial ventures. Some may involve formal exchanges, job transfers, or temporary internships. Others may include collaborative research or R&D funding. This emphasis on nurturing "open borders" between universities and other components of the ecosystem has been a critical success factor in the commercialization of technology, the formation of new ventures, and the effective deployment of knowledge worker talent pools.

3.3.2 The Knowledge Hatcheries

In order to commercialize new ideas and technical breakthroughs, entre-preneurs need catalysts that can help to "hatch" their ideas by providing risk capital and early feedback. Angel investors and venture capitalists are the crucial catalysts in this context. They provide the capital, the expertise, the discipline, the network, and ultimately the "runway", to help fuel the growth of new entities.

Risk capital providers are a crucial component of this knowledge eco-system (Kenney and Florida 2000). Although one can over-state the role of venture capital in creating new companies, the community is responsible for accelerating the growth of new ventures by providing management know-how and market feedback, particularly during the crucial early

---

[11] A well-known case is the Internet. It was originally started by research funding from DARPA in 1973, in order to facilitate defense-related work between business and aca-demic institutions.

stages. Armed with networks of relevant contacts, they augment founding teams, as a venture evolves through different stages of development.

Silicon Valley is host to 22% of all venture-backed US start-ups and has the world's largest venture capital cluster (Zhang 2003, p. 40). The vast majority of venture capitalists are, in the main, responsible for funding new ventures after the initial "seed" stage. Typically, co-founders and private investors provide the seed funding to kick-start new ventures. This enables a start-up to develop an initial prototype, although several rounds of financing are typically needed to ramp up its growth. Critical activities include forging distribution channels, generating reference accounts, developing product enhancements, and engaging in global expansion. The principal role of the venture capitalists is to provide the funds necessary to "ramp" the enterprise into a substantial business by providing the "runway" so it can take off.[12]

Start-ups typically require several rounds of financing before they are in a position to generate sufficient revenue and earnings growth to embark on a liquidity event, such as an initial public offering, or an acquisition by another company. The "lead" investor of the initial consortium may help with follow-on financing and the IPO or the acquisition process.[13] Moreover, forged relationships between entrepreneurs and venture capitalists may endure over and above any one venture. In certain cases, they may fund the entrepreneurs' next start-up, or invite them to join their venture firm as a limited partner, general partner or a venture partner. A number of established venture capital firms have "entrepreneurs in residence" programs, an opportunity to leverage the knowledge, the capabilities, and the experience of seasoned entrepreneurs who may be in-between assignments. They may be enlisted to review deals, to jump-start a portfolio company, or to provide ideas for hatching a new start-up.

---

[12] One of the driving forces behind the historically high growth rates is the structure of venture capital limited partnerships that have typically lasted for around 7 years. In order to raise a subsequent or follow-on fund from its Limited Partners, the General Partners need to orchestrate some from of "liquidity event" for portfolio companies within the time span of the partnership. Venture capitalists often hedge their bets by investing in several firms vying for dominance in a given arena. Even the most seasoned venture capitalists may be unable to spot winners early on, as witnessed by their initially unfavorable reactions to ROLM, Seagate, and Adaptec, among many other successful ventures.

[13] Venture capitalists rarely invest alone in a deal, but with a group of other venture capital firms. For a historical description of the role of venture capital in Silicon Valley see Hambrecht (1984).

3.3.3 The Knowledge Generators

Silicon Valley is well known for its track record in generating a critical mass of technology companies. By far, the most significant building block of this knowledge ecosystem is the broad variety of fledgling start-ups, mid-sized adolescents, and agile giants that make up the diverse pool of knowledge "generators". They bring together the talent pools, the ideas, and the technical breakthroughs in order to create new products and innovative services for global markets.

Successful ventures experience rapid growth and evolve through various stages of development in quick succession. The embryonic phase spans the time that the business idea is first conceived to the time that the prototype is developed. This stage is characterized by formation of the founding team, development of a plan of action to capitalize on a new product idea, a market opportunity or a technological breakthrough, raising capital from "angels", seed venture capitalists, family and friends, and developing the first prototype. Typically, there is a high level of optimism, focus on funding and prototype development, formation of a core team with complementary capabilities, and informal interactions. Many ventures are terminated during this phase, if they fail to get sufficient market traction.

During the emergent phase, successful firms experience "lead user" acceptance to signal future viability. Critical tasks include validating the business proposition, improving the product prototype, forging collaborative partnerships and stimulating market demand. The organization may expand rapidly, and begins to outgrow its informal procedures and face-to-face communication.

Ventures that do not experience market growth and acceptance face a different reality. Some recalibrate their business trajectory and target different market segments. Others seek partners that augment their own capabilities. Some may sell their core technology to an established player. There are also many instances of the "living dead" (Bourgeois and Eisenhardt 1987); companies that would not survive without an artificial life support system; venture backers or angel investors who continue to fund their operations.

The ability to introduce strategic change and redirect priorities may be relatively uncomplicated for a one-product company. However, the situation is somewhat more complex when a start-up reaches "adolescence". By this phase, a company may have introduced a second product line and would have typically broadened its sales efforts to cover additional market segments. It faces competition from both, new start-ups (at times its own spin-offs), as well as established companies that may be lured by growing market acceptance for pioneering products and demystification of new technologies. This competitive "pincer envelopment" can result in loss of strategic focus and fragmentation of management attention.

Depending on the prevailing conditions in the stock market, by this stage the typical adolescent company would have typically gone through a "liquidity event". This may be an Initial Public Offering (IPO) or an acquisition by another company. Organizationally, it has to digest its growth and instill a sense of uniformity and discipline. Informal procedures give way to more formal processes to accommodate its growth and diversity. The founding team may have been augmented or replaced by professional managers. While some members of the original team may continue to stay, it is unlikely that they all retain their original power and influence. Some may have "burnt out" from the earlier years of "100 hour weeks"; others may simply be unable to cope with new managerial (rather than technical) challenges, or may want to pursue other interests, especially when their financial goals have been realized.

When it reaches the established phase of an "agile giant", a technology firm would have consolidated its position, and diversified into related businesses. This does not mean that it has a guaranteed future. Many have to re-position and re-invent themselves to address emerging market needs, as indicated by the HP-Compaq merger in recent years, or Intel's exit from the memory chip business during the 1980s (Burgelman 2002). However, in general, established technology firms are viewed as significant industry players.

Evolution through each stage depends on several factors: industry growth rates, market acceptance of new technologies, managerial competence, luck, and timing. The challenge is especially complex because of compressed time frames, steep oscillation in growth rates, quick emergence of global customers and competitors, rapid evolution of technological know-how, short product and market life cycles, and high expectations of knowledge workers.

Close physical proximity between different categories of knowledge generators is a critical success factor in Silicon Valley. It provides opportunities for spin-offs, cross-fertilization, and the creation of flexible collaborative and partnering arrangements. Moreover, pioneering products and services do not develop in a vacuum, or in isolation from the user community. The diverse range of technology companies and the presence of various industry clusters mean that the ecosystem is also host to early adopters and lead users of new products and services. These players provide the crucial early feedback and help recalibrate the design features and market positioning of new products and services. They test pioneering products' feasibility and usability so that engineering and marketing plans can be fine-tuned for later introduction into the broader market.

3.3.4 The Knowledge Lubricants

Hatching a technology venture is a complex process requiring the contribution of several specialists. However, a young start-up cannot afford to recruit all the required experts full time, even when their expertise is needed urgently. Moreover, in many technology sectors, product life cycles are short and windows of market opportunity are narrow. A crucial feature of the Silicon Valley ecosystem is the presence of a sophisticated service infrastructure of complementary specialists. They provide the necessary "lubrication" to get a new venture off the ground and enable start-ups to focus on their chosen steeple of expertise, rather than dissipate their energies across a broad range of peripheral or supporting activities. Lawyers, accountants, market researchers, headhunters, real estate brokers, technical advisors, and others, provide variable, specialist advice, as and when needed.

Contract manufacturing services are available to develop prototypes, or to engage in high volume or "peak load" manufacturing of sub-systems and finished goods. Specialized public relations firms provide assistance with strategic marketing, product packaging, trade shows, company logos and other collateral. Accounting and law firms have specialized technology practices. Executive search firms scan for new talent and help augment management teams of growing ventures. Real-estate firms have expertise in the provision of facilities, especially designed for high technology firms. For example, some may require clean rooms or highly purified water supplies; others set out to create a "campus"-like environment for knowledge workers.

Law firms also play a crucial role in the creation of new ventures (Suchman 2000). A handful of prominent law partnerships has grown in Silicon Valley by specializing in high technology services. They undertake several tasks, including initial incorporation and company name search, stock allocations, patent filings, alliance and acquisition agreements, preparation of public offering prospectus, SEC filings, and litigation support.

Typically, investors collaborate closely with law firms during several rounds of financing. A new start-up may be offered favorable fee structures, in the hope that as it grows, it would need substantial legal assistance and can pay accordingly. Senior partners typically forge long-standing relationships with the venture capital community and refer entrepreneurs to venture capitalists who have expertise or prior experience with a specific type of venture, a business category, or a vertical industry.

The "lubricants", whether they are lawyers, accountants, headhunters or specialist contractors, provide a broad range of complementary services. If a start-up needs to prototype an integrated circuit to test a new design, it can be fabricated in a matter of days; if it needs a booth for a trade show, it can be put together over a weekend; if it requires specialized advice, it can be provided by a phone call.

3.4   The Ecosystem's "Climate"

Just as species in a biological ecosystem share a common climate, so do the various building blocks of the Silicon Valley ecosystem. We use the term "climate" to refer to operating norms and ground rules that characterize common practices within the ecosystem. Whereas the building blocks described earlier are analogous to the "anatomy" of the ecosystem, the "climate" represents its "personality". A cumulative result of historical precedents, successful business recipes, and legendary role models, these norms are about the business of technology venturing and the rules by which the game is played.

The ecosystem's climatic conditions are critical in understanding the macro processes that enable the ecosystem to achieve and sustain a certain measure of super-flexibility. Just like the climate in a natural ecosystem, Silicon Valley's climate is subject to continuous ebbs and flows; sometimes weather patterns can be predicted; othertimes they evolve unexpectedly. The following section describes broad climatic conditions that we have observed over time and that we believe characterize the ecosystem's *modus operandi*.

3.4.1 Goal-Driven Work Ethic and Eternal Optimism

A critical ingredient of the Silicon Valley ecosystem is the pioneering spirit and the relentless work ethic. The entrepreneurial culture was initially born out of a Californian history of pioneers making the perilous journey over the Rocky Mountains, coupled with the legacy of the Gold Rush (Kotkin and Grabowicz 1982). The culture ingrained over time and is characterized by hard work, goal-driven action, and focused specialization.

After World War II, many ex-servicemen moved to the Bay area, encouraged and subsidized to attend universities and undertake further education. This provided an educated and disciplined workforce for the early-generation companies, such as Hewlett Packard, Varian, Watkins Johnson and Lockheed. With the growing strategic importance of the Pacific Rim and the increasing technological intensity of the "Cold War", these educated GI's provided a disciplined and eager workforce that helped build many Valley companies during the 1950's and the 1960s. As this talent pool matured and rose to executive positions, the culture of many of the early pioneers was infused with strong work ethic, coupled with discipline and integrity.

This generation was later augmented by troops returning first from Korea, and later from Vietnam. Ironically the contrast between this "work hard/play hard" lifestyle was brought into sharp focus when contrasted with the rise of the "hippy" movement in San Francisco during the late 60s and the 70s. Initially, the two worlds collided, but, over time, the two ends of the generational spectrum gradually coalesced.[14] We suggest that the fusion of the two worlds has played a critical role in forging the disciplined, yet creative, spirit of Silicon Valley.[15]

Historically, Silicon Valley entrepreneurs have exhibited many of the qualities of the early pioneers. They have taken enormous risks, innovated in areas that many said couldn't be done, worked long hours over extended time frames, showed passionate commitment to their ventures, and even suffered personal problems, while developing a product or building an enterprise.

This is not to suggest that all entrepreneurs in Silicon Valley are so passionate about their ventures that generating wealth is not on their radar screen. Indeed, attitudes towards wealth generation changed considerably during the Internet boom years, with the influx of a younger generation and new talent into the area. Financial goals and a quick "exit strategy" became the critical motivational drivers. However, if financial rewards were the only or the ultimate goal, it would be difficult to explain the phenomenon of "serial entrepreneurs". It does suggest, however, that those who have become legends in Silicon Valley, or who are inspirational role models, do exhibit those "passionate" qualities. Their primary goal is not simply financial gain. There are emotional and intellectual drivers as well.

---

[14] When Remedy, an enterprise software company in the helpdesk business, took its public offering road show to Wall Street and the City of London, the theme from Led Zeppelin song "Stairway to Heaven" was used as incidental music.

[15] This blending of dual cultures is underscored by some of the anecdotal observations we have heard from long-standing Valley entrepreneurs. They describe effective teams as a combination of the "suits" and the "cowboys".

3.4.2 Limited "Safety Net" and Minimal "Life Support System"

Silicon Valley is a Darwinian ecosystem. There are no safety nets in that "only the fit survive". In this context, fitness is about competence, intelligence, adaptability and initiative, as well as prudent timing and luck. Fitness applies to both, individuals as well as enterprises, and can be assessed in terms of how well individual skills and capabilities, as well as enterprise products and services, match emerging opportunities. A limited life support system means that nothing can be sustained artificially for long. From the standpoint of super-flexibility, this climatic condition, while brutal at times, can also facilitate rapid adaptation. For example, the high cost of living in the area has led many companies to move, initially low-skilled jobs, out of Silicon Valley to other locations and countries. In recent years, even core activities are being moved offshore to countries such as India and China where technical talent is cheaper and readily available (Hagel 2004). There has also been a major shift in patterns of "cluster employment", reflecting market realities and changing conditions. According to 2003 Index of Joint Venture Silicon Valley, during 1992-2001, employment in defense and aerospace fell by 8%, reflecting reduced levels of defense expenditure after the end of the Cold War, while employment in software increased from 7% to 21%.

Another dimension of the adaptation process, boosted by the idea of a limited life support system, is the "swarm effect". Just like bees around honey, investors and entrepreneurs throng around the latest new idea, or the new "category". This swarm effect ramps up experimentation in innovative arenas rather quickly. However, since there are no safety nets, entrepreneurs and investors also "stampede" away from failed concepts and recipes. So if an idea goes out of favor, or does not pay off as initially promised, its demise is swift. The same principle also applies to new ventures. If a venture is no longer viable, disengagement can be measured in terms of weeks, not months or years. By the same token, if something happens to change an out-of-favor technology or a business concept, especially if justified by tangible market evidence, investors "re-brand" and quickly move back into the area. The emphasis is on pragmatism or "what works", rather than idealism or "what should work".

A limited "life support system", combined with an overarching quest for pragmatism, rather than perfection, is a critical catalyst for adaptation and entrepreneurship. This spirit is further reinforced by the success of "Davids" versus "Goliaths", the collapse of over-funded start-ups that have a great deal of initial credibility, and the dynamic evolution of large companies in the area. For example, as indicated in Table 5, half of those entities listed as the "forty largest technology" firms twenty years ago, no longer exist. Indeed "only four firms on the 2002 list are survivors from the 1982 list. More than half of the 2002 top firms were not even founded in 1982. Each year's list, on average, includes 23 new firms." (Zhang 2003, p. 6).

1982	2002
Hewlett-Packard	Hewlett-Packard
National Semiconductor	Intel
Intel	Cisco
Memorex	SUN Microsystems
Varian	Solectron
Environtech	Oracle
Ampex	Agilent
Raychem	Applied Materials
Amdahl	Apple
Tymshare	Seagate
AMD	AMD
ROLM	Sanmina-SCI
Four Phase Systems	JDS Uniphase
Cooper Labs	3Com
Intersil	LSI Logic
SRI International	Maxtor
Spectraphysics	National Semiconductor
American Microsystems	KLA Tencor
Watkins Johnson	Atmel
Qume	SGI
Measurex	Bell Microproducts
Tandem	Siebel
Plantronics	Xilinx
Monolithic	Maxim Integrated
URS	Palm
Tab Products	Lam Research
Siliconix	Quantum
Dysan	Altera
Racal-Vadic	Electronic Arts
Triad Systems	Cypress Semiconductor
Xidex	Cadence Design
Avantek	Adobe Systems
Siltec	Intuit
Quadrex	Veritas Software
Coherent	Novellus Systems
Verbatim	Yahoo
Anderson-Jacobson	Network Appliance

Table 5. Top twenty firms in Silicon Valley, 1982 & 2002 (Source Zhang 2003)

3.4.3 Collaborative Partnerships and Recombinant Innovations

The Silicon Valley ecosystem comprises several clusters of specialized en-terprises with multi-faceted collaborative relationships. Collectively, the groupings of knowledge originators, hatcheries, lubricants, and generators, provide "meta" flexibility at the level of the ecosystem. This is largely achieved through a process of "inter-linked specialization and complemen-tary collaboration"[16], Each firm focuses on what it does best and leverages others' capabilities for complementary activities. A start-up can focus on its technical design, and use other entities for prototype development, manufacturing, market research, public relations, advertising, and staffing, Established firms acquire young companies with breakthrough innova-tions, as indicated by Cisco's growth-by-acquisition strategy during the 1990s. Mid-sized adolescents become distribution channels for emerging start-ups.

Collaborative partnerships are the lifeblood of the ecosystem. They are forged between individuals when they coalesce into entrepreneurial found-ing teams; venture capitalists forge alliances in the form of a syndicate to co-invest in a new venture. Alliances are forged between established and emerging firms for marketing, manufacturing, development, or distribution purposes, and with contractors, vendors, and outsourcers for providing complementary capabilities.[17] These arrangements are helpful for small start-ups, wishing to penetrate challenging markets, or for larger firms, in-tending to fill their pipelines and maintain the flow of innovative products.

The innovation process in Silicon Valley reflects this emphasis on col-laboration and complementarities. It is as much about blending and com-bining, through collaborative processes, as it is about breakthroughs in new fields. Often an end-of-life technology can be refreshed and aug-mented by the addition of something new. Or something that was only possible to do in a given domain can be transposed to another.

---

[16] The notion of "diverse specialization" was first discussed by Piore and Sabel (1984).

[17] Global alliances have been a historic feature of Silicon Valley. For example, The now-defunct personal communications start-up, EO, had a number of global partners, includ-ing AT&T, Matsushita, Marubeni, amongst others, only 18 months into the venture's life-cycle, before being acquired by AT&T. 3DO, a multimedia firm founded by Trip Hawkins, the founder of Electronic Arts, was initially a joint venture between Time Warner, Matsushita and Electronic Arts. Similarly, General Magic, the personal com-munications software company and an Apple spin-off, was initially forged through an alliance between Apple, AT&T, Philips and Sony. Quantum Corporation, the disk drive firm, allied itself with Matsushita, as its manufacturing partner, during the 1980s. Aus-pex Systems, the file server company, forged an alliance with Fuji-Xerox in its forma-tive years, involving both investments and distribution agreements.

Consider, for example, how removable Winchester disk drives borrowed much from the technology of floppy disk drives and enhanced input/output controller, first with Syquest cartridges, and later with Zip drives; or how ROLM pioneered the digital PBX by applying minicomputer digital technology to the telecommunications equipment business.

3.5   Super-Flexibility and the Ecosystem

Silicon Valley's climate impacts the creation and demise of new enterprises as well as the dynamics of the adaptation process. It is not sufficient to create the anatomical building blocks, without considering the climate's impact on the ecosystem. Having venture capital, without the ability to "pull the plug" at the right time, is not conducive to creating viable, new ventures. Similarly, having world-class universities and research laboratories, without developing an open attitude to partnering and information sharing, does not lead to the generation of a critical mass of innovative enterprises. Silicon Valley should be understood in the context of both, its anatomy as well as its personality. Taken as a whole, it provides a dynamic and innovative laboratory for studying super-flexibility.

The constellation of knowledge originators, hatcheries, generators and lubricants in Silicon Valley, characterize a dynamic ecosystem of independent, yet complementary, entities, communities, and cultures. The ecosystem strives to be super-flexible by being robust as well as versatile. Since each component is modular and autonomous, the ecosystem can withstand shocks and perturbations. If one of its building blocks performs badly or goes out of business, its demise is not necessarily detrimental for the entire ecosystem. It is also versatile in that new competencies can be added quickly without going through extensive "re-modeling". This process can further enhance and upgrade the capabilities of the ecosystem as a whole.

During the past 30 years, Silicon Valley has generated a critical mass of global, knowledge enterprises, whose innovative products and technologies have transformed the global economy. The ecosystem provides an anchor of stability within which incumbent firms and new start-ups can flourish and become a source of innovation and employment. Yet it adapts to new realities through a process of "recycling" where failed ventures and terminated initiatives are re-configured, blended, and re-packaged in order to adapt to emerging challenges and opportunities. The dynamic concept of "recycling", our first action principle, will be explored in further detail in Chapter 4.

4 Recycling: Life after Death in the Ecosystem

How do entrepreneurial firms interact with this versatile ecosystem? How does the ecosystem adapt to the ups and downs of business cycles and innovation loops? How does it enhance an enterprise's capacity to become super-flexible? The principle of "recycling" may be a partial explanation. It describes how talent, ideas, products, and technologies are re-blended, reconfigured, re-packaged, and ultimately recycled. Recycling, we propose, is the cornerstone of the adaptation process in Silicon Valley. It enables the ecosystem to harness "failures" and to become revitalized in the process.

The principle of recycling is a critical feature of Silicon Valley's ecosystem dynamics, and its ability to provide a super-flexible context for entrepreneurs and enterprises. During periods of rapid growth, there is a need to capitalize on market opportunities and technological innovations with considerable agility and versatility. During economic downturns, it is important to degrade gracefully, leverage failed initiatives and learn from setbacks. As indicated in the next four chapters, "recycling" is an important meta principle to understand since it has a catalytic impact on the adaptive capacity of business enterprises. This chapter focuses on the enabling mechanisms that facilitate recycling. It is a precursor to our discussion of the core principles, discussed in chapters 5 through 8 that facilitate super-flexibility at the enterprise level.

The rationale behind "re-cycling" is easy to comprehend. Operating in knowledge-based arenas is analogous to being a pioneer, where there is no perfect information and there are no pre-existing blueprints for success. Ultimately, business propositions have to be tested "on the ground", pass the market traction test, and respond to lead-user feedback. Just as pioneers may go down many "blind alleys", entrepreneurs often pursue business propositions that may not succeed and become branded as "failures". This situation presents a dilemma: How to nurture, encourage, and facilitate rapid experimentation and prototyping, while minimizing the negative stigma and the waste of resources typically associated with failed ventures.

We propose that "recycling" facilitates "empirical pragmatism", enabling varied and novel re-configurations of knowledge, talent, technologies, and resources. The process makes it possible for new firms and novel products to rise from the ashes of "failed" initiatives. Failure is a necessary feature of the entrepreneurial, risk-taking process, and there is a high mortality rate associated with new ventures. However, it is also crucial for adaptation. Just as plants and animals adapt to their surroundings through evolutionary processes, so do entrepreneurs and knowledge workers. There is life after death in this ecosystem in that the demise of a firm, or the failure of a product, may lead to the formation of other entities, and the development of innovative products and services. The remainder of this chapter describes different mechanisms used to facilitate recycling and illustrates their use in the context of the Silicon Valley ecosystem.

4.1 Recycling Mechanisms

Several mechanisms explain how recycling takes place in Silicon Valley and why it is a valued contributor to super-flexibility. It is difficult to disentangle these into separate categories. They typically overlap and are closely related to one another. The important point to note is that "recycling" applies to products, technologies, and resources, as well as talent, information, and know-how.

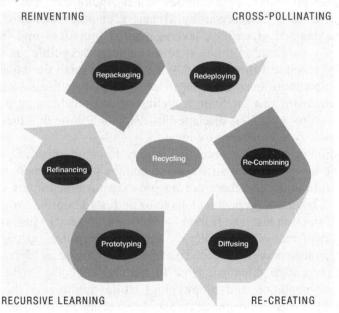

Figure 4. Recycling mechanisms

We have observed four categories of recycling mechanisms at work. As depicted in Figure 4, these include: recycling by "re-creating", inducing high birth rates for new ventures; recycling by "cross-pollinating" through talent mobility and "information diffusion"; recycling by "recursive learning" through exploring, prototyping, and failing; and recycling by "reinventing" through re-financing, re-combining and re-packaging.

4.1.1 Recycling by Re-Creating: High Birth Rates for New Ventures

A striking feature of Silicon Valley is the high birth rate for new ventures. According to a recent study, 29,000 high tech companies were founded in Silicon Valley from 1990-2000 (Zhang 2003). During the same time frame, new ventures, or those started after 1990, accounted for most of the employment growth in the area.[18] We suggest that this high birth rate facilitates the recycling process, in that the most successful elements of failed ventures can be blended into new ones.

New ventures are founded in several ways. They may be induced by venture capitalists, recognizing growth opportunities presented by emerging technologies. They may also start accidentally, through the efforts of enthusiasts and hobbyists. Venture formation may be triggered by collaborative research programs, or by graduate students' doctoral studies. Some are formed by intact teams, spinning off from existing companies, by "serial" entrepreneurs, or by complementary experts from different entities.[19]

As indicated in Chapter 3, the ecosystem is a catalyst for networking among founding teams. Many initially get to know one another at universities, or are introduced to each other by investors. They may have also forged collaborative relationships in their previous relationships as customers, vendors, colleagues, or even competitors.

Historically, the birth of many well-known technology companies has been linked to technology enthusiasts. They may have developed the initial prototype for their own use, or because of their personal interest. Well-known examples include HP and Apple Computer. Yahoo is a more recent example. The business idea started as a "hobby" for Jerry Yang and David Filo, its two founders, while they were still graduate students at Stanford. Called "Jerry's Guide to the World Wide Web", it was an informal mechanism for Jerry, David and their friends to navigate the net: *"In the early days, it was clearly something for our own use ... then after other people started using it, it became something for them to use ... nothing more than just kind of a hobby."*[20]

"Serial" entrepreneurs also contribute to high venture birth rates. As depicted in Figure 5, and discussed later in the chapter, Alan Shugart parted

---

[18] In 2001, start-ups less than five years old employed 159,300 people in the area (Zhang 2003, p. 11).

[19] Every year, venture capital firms fund approximately 300-500 new ventures in Silicon Valley. However, this is only a fraction of new ventures. Many are "boot-strapped", self-funded, or kick-started through financial assistance from family, friends, and business "angels".

[20] Source: Video case study "Yahoo: Jerry and Dave's Excellent Venture", Stanford University, October 1997.

company with Shugart Associates during the mid-1970s. He went on to co-found Seagate Technology in 1979 with another Shugart co-founder, Finis Conner. Conner left Seagate to found his own company, Conner Peripherals, during the mid-1980s. It became one of the fastest growing companies in the US business history Similarly, Larry Boucher, left his first entrepreneurial venture, Adaptec, to co-found Auspex Systems in 1987, and then moved on to start a new company, Alacritech, in 1997. Other well-known "serial" entrepreneurs include Jim Clark (SGI, Netscape, Healtheon, My-CFO), Steve Jobs (Apple, Next, Pixar), Trip Hawkins (Electronic Arts, 3DO), and Tom Siebel (Gain Technology and Siebel Systems).

Another source of new ventures can be best described as "re-starts". These refer to ventures that are acquired by larger firms but later flounder. They can also be venture-backed start-ups that do not receive follow-on funding; or they may be ventures where the original founders and investors are "washed out" during later rounds of financing. Some are able to rise from the ashes of the failing parent or may be bought out to achieve independent viability.

Re-starts are an important source of new ventures. It is rare to get a start up right the first time. Innovations take time to mature and may be too early for the target market. As we argue in chapter 6, a critical entrepreneurial skill is the willingness and the ability to recalibrate product features and marketing recipes until they address user needs. Re-starts are a good illustration of the recalibration process at work.

Scientists' desire to commercialize pioneering ideas is yet another trigger for venture formation, especially in biotechnology and life sciences. Well-known examples are Boyer and Cohen, the co-founders of Genentech, and Thomas Fogarty, the inventor of the catheter, who later founded a venture capital firm, specializing in life sciences. Nelcor was founded by Bill New, who left Stanford Medical School during the late 1980s to commercialize the oxymeter as an aid to anesthesiologists. Carver Mead, a professor at Cal Tech, and a pioneer in the field of neural processors, joined forces with Frederico Fagin, founder of Zilog, to start Synaptics. Syntex commercialized Carl Dersai's Nobel Prize winning discovery of the contraceptive pill. William Sharpe, the Noble Prize winner and Stanford professor, co-founded Financial Engines, during the late 1990s.

Spin-offs from existing firms are also a significant source of new venture formation. A recent study (Zhang 2003, Table 6) confirms Silicon Valley's relatively high birth rates, in terms of venture-backed spin-offs from established companies: *"...leading firms in Silicon Valley significantly outperformed their counterparts in the Boston area in terms of producing entrepreneurs ... together DEC and Raytheon spun off 48 venture-backed start-ups ... about half of the 99 spin-offs from HP ... Apple has spun off 71 venture-backed start-ups, whereas Lotus in the Boston area (has) 26 spin-offs... Even IBM ... with a presence in both areas, has 77 spin-offs in Silicon Valley, compared to 23 in the Boston area."* (Zhang, pp. 50-51).

The point to note is that irrespective of their origin or backing, the high venture birth rates, and the blending of talent and ideas from "failed" ventures into new ones, boosts the innovation process, leverages existing know-how, generates new insights, and creates an environment that is conducive to enterprise creation.

Silicon Valley	Employee Founders	Venture Capital backed Spin-off Start-ups	Boston Area	Employee Founders	Venture Capital backed Spin-off Start-ups
Apple	94	71	Data General	13	13
Cisco	41	35	DEC	52	41
HP	117	99	EMC	9	6
Intel	76	68	Lotus	29	26
Oracle	73	57	Prime	5	5
SGI	50	37	Raytheon	7	7
SUN	101	79	Wang	11	11
IBM	82	77	IBM	23	23

Table 6. Spin-offs from leading firms in Silicon Valley and the Boston area (Source: Zhang, 2003, p. 50)

4.1.2 Recycling by Cross-Pollinating: Talent Re-Deployment and Information Diffusion

Silicon Valley enjoys a "regional advantage" partly because its culture encourages knowledge workers to move between entities (Saxenian 1994). Indeed, there is considerable talent mobility and re-deployment between the different building blocks of Silicon Valley. Executives move from high tech companies into venture capital and consulting. Engineers change jobs by moving just "down the road" to another firm. Consultants take on new roles as investors and executives. Many leave the relative security of an established firm to join a small venture, or to start their own companies.

There are many examples of this mobility in Silicon Valley, dating back to its pioneering days. For example, Gene Kleiner, founding partner of Kleiner Perkins, Caufield & Byers (KPCB), one of the Valley's leading venture capital firms, was previously at Fairchild Semiconductor. Tom Jermoluk, the former CEO of Silicon Graphics, moved to Excite@Home, the venture-backed start-up during the early 1990s, and went on to become a partner with KPCB. He joined other entrepreneurs, @Home's co-founder Will Hearst, Oracle's former COO, Ray Lane, and SUN's co-founder, Vinod Khosla, who had also joined the firm. George Sollman, the former President of the American Electronics Association, moved from Shugart, the disk drive company, to the venture capital community, and later became the turnaround CEO of a voice-messaging firm, Centigram, before starting his own venture, @Motion, in 1997.

This high degree of mobility is not limited to the venture community. For example, Stig Hagstrom, who was responsible for one of the research labs at Xerox PARC, moved to Stanford University's Material Science Department and later founded the Center for Innovations in Learning at Stanford in 2002. Mario Rosati, the co-founder of the technology law practice, Wilson Sonsini Goodrich & Rosati, became an adjunct professor at the Haas School of Business, University of California, Berkeley.

Mobility is just as common among executives who may work for competing firms. For example, after stepping down as the Chief Operating Officer of Seagate Technology, Tom Mitchell became a co-founder of the competing disk drive firm, Conner Peripherals, and returned to Seagate, after it acquired Conner. Jim Bagley and Steve Newberry, the CEO and COO of Lam Research, were both members of the top executive team at Applied Materials, Lam's competitor.

At its core, the ecosystem operates through an inter-connected network of personal relationships, a long-standing feature of Silicon Valley. Shugart, the pioneering disk drive company, was co-founded by eleven former colleagues. They had worked together for IBM and Memorex. Shockley Laboratories was the initial setting that brought together Fairchild's founding team.

As indicated in Figure 5, informal networks are forged in several ways. They may be forged accidentally, among those with the same hobby or even those attending the same sports or social clubs. Universities, research labs, and established firms, like HP, Intel, or Oracle, may be the initial setting for bringing entrepreneurial teams together. Relationships may be forged deliberately through referrals from lawyers, accountants, venture capitalists and other ecosystem members. Overall, networks are the hub of activity in Silicon Valley. They facilitate talent mobility and ultimately, recycling, in a dynamic ecosystem.

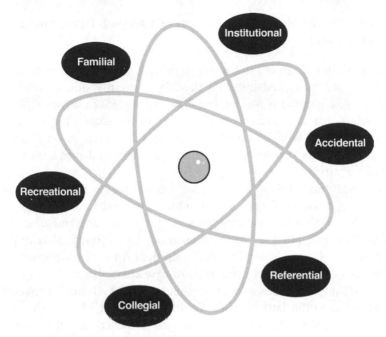

Figure 5. Antecedents for forging informal networks

Cross-pollination is not limited to talent mobility. It also applies to rapid diffusion of information. It is difficult to keep secrets in Silicon Valley due to several factors. These include close physical proximity between companies, early adoption of new technologies, fast moving nature of high technology industries, inter-firm mobility of knowledge workers, and extensive reliance on contractors, partners and vendors. Ideas are quickly picked up, transferred and bounced around in formal as well as informal exchanges. The center of gravity of the strategic problem is not just knowing what to do, but also how and when to do it.

In addition, information has a short "half-life" in high technology industries. New products are alpha and beta-tested by early adopters. Pioneering firms have to release technical information to their vendors, contractors and partners. Moreover, due to the rapid pace of change, information about products, markets, and competitors become quickly obsolete. Formal and informal exchanges among "techno-evangelists" are another source of information diffusion. These individuals have a passion for their technical interests and often interact on the Net, at user group meetings, conferences, trade shows, and other industry or networking forums. The ecosystem provides the setting within which knowledge workers can exchange information and ideas. An idea that may have failed at one time in a particular context may be re-used later in a different setting and eventually pay off.

4.1.3 Recycling by Recursive Learning: Exploring, Prototyping, and Failing

In Silicon Valley there is little or no stigma attached to honest failure. Entrepreneurs are measured by what they are currently doing, not by what they did in the past. This means that they can engage in novel experiments in the belief that it is immeasurably better to try something risky and to fail, rather than to wonder about what might have been. Even if a venture fails, entrepreneurs can learn from the experiment and move on to start a successful entity.

Positive attitudes towards failure are critical to the ultimate success of the recycling process. Many new products succeed because they are refined as the result of a learning process, during which innovators clearly learn by "doing"; but they learn even more by "failing" (Maidique and Zirger 1984, 1985). These "failures" may lead to a re-assessment of the original concepts and the development of new alternatives.

Apple III and Lisa are two classic examples of "failed" products that eventually led to the launch of the highly successful Macintosh. Intended to be a successor to the Apple II, Lisa was launched in 1983, as the first downturn of the PC era began to bite in Silicon Valley. While it was a technologically sophisticated computer, it was expensive and did not sell well. The design was later recalibrated and the technology was recycled into a smaller, simpler, and cheaper product. The new product, called Macintosh, was introduced in 1984 and has been a major industry success, as was its later successor, the iMac. Similarly, after Handspring merged with its competitor, Palm, in 2003, the combined teams rapidly repackaged the Treo communicator/organizer as a Palm product and re-launched it.

The ability of the ecosystem to recycle know-how is closely linked to a tolerant attitude towards failure. Many entrepreneurs do not even use the word "failure" as part of their vocabulary. Instead failures are viewed as "setbacks", temporary challenges to be solved, and critical learning opportunities. Today's failure becomes the crucial ingredient for tomorrow's successful recipe. Knowledge workers who participate in failed start-ups, learn from their mistakes and apply the lessons to their later assignments. Many seasoned venture capitalists prefer to fund entrepreneurs who have lots of "scar tissue" from previous "failures". The assumption is that it is unlikely that they would repeat the same mistakes twice. Past success, on the other hand, can breed arrogance and over-confidence. It can limit an entrepreneur's ability to learn from tangible market feedback.

The essence of recursive learning is exploring, prototyping, generating feedback, experiencing setbacks, and recalibrating. Attitudes towards failure are especially critical when there are no historical precedents or success recipes for a given product or market segment. Even with the most elaborate planning and focus group meetings, it may not be clear, ahead of time, how customers are likely to react to a new class of product. The related principle of "recalibration", that facilitates recursive learning, will be further discussed in Chapter 6.

4.1.4 Recycling by Re-Inventing: Re-Financing, Re-Packaging, and Re-Combining

Another approach to recycling is through re-invention. The process entails selecting the most effective ingredients of an unsuccessful business proposition, or a failed product or a venture, combining these with some novel ingredients, and re-introducing the previous "failure" in a new form. Several mechanisms facilitate the re-invention process. These include re-financing a venture with new investors and revised valuations, re-packaging a product with new features, a new name and a new logo, or even combining a number of ventures in the same arena, under a new corporate umbrella, giving it a new identity and a new focus.

The move to repackage is most evident during the down-cycles of the Valley. It is also a low cost method of developing new products. An early example was the development of hard cards by Quantum in the 1980's, at a time when most users increased their computers' storage capacity by adding a disk drive and an I/O controller card. Another example was the fusion of Winchester technology into a removable disk storage device. The product that won at the end was the Zip drive from Iomega. It evolved from the Bernoulli drive and removable Winchester, fused together with I/O controller technology.

Other well-known examples of product re-invention are the repackaging of the Macintosh as the new iMac during the late 1990s, and the evolution of the PalmPilot. The latter was first developed as a hand held game console called the "Zoomer". Due to cost constraints, the developers adapted the device and turned it into what later became the "Palm Pilot". US Robotics acquired the company just as the product began to take off. US Robotics was itself acquired by 3Com for its networking technology. Palm was later spun off by 3Com as an independent company. The original developers of "PalmPilot" left to found Handspring, and developed the "Visor". In the wake of the most recent Valley downturn, Palm merged with Handspring in 2003.

Re-invention can also be achieved by combining ventures that compete in the same arena. Venture capitalists, for example, often combine several ventures in order to get "critical mass", to gain credibility, to reduce overhead, to expand product portfolios, to put together an effective marketing team with a solid technical team. or to combine balance sheets in preparation for a public offering or an acquisition. A case in point is the merger between Palm and Handspring in 2003, or the merger between Macromind and Authorware, now Macromedia, during the early 1990s.

This trend was further amplified during the downturn of 2002/3 for ventures with common investors. A good example was the merger between Cross-Weave and AmberPoint, funded by Sutter Hill Ventures and Norwest Venture Partners.[21] Cross-Weave had received $10.6 million in 1999 in two rounds of financing. AmberPoint raised $9.1 million in 2001 and a second round of $13.6 million in November 2002. While in some senses this could be seen as an acquisition, in that only a handful of CrossWeave's employees joined AmberPoint, the benefits for the investors were substantial.

Re-packaging often requires a new management team, new investors, and new valuations to kick-start languishing ventures. During the growth cycle, a venture capital firm's portfolio will expand, either by focusing on early stage deals or by accelerating Series B & C stage companies ready for an Initial Public Offering. During downturns, however, the situation changes considerably. Venture capital firms usually have insufficient funds to expand all the enterprises in their portfolio. The poorer performers, or those with limited prospects, are discontinued. Even those that receive follow-on funding during downturns are often "washed out" through a re-valuation of previous equity distributions. The objective is to take a fresh look at the portfolio and to be factually objective, minimizing the psychological and emotional commitment that former investors may have to the "original" business direction and value proposition.

Although the original investors may be "washed out", new executives and new investors are brought in, and a "refreshed" trajectory for the business may follow. This is yet another mechanism for adaptation. However, although the process enables a new team to take a fresh look at the business prospects and minimizes potential escalation to a failed course of action, the challenge is to ensure that re-valuation does not negatively motivate early employees who may still be critical to its eventual success.

---

[21] Source: The Venture Capital Analyst, Venture One April 2003 ,p. 7.

4.2 Case History

The following case vignette partly illustrates recycling at work. Our intention is to show how the demise of a company does not necessarily go to
waste, and how its talent pool, technologies and products can be re-cycled
into the broader ecosystem. Our focus is on a pioneering company in the
disk drive industry that no longer exists. However, its demise led to the
formation of other disk drive entities and to the migration of its talent pool
to several other ventures. Fundamentally, the vignette shows adaptive
processes that can be facilitated by recycling.

Shugart Associates was a pioneering disk drive company in Silicon Valley during the mid-1970s and early 1980s. Its eleven co-founders had previously worked together at IBM and Memorex. Each co-founder invested
$5000 to start the company in 1973, and later received venture capital
backing from Bill Hambrecht of the venture firm Hambrecht & Quist, and
John Friedenrich at Donaldson Lufkin and Jenerette.

At first, the company was engaged in the parallel development of three
products: an OEM disk drive, an OEM printer and a desktop computer system. The founding CEO, Alan Shugart, left the company shortly afterwards to be succeeded by another member of the co-founding team, Don
Massaro, who re-focused the business on disk drives.

Shugart's first product, an 8-inch floppy disk drive, was introduced in
May 1973 with volume shipments beginning in July 1973. It introduced
the double-density 8-inch floppy disk drives in April 1975. This was followed by another innovation that has become part of Silicon Valley folk-
lore. As discussed in Chapter 5, the SA400, 5.25-inch floppy disk drive
was introduced in September 1976 and became a major success. It accelerated the company's growth, with revenues rising to $18.14 million by
1977. Shugart augmented its product line by developing an 8 inch Winchester disk drive. Much like the earlier SA-400, its development was
funded by two of its customers.

As recounted in Chapter 5, the 5.25-inch floppy disk drive became an
industry standard, fueling the meteoric growth of word processing systems
during the late 1970's and early 1980's. Shugart was ideally positioned to
exploit the soon-to-emerge personal computer market. At this time, market
conditions precluded a public offering so it was not a favored "liquidity
event".

Xerox acquired Shugart in 1978 together with other companies specializing in related products, including printing pioneers, Diablo and Versatec.
The acquisitions were an important element of Xerox's focus on its office
automation strategy. Fueled by increasing demand for the 5.25-inch floppy

and other product lines, Shugart's revenues continued to grow rapidly. Even before the acquisition, however, several members of its management team and engineering staff had left the company; some to form "niche" disk drive start-ups, others to join competing firms. For example, two members of Shugart's core team, Jim McCoy and David Brown, joined forces with System Industries' Jim Patterson, to co-found Quantum in 1980.

In 1981, not yet weakened by these spin-offs and Japanese competition, Shugart continued to innovate and prosper. It pioneered, among others, the Shugart Associates Standard Interface or SASI, so that systems integrators could quickly develop the micro-code to allow Winchester disk drives to meet the unique operating systems requirements of different computer system manufacturers. Eventually, this product became an industry standard, enabling the interchangeability of disk drives between different and previously incompatible computer systems.

SASI was the forerunner of what became the widely accepted SCSI standard, "controlling" both, IBM PCs (along with PC-compatibles) and the Apple Macintosh. Ironically, the team who pioneered the SASI innovation had previously proposed creating a disk drive controller business as part of Xerox's efforts to stimulate internal ventures. However, at the time the business proposition was rejected. The "controller" team, led by Larry Boucher, left Shugart and founded Adaptec in 1981. During this period, Shugart was also engaged in other product development initiatives, including the optical disk drive technology. In this case, a subsidiary unit, Optimem, was established as an international strategic alliance between Xerox and SGS Thomson of France. Another venture unit was also created to develop the 3.5-inch floppy disk drive, destined for portable computers.

Between 1981 and 1983, Shugart's revenues grew considerably, although at the same time, industry and competitive dynamics were being transformed. Several niche spin-offs, together with other start-ups, began to erode selected parts of its business. Japanese manufacturers had made aggressive inroads into the low-end floppy disk drive market by competing on the basis of low price and high quality. IBM sourced the floppy disk drive for its new PC from Tandon, whose Indian founder had established low cost manufacturing operations in India. Yet Shugart was still, at this stage, the leading "across-the-board" supplier of rotating memory products. Cost reduction strategies, especially related to "offshore manufacturing", would become the decisive competitive battle.

Following an abrupt industry downturn that resulted in two years of consecutive losses, Xerox divested Shugart between 1985 and 1986. By this time, Xerox was facing the cash needs of its new acquisition in the insurance industry, Crum and Forster. The floppy disk business, accounting for about one third of Shugart's revenues, was sold off to its Japanese joint venture partner, Matsushita. Its Winchester disk drive division was dissolved, and its optical disk drive unit, Optimem, was sold to Cipher Data, itself later acquired by Archive. The much paired down Shugart, stripped of its 5.25-inch and pioneering 3.5-inch floppy and Winchester lines, was sold off to a group of investors. It continued to operate for some time as a service and distribution center in Los Angeles, focusing on drive-refurbishing and end-of-life products.

Interestingly, Don Massaro, who replaced Alan Shugart as President of Shugart, became CEO of Xerox Printing Division. He left Xerox to co-found Metaphor Computers with Dave Liddle, the co-inventor of Ethernet at Xerox PARC. Massaro later became VP of Marketing at Conner Peripherals and then spun off with a Conner co-founder, Bill Schraeder, to start Diamond Multimedia. Massaro then went on to re-start Array Networks, funded by US Venture Partners and his former partner, Dave Liddle. Array Networks was later fused with Inetd.com and re-started in Massaro's garage as Reconnex in 2003.

Most analyses of Shugart would typically end with its disengagement. Using our traditional optic, the company would be viewed as a failure, a star that shone brightly for a short time and disappeared. However, although it ceased to exist in its original form by 1986, its people, know-how, intellectual capital, and market relationships have since been extensively recycled. It partially gave birth to a new generation of entrepreneurial companies, even before it floundered. In Silicon Valley, the firm's legacy continues to this day. In view of the knowledge-intensive nature of technology businesses, a firm's technical demise, we suggest, is not necessarily detrimental as long as the ecosystem can flexibly re-cycle its critical know-how and human assets. Shugart's demise resulted in the re-configuration and re-cycling of its people, their know-how, and their capabilities. As indicated in Figure 6, many of Shugart's employees joined its spin-offs, started new companies, and in some cases, re-vitalized other entities.

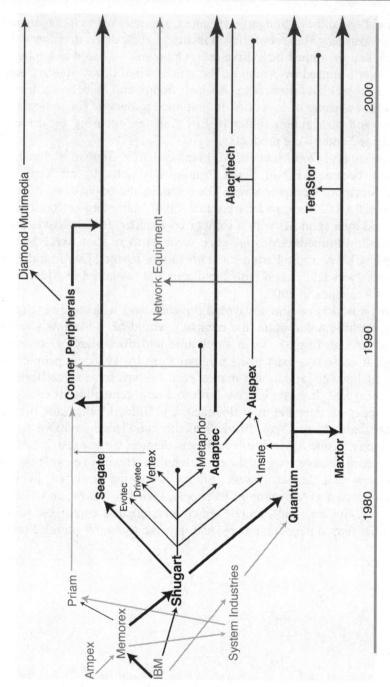

Figure 6. Spin-Offs from Shugart in the disk drive industry

Its co-founder, Alan Shugart, left the company early on, and moved to Santa Cruz to pursue other interests. Meanwhile, one of his former IBM colleagues and Shugart co-founder, Finis Conner, kept in touch and later left Shugart to co-found Seagate Technologies, together with Alan Shugart and two others. In 1980, another disk drive company, Quantum, was co-founded by an ex-IBM'er from System Industries, Jim Patterson, and several Shugart engineers, including Jim McCoy and David Brown, who later became Quantum's president and CEO. Both had played major roles in product development at Shugart. Quantum focused on developing 8-inch Winchester disk drives. Jim McCoy later left Quantum and went on to found Maxtor, a leading disk drive company.

Former Shugart employees also started the disk drive controller industry. A team of three, under the leadership of Larry Boucher, left Shugart in 1981 to found Adaptec, pioneering the SCSI Interface. Its first product was a SCSI interface chip set that was developed by Larry Boucher and two of his colleagues while still at Shugart. In order to get funding for the new project, they presented an internal business plan to Shugart's executive team. When their proposal was rejected, Boucher and his two colleagues left to found Adaptec, focusing on input-output controllers. The founders mortgaged their homes in order to pay for prototype development. Later, the venture capital firm, TVI's General Partner, David Marquadt, a former employee of Shugart's sister company, Diablo, invested in the first round of Adaptec's venture funding. TVI had been co-founded by Jim Bochnowski, who was DLJ's representative on Shugart's board and later became Shugart's President for about a year. Today, Adaptec is a successful public company, specializing in storage infrastructure solutions.

The recycling story is even more intricate. Following a downturn and a spell as Adaptec's Chairman, Larry Boucher co-founded Auspex Systems in 1987, together with Jim Patterson, Quantum's co-founder. In this case, David Marquadt was again an early investor. Auspex pioneered the concept of file servers during the late 1980's. Interestingly, an Auspex spin-off commercialized the file-server technology for the broader market during the 1990s, when two engineers and a consultant left Auspex to start Network Appliance. While Auspex had a "Cadillac" product, NetApp, as it became known, pioneered the "Chevy" version of file servers, just as the internet/local area network explosion was taking off. Today NetApp is a $1 Billion company in the net storage business.[22] Ironically, Shugart's Vice President of Human Resources, Chris Carlton, later became NetApp's SVP

---

[22] See Network Appliance (A), Case study #S-E-55A, Stanford Business School, April 1998 for a history of the company and the industry.

of HR. The story of this stream of spin-offs does not end here. Larry Boucher left Auspex to found a new start-up, Alacritech, in 1997. Recycling the Shugart talent pool was not limited to the disk drive industry. George Sollman, who joined Shugart from Control Data in 1976, as the Product Manager of the 51/4-inch floppy disk drive, later became Shugart's Vice President of Sales and Marketing. In 1984 he moved on to the venture community and was later persuaded to join a "re-start", Centigram, at the time, a languishing voice-messaging company. In an ironic twist of fate that displays the ethos of Silicon Valley, Sollman was previously responsible for reviewing the internal business plan that Larry Boucher had submitted, while at Shugart. Notwithstanding, Boucher became Sollman's first customer at Centigram. He placed an order for a voice messaging system for use at Adaptec. The voice messaging system at this time was a PC with a number of disk drives, so Sollman's knowledge and contacts in this arena were major assets. For example, he invited Jim McCoy, Quantum and Maxtor co-founder, to join Centigram's Board of Directors. The relationship had been forged much earlier at Shugart. Sollman took Centigram public and after a spell as the President of the American Electronics Association, he founded Arabesque, later re-named @Motion, a wireless telecommunications company, in 1997. Phone.com (later to become Openwave when it merged with Software.com in November 2000) acquired @Motion in 2000.[23]

4.3   Recycling and Super-Flexibility

As illustrated by Shugart's case history, the Silicon Valley ecosystem thrives on the process of recycling, as start-ups and spin-offs are formed, and as "failures" are constantly blended and reconfigured into new ventures. The Shugart case illustrates the dynamic forces that drive the recycling process. Recycling occurs by creating new firms, by moving people between entities, by cross-pollinating information and know-how, by recursive learning, and by re-inventing a venture in a new form. The process works more effectively during the Valley's down cycle. The ecosystem experiences what we characterize as the "wash effect", whereby the "beach" is cleared of "flotsam and jetsam" and the nutrients are re-cycled

---

[23] Many seasoned venture capitalists have historically preferred to fund entrepreneurs who have had the "scar tissue" of a previous failure, and who have worked for a professionally managed firm such as IBM, Intel, HP or some other large Valley company because they can learn how to scale and manage a complex business. This is of immense value for a start-up, as the founders understand what is to come, and what the organization may evolve into, if it scales.

for the next generation of firms to grow. The recycling process, we suggest, extends Schumpeter's (1934) notion of "creative destruction", and provides a practical framework for benefiting from setbacks and failures in contemporary knowledge-based arenas. The recycling process is enhanced in the absence of the typical stigma associated with failure.[24] Indeed, the high failure rate associated with start-ups increases experimentation and the speed of recycling. In the Popperian sense of "falsifiability" (Popper 1972), entrepreneurs learn, just as scientists do, much from failed experiments. Since organizational death is not viewed as a finite expression of failure, entrepreneurs are able to entertain, what would normally be considered, "outlandish" risks. Prospects of failure and mortality can also reduce feelings of over-confidence and invulnerability among successful incumbents and keep them on their toes. In such a setting, incumbent firms strive to become "agile giants", capable of rapid maneuvering and recalibrating.

Operating in conditions of kaleidoscopic change, a firm's technical demise, we suggest, is not necessarily detrimental as long as the ecosystem can re-cycle its critical know-how and human assets.[25] The short life cycle of many high-technology firms may also be helpful for sustaining the long-term innovative capability of a knowledge ecosystem. In addition to maintaining the stream of new firms, that in turn provide job opportunities and create new products and services, ephemeral firms increase the variety of experiments, and, when acquired, can help rejuvenate other entities, or become reconfigured in the form of new entities. This variety can also facilitate the development of new ventures. Recursive learning is crucial, given that it is difficult, if not impossible, to know the "winning formula" ahead of time. Recycling, we suggest, enables continuity and change to co-exist. The ecosystem provides a stable anchor within which talent pools, ventures, products, know-how, and relationships can be re-cycled, reconfigured, and re-deployed. Taken together, the recycling mechanisms described in this chapter provide the broader context within which business entities can strive for super-flexibility.

---

[24] A rule of thumb in the venture community is that the number of successful start-ups is around 1 in 30, as a "ball park" figure.

[25] Another illustration of recycling is the story of ROLM Corporation, the pioneer of the digital PBX, acquired by IBM in 1984. Ken Oshman, its co-founder and Chief Executive, moved on to lead Echelon, a pioneer in the networking field. A number of former employees of its Mil-Spec Division founded Ultra, a firm working on high-speed local area networks. Richard Moley, its former Vice President of Marketing and its first PBX product manager, became the CEO of Stratacom. He orchestrated Stratacom's turnaround and its eventual sale to Cisco during the 1990s.

5 Maneuvering: Navigating a Dynamic Trajectory

How do technology companies manage for the moment and develop strategies to prepare for the future? How do they balance short-term actions and long-term intentions? How do they change strategic direction and revise expectations when their reality is about catching, riding, and descending successive waves of opportunity? How do executive teams carve out an organic vision in the fog of competitive battle and modify it as events unfold? This chapter is about how technology firms devise and execute strategies, maintain momentum, and revise their business trajectory, in other words how they navigate real-time.

Super-flexibility is the hallmark of effective strategies in high tech companies. It provides the "degrees of freedom" to modify strategies "on the fly". Super-flexibility is clearly critical when soaring through the heights of mercurial growth, yet it is just as crucial when sliding into the abyss of a sudden downturn. Knowledge-based entities need fluid strategic trajectories, as products rapidly become obsolete, new markets quickly open up, and technological breakthroughs create unanticipated opportunities. Furthermore, financial markets are often quick to turn a high-performing "quasar" firm into a black hole of a moribund enterprise. In such turbulent settings, super-flexibility is highly prized.

Effective firms we have observed navigate by maneuvering. Maneuvering encompasses both, offensive and defensive moves, synchronous deployment of multiple approaches, and operating "on the fly" where speed of action is critical. Maneuvering a technology firm is analogous to steering a yacht in unchartered waters, with volatile weather conditions and unpredictable ocean currents. Effective maneuvering enables knowledge enterprises to either bring about new situations, or to adapt to new circumstances. Technology enterprises without the capability to maneuver are often unable to override the inertial forces of their environment.

5.1 Conceptual Underpinnings

The term "maneuver" is derived from military strategy. We describe it as the dynamic manipulation and deployment of assets, capabilities and resources, targeted towards capturing value and generating wealth on the shifting sands of market opportunities. Historically defined as the means of executing strategy in the midst of an engagement, we draw on the term to describe how to navigate the fluid trajectory of a knowledge enterprise over time. We suggest that knowledge enterprises need super-flexibility in order to instigate, lubricate, and extend their scope of maneuvers.

Military thinking about flexible maneuvering developed over many centuries and, until the 19th century, largely consisted of the insights of a few pioneering figures. In classical warfare, enemies lined up facing each other and the larger force typically prevailed. In 1760, the French nobleman, Bourcet (whose work was published later in 1888), implemented a divisional structure in the monolithic, pre-revolutionary French army. This was later augmented by the innovation of drilling troops on a functional, rather than a ceremonial, basis. Instituted by Compte de Guibert, he increased the pace of marching from 70 to 110 paces per minute, preparing the troops for real battle.

With these changes in place, Napoleon (supported by many of his friends as field commanders) was able to put together a military force that relished in the art of maneuver. Even Carl von Clausewitz, the grand father of military strategy could only marvel at the skill deployed by Napoleon (von Guyczy et al 2003). As Clausewitz remarked: *"Battle is money and property, strategy is commerce; it is through the former that the latter becomes significant"* (Hahlway 1966, p. 647). Ironically he became bogged down in marshes and was unable to join his commander, Blücher, in tipping the balance during the final stages of the Battle of Waterloo.[26]

Decades later, during the American Civil War, General Sherman (1875) deployed the art of maneuver with devastating impact. By lessening the load of his troops to a bare minimum, and deploying scouts to act as foragers for food, he was able to move with speed and outflanked his opponents. With the onset of mechanized warfare, the situation changed yet again.

Fuller (1946), who oversaw the development of the tank, described some of these impacts and extended the idea of maneuver through his dictum of "strike, dislocate and consolidate". The notion of flexibility was further developed by Liddell-Hart (1929, 1954) as a fundamental principle of warfare. He emphasized the value of the "indirect approach" as the essence of flexibility.

As Foch observed we *"should give up talking about maneuvers a priori…it can only be valuable if it leads to fighting under advantageous tactical conditions, if it permits the most favorable utilization of our forces"* (1921, p. 42). It is in the execution of maneuvers that super-flexibility is

---

[26] Marshall Ney, together with his revered Swiss strategist, Jomini, attacked the center of Wellington's forces, misreading Napoleon's order to strike the left flank. Even the grandfathers of strategy, Clausewitz and Jomini, made mistakes.

required. The objective is to continuously juxtapose several actions and to deploy disparate assets and multiple capabilities to deal with complex and evolving situations, as they are actually confronted. As Jomini argued: *"the more simple a decisive maneuver, the more certain will be its success."* (Hittle 1947, p. 15). Simplicity, as discussed in chapter 2, is a critical cornerstone of super-flexibility.

Management scholars have invoked maneuvers as a conceptual construct to help understand the dynamics of business (Evans 1991, D'Aveni 1994, Clemons and Santamaria 2002, von Ghyczy, Bassford and von Oetinger 2003). The focus has been on strategic management in hyper-competitive and fast-moving industries, where business leaders have to balance the need to act and respond real-time, in the context of broad strategic guidelines and long-term intentions.

5.2 Triggers

In embarking on maneuvers, enterprises seek to inflict and respond to change. Change comes in many shapes and guises. Sometimes it follows a stable linear course, othertimes it is stochastic or "kaleidoscopic", where small insignificant changes coagulate into an unpredictable, paradigm-breaking shift. Several categories of stimuli might cause a firm to instigate a maneuver, to revise a maneuver during its execution, to abandon it all together, or even to start from scratch again.

For our purposes, we can aggregate these stimuli into "triggering events or episodes". The term "trigger" is used to describe the underlying forces that precipitate a transformed situation. These may encompass revolutions, innovations, natural disasters, and the emergence of new competitors.[27] Serendipitous events, such as windfalls, luck, fashion or even the unique conjunctions of singularly unimportant factors, can also precipitate the need for instigating maneuvers.

Other equally significant types of trigger include changes in the composition of, or chemistry among, management teams, and the discovery of new market segments. Natural occurrences, such as extreme weather variations, earthquakes, volcanoes, or medical epidemics, also require the de-

---

[27] Consider the magnitude and impact of radical geo-political changes experienced in recent years. Examples include the 1979 revolution in Iran, the fall of the Berlin Wall and the demise of the former Soviet Union, the tragedy of September 11, and the wars in Afghanistan and Iraq. High profile examples of major disasters include Exxon Valdez, Bhopal, and Chernobyl.

ployment of rapid maneuvers. This is clearly illustrated by the SARS crisis during 2003. It seriously impeded the ability of many Silicon Valley companies, with extensive manufacturing facilities in China, to get new products out of engineering into production.

In high technology ecosystems, it is clear that scientific innovations and new ways of doing things result in the creation of new business sectors and the redrawing of competitive dynamics in existing domains. In knowledge-intensive industries, the susceptibility of firms to "innovation" triggers is very high. The dilemma is that the impact of innovations is difficult to forecast with much accuracy. Sometimes breakthroughs come from directions least expected (Christensen 1997). As the experience of Silicon Valley has conclusively demonstrated, a nimble start up may overcome the entrenched Goliaths of the industry, and unknown research students may become the next generation of successful entrepreneurs.[28]

Another source of uncertainty is that new innovations often fail to deliver on early promises or, almost inevitably, take longer to come to fruition than originally envisioned. Consider the high expectations surrounding artificial intelligence during the late 1980s, B2B exchanges during the Internet boom years, as well as synthetic fuel and electric vehicles. Technological innovations also force pioneering "first mover" firms to go through "knot-holes" before becoming viable. Examples include Palm Pilot, object-oriented software, G3 telecommunications infrastructure, robotic manufacturing, solid-state data-storage, and sputtered media for Winchester disk drives. There are considerable uncertainties and commercialization is typically a complex process, with lead-users and developers inextricably intertwined until standards emerge.

In knowledge intensive sectors, the organizational climate changes as entrepreneurial firms go public and raise their profiles. This clearly heightens the level of exposure to external events beyond a firm's control. Changes also occur in the motivational profiles of founding teams and early employees. Founders may even be sidelined as a firm becomes "professionally" managed. In addition, being in the public glare, also imposes legal restrictions resulting in the formation of insiders and outsiders. The ultimate source of consternation is that once a firm is public, it can become the target for upstart fledgling companies.

Public companies are also subject to sudden takeover moves. Well-publicized examples that clearly change competitive dynamics are Ora-

---

[28] Well-known examples include Jerry Yang and David Filo, the co-founders of Yahoo, Marc Andreessen, the co-founder of Netscape, and the founding teams of ROLM, SUN Microsystems, and Google.

cle's attempt to purchase PeopleSoft, the merger between HP and Compaq, or Vodaphone's acquisition of Mannesmann. Uncertainties unfold during the acquisition/ merger process, and afterwards, during the post-acquisition digestion stage, or even when the dust settles from a failed attempt. Post-acquisition uncertainties abound since most of the "knowledge", on which the acquired companies have been built, resides in their people. As many large multinationals have found to their chagrin, buying a company without courting the hearts of the key employees, is often a recipe for failure. Disgruntled employees may leave and join, or even form, a rival competitor.

An interesting case in point was Xerox during the 1980's. Arguably it had the potential to dominate the disk storage business via acquisitions of Shugart and Century Data, printers via the acquisition of Diablo Systems, and computer communications and interface technologies, through its Palo Alto Research Center (PARC). As described in Chapter 3, Shugart was disbanded and sold off in the mid-1980s, and PARC technologies later became the foundations of 3Com and Adobe, both founded by former PARC scientists.

While each individual trigger is a stimulant for change, the problem of adaptation becomes much more complex when several triggers occur concurrently. Collectively, triggers create a multitude of uncertainties and transform competitive landscapes on which hot spots randomly appear and disappear. Inside a firm, they can generate pain points when things are not working out or when fleeting opportunities go by unexploited. The conjunction of these triggers produces pressure points that require "out of the ordinary" or non-standard responses. It is the role of super-flexibility to reduce these friction points as a firm maneuvers.

Before describing the various types of maneuvers induced by triggering events, it is essential to specify the object of a maneuver in terms of the "why" and the "when", so that the "how" can make sense. The "when" dimension is about timing, the "why" dimension is about intent. These two dimensions are further explored in the following section.

5.3 Maneuvering: The Time Dimension

An enterprise acts based on the reality it faces today and the expectations it may have about tomorrow. Sometimes action can be taken ahead of time. In these cases, forecasts, scenarios, predictions, and even hunches, are helpful in devising a desired course of action. At other times, action is initiated after the fact, in response to a technological breakthrough, an accident, a revolution, a competitive surprise, legislative initiatives, or even fashion. These "*ex post*" and "*ex ante*" temporal dimensions are useful distinctions when forging an enterprise's trajectory, before and after a triggering event.

Action is typically initiated at a point of engagement at a specific time. This state of affairs may endure for an instant, a week, a month, a year, or as long as the particular equilibrium unleashed by the trigger remains in place. In knowledge-intensive settings, an enterprise must maneuver constantly because kaleidoscopic changes, induced by the triggers, can rupture short-lived periods of stability and transform these into novel situations. Earlier, we referred to this state as a "Kuhnian inversion". This provides the stimulus for changing the direction or even the nature of a firm's maneuvers.

It is difficult to know ahead of a triggering episode what must be done in the new circumstances. All eventualities cannot be imagined before situations unfold, and actual rather than imagined preferences cannot be anticipated until outcomes have been experienced (March 1981). Novelty and spontaneity are forces to be reckoned with.

Actions initiated ahead of time, are typically taken in anticipation of certain events, or in an attempt to change the rules of the game. When expectations are not met, or when events occur that have not been predicted, a firm may require flexibility after the fact. In these cases, attempts are made to correct a mistake or to capitalize on an unexpected opportunity.

Knowledge enterprises try to predict the future in different ways. Even new start-ups produce detailed financial projections and prepare business plans about their fledgling businesses in order to get equity funding. Larger enterprises must forecast sales volumes to ensure that manufacturing capacity, inventory and cash are all balanced. Some companies engage in elaborate scenario planning (Schwartz 1991) to develop long-term strategies.

Although forecasting techniques have become much more sophisticated, the problem is that we are continually surprised at how the future unfolds. Things that were previously unthinkable or unimaginable, do indeed occur. These events seem obvious with hindsight, but are somewhat shielded from view ahead of time. There are many reasons for these disconnects. Clearly, when moving in unchartered territory, surprises inevitably do occur.

Entrepreneurs in knowledge enterprises often rely on intuition or hunches, triggered by their experiences close to the point of action. Economists use expectations of the future as a pivotal dimension of their models. Sometimes, things can be done before the triggering episode unfolds, as was the case with de-regulation of electric utilities in the UK, or the introduction of the Euro.

However, when engaging in high-risk activities, serendipity, luck and freak occurrences also play a role. For example, innovations often go through several "knot-holes" before crystallizing into workable products. The challenge is to figure out the appropriate adaptive actions, when situations deviate from prior expectations.

While pioneering firms can inflict triggering episodes, many enterprises are typically forced to adapt due to changes beyond their control. In these cases, they can either act ahead of time, by forecasting and anticipating, or they can respond after the fact. Sometimes it is better to wait and see how situations turn out before initiating action. Other times it is best to act quickly to capitalize on an unexpected opportunity, or to move out of the way of potentially harmful threats. So the "time" or the "when" optic is the first dimension of our framework.

5.4 Maneuvering: The Intent Dimension

Maneuvering depends on what has to be achieved and why it needs to be done. In sports, competing teams know the rules and there is usually some official, a referee, to ensure adherence to those rules, However, the objective, for example in soccer, is not simply to score goals, but to prevent the other team from scoring goals. The formation and the tactics are different for offensive and defensive play, although they should work together; the real art is shifting the balance from one to the other at the right time; for example, by moving out of defense into an attacking position. The sporting analogy may be overly simplistic. The rules are clear, the objectives are well defined, and the parameters are stable. Yet there are clear parallels to business.

Similarly, in the military arena, there are several parallels to business that have long been noted. While the complexity and stakes of warfare are very different, the parallels with business are strong in that a business is an organized grouping of people, capital and knowledge brought together to satisfy consumer needs, locally and globally. So while the ends differ, the means of achieving them may have more in common than expected. A military force must move to find an advantageous position in which to successfully engage the enemy. The opponent attempts the same. Sometimes an enemy may be stronger and may force its opponent onto the defensive. Irrespective of the situation, the means of attack and defense are by movement and by clustering assets to achieve a given objective. In other words by maneuvering:[29]

It is in playing the game against adversaries that the concept of intentionality enters our framework. Drawing on the sporting and the military analogies, a firm can either go on the offense, for example by attacking a new market segment, or it can go on the defense, by regrouping to repel an attack, or by consolidating in a given arena. It may attack by acquiring firms or by capitalizing on its own capabilities. Sometimes an attack may involve a "feint" where a threat is made in order to divert competitors' attention and resources, making the real target easier to attack. Even when all this is done successfully, victory is only achieved when the dislocation produced by the attack is hammered home, just as a crop must be harvested and taken to market in order to produce profits.

In a similar vein, knowledge enterprises engaging in high-risk activities often fail to realize their mission. This may prompt them to go on the "defensive". Sometimes, the problem can be foreseen. A super-flexible firm may inoculate or immunize itself against risk or potential failure, for example, by hedging or by buying insurance. Other times, it may regroup and take stock after a failed initiative, and refocus its efforts on achievable goals. When faced with a threat, it may also seek cover, attempt to buffer itself, or absorb the shock in some other way.

---

[29] Becoming flexible by means of maneuvers was an essential cornerstone of Napoleon's approach to warfare. This is somewhat reflected in the following anecdote recollected by Gohier commenting on the meeting of Generals Bonaparte and Moreau: Bonaparte told Moreau how anxious he had been to make his acquaintance. "You have just come from Egypt as a conqueror", answered Moreau, "and I am just home from Italy after a great defeat…" ..he concluded: "It was impossible to prevent our army from being overwhelmed by so many combined forces. Big numbers always beat small ones." "You are right", said Bonaparte, "big numbers always beat small ones." "Still General", said I to Bonaparte, "you have often beaten big armies with smaller ones." "Even in that case", he said," the small numbers were always beaten by big ones." This led him to explain his tactics: "When with inferior forces, I was met by a large army", he said, "having quickly regrouped my own, I fell like lightening on one of the wings, which I routed. I then availed myself of the disorder this manœuvre never failed to produce within an enemy army, so as to attack it in another part, and again with all my forces. I thus beat the enemy piecemeal; and the ensuing victory was invariably, as you can see, a triumph of the larger over the smaller." The art consisted in *securing the numbers*, in having the numbers on the selected point of attack; the means of doing this was: *an economy of forces*. Such mechanics ultimately led to the utilization to the utmost disorder this manœuvre produces within the enemy army, as well as the moral superiority created by the same manœuvre within one's own army." That was Napoleon's War (Foch 1921, pp. 95-96).

Unlike sports, however, in business, the balance of play between offense and defense is not binary. Even a "simple" start-up has to fight many battles simultaneously to win in the market. Some of these involve attack, like pushing the limits of a new technology; others entail defense, explaining to investors why revenue or profit targets are not met, but these moves have to be undertaken at the same time. The degree to which a firm is aligned determines how effectively it can maneuver by deploying all its resources to concentrate on a decisive point, to achieve its objectives, and ultimately to move on and refocus on the next decisive point.

It is this constant shifting of the center of gravity of a strategic problem, generated by triggers, that highlights the importance of super-flexibility. Moreover, like shifting sands, change evolves continuously. What is "right" one day, may be wrong the next. An army on the move faces unpredictable consequences when engaged in battle. Similarly in knowledge businesses, initiatives and actions seldom work out exactly as planned. So the "intent" or the "why" dimension, and the need to engage in offensive and defensive moves, is the second dimension of our framework.

5.5 Maneuvering to Achieve Super-Flexibility: A Conceptual Framework

In terms of achieving super-flexibility to maneuver a firm's fluid trajectory, it makes little sense to focus exclusively on optimal, planned moves "*a priori*". Nor is it sufficient to rely exclusively on "*ex post facto*" actions initiated after uncertainty is resolved. There is a need to engage in both, offensive and defensive moves simultaneously. The conjunction of the "time" and the "intent" dimensions allow us to identify four generic maneuvers for achieving super-flexibility.

Figure 7 sets out the four operational maneuvers for achieving super-flexibility; these are categorized as "pre-emptive", "protective", "corrective", and "exploitive". For the sake of clarification, each type of maneuver is described individually, although it must be emphasized that their effectiveness largely depends on their collective deployment. The challenge is to select and execute the right combination of maneuvers at any given point in time, and to continually re-assess their relevance. For practitioners, these maneuvers should be viewed as conceptual coat hangers, so that they can analyze their current trajectories, initiate action, and engage in suitable balancing acts.

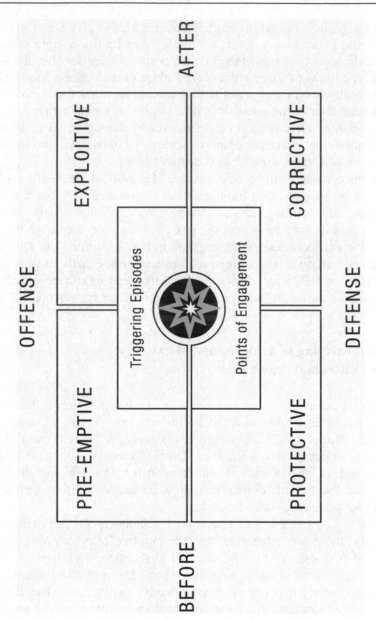

Figure 7. Maneuvering: A framework

5.5.1 Pre-emptive Maneuvers

Pre-emptive maneuvers are deployed in order to precipitate a transformation by seizing the initiative to induce a triggering episode. The intention may be to inflict a surprise on competitors, or to create new rules of engagement. In a technology setting, this form of maneuver typically involves what Heidegger (1977) termed "enframing" in order to "bring forth" novelty, such as a radical innovation, or a novel distribution channel, by altering the rules of the game or the nature of a domain.

Pre-emptive maneuvers often create a range of options before they are needed. This has two benefits; the first is the intrinsic value of the options themselves; the second is the capability base developed in pursuit of different alternatives. Policies, such as not discussing or pre-announcing new products, or being constructively ambiguous about future intentions, can facilitate the use of pre-emptive maneuvers.

There are several examples of these maneuvers in technology settings. Stealth start-ups, as discussed in chapter 4, are a case in point. They can keep their options open and increase their chances of being first to market by expressing their intentions in broad, general, terms early on. This approach does not alert potential competitors to their business proposition. Another benefit is that a management team can change its mind and adopt a different approach if the original business proposition turns out to be untimely, unrealistic, or simply wrong. Entrepreneurs can shade their activities from public view and retain the option to recalibrate and change their trajectory. Revisions can therefore be made without appearing "inconsistent" or having to spend much time and energy explaining and justifying the change to the various stakeholders.

There are other ways of being pre-emptive, in addition to creating options. One example is the deliberate use of targeted acquisitions to position a knowledge enterprise as a leading-edge provider of new products and services. This is illustrated by Cisco's growth-by-acquisition strategy. It acquired more than 80 companies between 1997-2003, including 23 in 2000. The businesses were, in the main, acquired to provide early access to emerging technologies. They also gave Cisco the opportunity to recruit a number of technology pioneers.[30]

The company used different acquisition formats, including pooling of assets, "spin-in's", subsidiary purchases, asset purchases, and "recruit-

---

[30] For example, Howard Charney became Cisco's EVP of Strategy, after Cisco acquired Grand Junction during the 1990s. Similarly, Judy Estrin became Cisco's Chief Technology Officer in 1995, after Cisco acquired Precept.

ment" acquisitions. As of March 2003, 1 in 6 Cisco employees were from acquired companies. Most of the deals were closed in 45-60 days, and the IT systems of the acquired firms connected to Cisco's within 2 weeks of purchase.

Cisco used its acquisition strategy as a significant pre-emptive maneuver. It proactively screened, selected and targeted acquisition candidates that best fitted its product and service portfolio. The acquisition strategy was augmented by a rigorous due diligence process, as well as a well-defined post-acquisition integration strategy. Both pre and post acquisition processes focused on identification and assimilation of key talent, targeted communication to the acquired company employees, and reliance on a dedicated core team of experts to guide and monitor the integration process throughout its various stages.

The speed of this pre-emptive maneuver, both in closing the deals and, more strategically, in integrating the selected parts of acquired firms, contributed to Cisco's leading position in its industry, at a time when its technological leadership was being challenged by other competitors, such as Juniper Networks. By ensuring the continued flow of new technology through its pre-emptive acquisition strategy of series B and C venture-funded companies, Cisco was able to scale itself, without relying exclusively on internally generated products.

At a more tactical level, pre-emptive maneuvers can also be embedded into products or processes. For example, it is standard practice in the disk drive industry to design a product so it can be upgraded at a future date to take account of anticipated advances in technology. This approach can leverage the early design activity over a longer product-life cycle, and is especially helpful if the product becomes an industry standard. Moreover, "upgradeability" is also a desired attribute in the acquisition of IT products. This theme is further underscored by echoing the "mantra" of agility in IT systems.

Finally, as illustrated in the following example, pre-emptive maneuvers often require the swift execution of a number of actions at the right time. Consider pre-emptive maneuvers of Shugart Corporation in developing the standard setting 5.25-inch mini-floppy disk drive. In 1976, 8-inch floppy disk drives were the *de jure* industry standard. However, by this time a group of lead users, including manufacturers of word processors and hobby computers, were dissatisfied with the available options for storage devices.

The product idea was initially conceived on the fly during a meeting between a Shugart sales executive and a large European customer.[31] Voicing

---

[31] Personal communication with the former head of Shugart's East Coast Sales Operations.

their dissatisfaction with the only available alternative to the 8-inch floppy disk drive used in word processing systems, a cassette tape drive, the customer expressed a need for a smaller removable storage device for the next generation of desk-top products under development. Shugart's sales executive, having heard similar concerns from other customers, picked up a cocktail napkin and asked if that was about the preferred size of the media. Having received a positive response, he made up a cardboard mock-up and sent it back to the headquarters.

The idea was initially dismissed at the headquarters because the then dominant player, IBM, had historically set the industry standard "form factor" for new disk drives. However, when another large customer expressed dissatisfaction with the available alternatives, Shugart spotted a major opportunity to depart from tradition and acted swiftly to develop a new product. The president developed product specifications when returning from a customer visit, and assembled the development team the following morning, a Saturday, to work out detailed design criteria and to draw the blueprints. In a bold pre-emptive move, intended to erect entry barriers, the team set an unusually aggressive manufacturing cost target of $100 for the proposed product.

This was the first time in the development of an OEM disk drive that cost considerations had played a critical role in the development process. Moreover, in a significant departure from standard industry practice, a young engineer autonomously set out to meet the aggressive cost targets by using off-the-shelf components. For example, a motor was used from a vending machine and other parts were taken from a cassette drive, with the result that the material cost came to within $5 of the target cost. This move also reduced the development cycle time. The first prototypes were ready in less than six months.

While the product was under development, the company deployed yet another pre-emptive maneuver. A general practice amongst disk drive manufacturers in the OEM (Original Equipment Manufacturer) business was to communicate new product specifications early in the design cycle. The intention was to ensure compatibility with their customers' products. In signing up large OEM orders, Shugart was expected to show its proposed drive (and its new media) to prospective customers. In the process, it would have to divulge valuable intelligence to competitors who would then be in a position to emulate the product design. In this case the critical piece of information concerned the size of the diskette. From this information the size or the "form factor" for the new product could be deduced, and a valuable time advantage would be lost.

The dilemma was resolved by Shugart's decision to send out five or six different sizes of media to potential customers, all within reasonable proximity to the intended 5.25-inch form factor under development. This "constructive ambiguity" gave the firm more lead-time to develop its new product. In this case, volume production started within 18 months, enabling Shugart to capture 70% of this market segment. The product became the first non-IBM industry standard OEM peripheral, and some 14 million units were produced worldwide in 1987.

In this case, the pre-emptive maneuver consisted of three complementary, components; first, in developing a standard-setting product initiated as a pre-emptive response to lead customers' dissatisfaction with existing products; second, in using available off-the-shelf components to build the product, reducing its manufacturing cost and positioning the company for long-term cost advantage over competition; third, in confusing the competitors about the size of the media diskette and gaining a time advantage with a standard-setting product. Moreover, speed of action in executing all three maneuvers proved to be critical.

Pre-emptive maneuvers have the potential to be the most "equilibrium shattering" weapon at a firm's disposal, but they can also be highly risky due to the multitude of uncertainties. Keeping intentions ambiguous can result in surprising competitors, but it can also limit market feedback. In addition, pre-emptive maneuvers can inspire people to perceive change as an opportunity, not a threat. As the lead engineer of Shugart's 5.25-inch floppy drive, who later co-founded a major disk drive firm, commented: *"(In this business) you always have to be pre-emptive and selectively use other maneuvers as needed."*

5.5.2 Protective Maneuvers

While seeking sustainable advantage through pre-emptive maneuvers, a knowledge enterprise must also guard itself against potentially damaging implications that it may face when entering new domains, or when addressing competitive moves, industry dynamics or geo-political conditions. In these circumstances, it is prudent to get some form of insurance, and adopt a hedging strategy; or drawing on a military analogy, to maintain a protected line of retreat.

In a defensive sense, protective maneuvers seek to deflect, absorb, cushion or immunize against the impact of potentially harmful forces. The actions are defensive moves, deployed ahead of a potential or probable triggering event. The old adage of "not having all eggs in one basket" encapsulates the sentiment of this type of maneuver. The objective is to guard against the potentially damaging outcomes that may occur when engaging in high-risk actions, or when moving into unchartered territories.

Consider the case of an innovative semi-conductor packaging firm. Its founder, an entrepreneurial scientist, had developed and patented a novel technology, implanting spring loaded probes, for improving the testing process for a new type of integrated circuit. Having raised several rounds of venture funding, its business portfolio was a combination of the conventional, older "test probes", as well as its path breaking newer product.

As the recession in the technology sector began to bite in 2001, its executive team realized that orders for the new products were much lower than originally expected. The recession intensified, especially in the semi-conductor manufacturing sector, historically a leading indicator of change in Silicon Valley. Faced with the reality of limited revenues for an innovative product early in its life cycle, the executive team decided to put the new product line on hold, concentrating attention and resources on the older test probe business.

After a couple of downsizing rounds, aimed at reining in costs and adjusting headcount, the economy did not improve and the move to stem the flow of cash proved justified. The company then started to see murmurings of growing demand from its customers for the latest technology. At the time, the semiconductor industry was in a cyclical downturn but OEM customers by now had shifted gear and began ordering the most innovative technology to push the capabilities of their products, such as mobile phones and personal computers. Seeing the "skies clearing", it began to ramp up the production of its new test packages to address growing customer demand. As the sales numbers continued to improve, the impact on the bottom line was amplified by the fact its cost base had earlier been reduced significantly. This enabled it to remain viable during very challenging times.

In 2002 the situation on Wall Street had made the prospect of a public offering unlikely. Notwithstanding, investment bankers prepared the way in 2003 for capitalizing on any limited window of opportunity that might open for an IPO. This preparatory action reduced the lead-time to promote the offering to prospective institutional investors. The combined impacts of reduced cost base, positive cash flow, new testing technology, and a strong customer base and order book made it possible to execute the offering during a limited "break in the clouds" on Wall Street in 2003. In addition, key shareholders signed a pledge not to sell the stock for 6 months in order to minimize wide oscillations in share price that typically accompany a public offering.

There are other types of protective maneuvers. For example, expectations of rapid market growth, or impending changes in industry standards, may prompt a firm to augment its internal technological capability by acquiring another firm, or by licensing a proprietary design. Another protective move in technology settings is to ensure continuity of supply of critical components by securing back-up sources, in case any one vendor is faced with potential disruptions, or if the market grows faster than expected. Yet another example is to select critical systems ahead of time and to install the ability to degrade gracefully if damaged. This would give a firm sufficient time to switch over to back-up systems, if needed.

Protective maneuvers in knowledge intensive firms also apply to people, policies and organizational infrastructures. For example, during the recent recession in Silicon Valley, a number of the larger companies adopted innovative approaches to "down-sizing". Many firms had twin, yet seemingly contradictory, goals of reducing cost by lowering headcount, while retaining their highly specialized technical talent pools. Instead of adopting the usual lay-off policies, a few firms offered key employees the option of taking up to a year's leave of absence to do community service or work for non-profit organizations, while retaining health and pension benefits and rights to stock options. In some cases they were paid a percentage of their salary. A review would be done after a year and the employees in question would be either offered full-time employment or be allowed to pursue other options. This protective maneuver allowed a number of technology firms to downsize without losing key technical talent. It also positioned them to ramp up quickly when the market conditions improved.

However, as is the case with other types of maneuver, protective moves often require the juxtaposition of several different actions. These include anticipating and planning for the worst case, reinforcing parts that may be especially vulnerable, and storing critical items, especially financial resources, in reserve. Consider the case of a pioneering technology company in the storage business. During a period of rapid growth, early signals of an impending market transformation prompted the firm to embark on a series of protective maneuvers. Sources of potential concern included rumors about the second sourcing practices of a major customer, and a significant build-up of capacity by offshore manufacturers, enjoying a considerable cost advantage. In a surprise move, the company reduced its domestic employees from 2200 to 900 within a few weeks, and relocated all its manufacturing operations to Asia, where it would benefit from an abundant supply of skilled workers, as well as lower component and labor costs.

A few months later, the storage industry entered a period of severe recession. Less than 10 of the 50 or so venture-backed start-ups managed to survive, and disk drive operations of several large corporations were disengaged or divested. Despite major problems in the industry, the company in question was able to avoid a major catastrophe. The protective maneuver had two benefits. First, it built up its customer base among the emerging PC makers (many were already based in Asia). Second, it consolidated its US customer base, largely because of its low cost position. These helped the company re-emerge later as a major force in the industry, with a commanding position in its market.

Although the short-term impact of its protective maneuver may have been brutal, had the firm failed to act quickly and decisively, it may well have gone out of business, along with many of its US counterparts. In embarking on an aggressive cost reduction strategy, before it was needed, the company was positioned for long-haul effectiveness. The protective maneuver installed a degree of robustness, enabling it to withstand shocks and to recover from the recession quicker than its competitors.

5.5.3 Corrective Maneuvers

In dynamic, fast-moving domains, damaging events occur from time to time for a variety of reasons. For example, there may be accidents, mistakes, or competitive challenges. In these situations, defensive actions, in the form of corrective maneuvers, must be taken after the fact. These moves are typically invoked when something goes wrong, when an initiative leads to an undesirable outcome, or when external events generate unfavorable consequences. Corrective maneuvers are about damage control, intended to minimize the negative impact of undesirable situations or outcomes. Maneuvering, in this corrective sense, refers to regenerative and recuperative practices needed to recover from traumas, accidents, mistakes and unworkable actions and initiatives.

Several guidelines should be taken into consideration when embarking on corrective maneuvers.

- Instead of pointing fingers and assigning blame, attention should be focused on admitting that the problem exists, and facing the facts as they are, rather than "as we wish them to be".
- The second requirement is to act quickly and apply the brakes early on, using bite-sized measures that can restore confidence and credibility.
- Third, time and attention should be focused on generating workable solutions, not just analyzing the problem. As is the case in first aid, if a patient is bleeding, a tourniquet must be applied, or, if a bone is broken, a splint can bring immediate stabilization.

Consider, how Steve Jobs turned Apple Computer around after re-assuming its leadership during the late 1990's. At the time, many experts had written off the company and did not view it as a significant market player. Instead of embarking on a new "grand strategy", Jobs concentrated on rapid, bite-sized, rollout of new products, every 90 days. He focused on what could be tangibly done to fix its problems, areas that were within the company's direct control. They re-packaged and re-branded their products, targeted new users, and opened their own retail stores to attract new customers and provide expert pre and post-sales advice in the form of "Genius Bars".

Another example of a corrective maneuver is how Intel fixed a bug in its "Pentium processor" after its initial introduction during the mid-1990s. Although the company initially dismissed the problem as "minor", many early adopters, including Wall Street traders, became vocal about their lack of confidence in the new processor. Intel quickly changed its posture, admitted that there was at least a perceived problem with the processor, recalled the shipped units to be replaced, and apologized for the inconvenience. This rapid corrective maneuver created a favorable image among the user community. They admired the firm for its honesty and integrity, and for demonstrating its commitment to end-users.

The re-integration of Palm and Handspring, two leading providers of hand held computers/organizers, is yet another example of a corrective maneuver. Palm was initially acquired by US Robotics, which itself was later acquired by 3Com, Palm was spun out of 3Com before the company was floated as an independent entity. Meanwhile, the co-founders and developers of the original Palm Pilot, had left 3Com/ PALM to co-found a new company, called Handspring. They focused the new company on producing a Pilot like device, called the "Visor", and migrated the product into the cell phone business by integrating the "organizer" and the "scheduler" components of the Palm Operating System and software into a larger than normal mobile phone. Faced with approximately a 40% drop in demand for both firms' products, and dwindling share prices, the two firms finally merged in 2003. Subsequently, the cell phone business was revamped and re-branded and the new entity became a stronger competitor.

Corrective maneuvers can also be observed amongst some of the leading venture capital firms during the Valley's "post dot com bubble" downturn. A case in point is the initiative taken by the firm of Mohr, Davidow Ventures. The esteemed firm trimmed its $850 million fund back to $650 million in 2002, returning the cash to their limited partners. In early 2003 the fund was paired down, yet again, to $450 million. In addition, the firm closed its offices in Reston (Virginia) and Seattle, and reduced the number of its general partners. The rationale was simple. According to its Managing Partner, the ideal size fund for an early stage investor is between $350-$500 million. Given the reduced levels of investment in the post-dot com era, and the number of deals in which a partner could comfortably invest, the firm wanted to reduce expectations of its limited partners and free up the general partners so they could focus their time and attention on fewer ventures where they could have a significant impact.[32]

A classic example of a corrective maneuver is the case of a disk drive controller company that made a U-turn in its strategy in order to stay in business. When it was founded in 1981, the company had targeted multi-user computer manufacturers, mainly those using the Unix operating system, as its customer base. The founders had pioneered an advanced input/output controller technology, termed SCSI or small computer standard interface. However, the target market did not materialize as initially projected because of the rapid diffusion of personal computers.

The industry standard IBM-PC diffused surprisingly fast. However, it used a controller that was a variant of an earlier interface, developed for single-user systems. In order to compete in the PC market, the company faced a clear choice: either to emulate the new standard controller product for the PC or to downsize its more powerful controller for the single-user desk-top environment. Its executives opted for the second option, and were able to capitalize on short-term opportunities generated by growth in PC's, and PC-compatible systems.

The decision to adapt the technology for use in IBM-compatible personal computers was more complex than expected. Since many of its customers were "cloning" IBM's systems, each had developed somewhat unique methods to ensure MS-DOS software compatibility. Therefore, the controller company had to design and develop "semi-custom" controllers to meet these compatibility requirements.

When in 1984 a dramatic shakeout occurred in the domestic personal computer industry, the firm lost over 70% of its customer base in just a few weeks. There was little forewarning of the impending crisis. The problem was made worse because during the initial growth phase, its customers had placed substantial orders, in excess of their requirements, in order to guarantee the timely flow of parts. Needless to say, the impact of the crisis was traumatic and almost terminal. Faced with this situation, another corrective maneuver was deployed.

The company quickly converted its un-saleable customized inventory of finished goods to "liquid" industry standard products, and offered these goods at substantial discounts. This move kept the firm afloat and gave it time to regroup. It was able to follow this strategy, in part, because it had already built up good will and credibility amongst its own vendors, granting them favorable credit terms for some time. The value of this good will was immeasurable during the traumatic adjustment period. It sustained the

[32] Source: The Venture Capital Analyst: Technology Edition, February 2003 Vol. VI (2), Venture One.

flow of critical components needed to convert the customized inventory into standard products. The point to note is that action taken ahead of time, even in the absence of a specific goal, can create options that can be used at a later stage. The corrective maneuver was effectively executed by rapidly reworking products, and selling them at considerable discounts, a move that surprised its competitors. The founder/CEO even took personal responsibility for sales and used every opportunity, including user group meetings, to sell the "converted" products.

This example has the hallmark of a super-flexible response, in that it needs several actions for effective execution. It also shows that speed of action, and the willingness to back down from the original intent, are sometimes critical for taking corrective action.

5.5.4 Exploitive Maneuvers

Technology firms often find themselves in situations where circumstances or preferences may not unfold as expected, both in a positive as well as a negative sense. A stroke of luck or being at the right place at the right time, are unpredictable events that nonetheless have to be capitalized on. Super-flexibility, in this opportunistic sense, is achieved by means of exploitive maneuvers. This type of maneuver is critical, for example, when a new product unexpectedly becomes an industry standard, resulting in rapid expansion of market demand. Apple's iPod is a good example.

Exploitive maneuvers are about focusing resources to rapidly capitalize on spontaneous opportunities. The objective is not to scan for opportunities; but to concentrate effort and resources to bring about effective execution around the opportunity "here and now". The "speed" factor is critical and may even partly account for the relative failure of many corporate "venture capital units" in generating new growth avenues inside established corporations (Campbell *et al.* 2003).

Exploitive maneuvers require rapid decision-making and swift concentration and deployment of resources. This is as much a function of executive will as well as availability of liquid resources. Consider how Microsoft made a dramatic shift in its Internet strategy in the aftermath of the success of Netscape and its Navigator browser in 1995. Within a matter of weeks, Microsoft had transformed its Internet focus, from a handful of people to several hundred.

Speed of action is critical since exploitive maneuvers are largely about harvesting the fruits of opportunities, or side-stepping threats that may be presented suddenly. In military strategy, victory is achieved when the dislocation produced by fighting is consolidated. Many firms fail to achieve this "final victory" because even though all the right ingredients have been put in place, that final consolidation is ignored.

Consider the controller company discussed earlier. It learned a valuable lesson from its earlier experiences, gradually diversifying its customer base to include manufacturers of disk drives, engineering workstations and super-microcomputers. The industry standard eventually migrated upward to the SCSI (small computer standard interface) product that it had earlier pioneered. Although the earlier corrective maneuvers kept the company afloat, it positioned it for its later success as a technology leader in its industry.

By this time, some of its competitors had begun to integrate forward into the disk drive sector, propelled by the trend toward "embedding" the controller directly onto disk drives. During the course of this industry evolution, the company had devised a computer-aided design system for developing SCSI controllers. These were intended for its own internal use. The objective was to reduce its product development lead-time, and to improve customer service by providing sophisticated test procedures.

As the end-user market became more memory-intensive, (as a result of the diffusion of local area networks, desk top publishing, and computer-aided design) the new standard became dominant. By this time, disk drive manufacturers also started to embed controllers in their products. Their goal was to optimize the higher capacity drives, and to reduce costs. Additionally, embedding a controller directly onto the drive electronics, removed the need for a slot to house a controller printed circuit board inside a desk-top device.

This industry trend provided the company with a fleeting opportunity. It packaged the design tools for sale to drive, peripherals and system manufacturers as a complete SCSI computer-aided design system (CAD). The CAD system allowed drive engineers to debug and test a SCSI product and also enabled a test or quality engineer to generate complex and repeatable tests and documentation for quality control of SCSI peripherals.

Revenues from the sale of these systems were not significant in themselves. However, this move positioned the company for the long haul by tying its customers to its own in-house design and prototyping processes. The move was only possible in this case because of the earlier corrective maneuvers; first, in deciding to downgrade its SCSI controller for the PC environment, second, in diversifying its customer base.

In summary, a firm needs to engage in exploitive maneuvers by rapidly recognizing opportunity and threat signals, and by mobilizing liquid resources quickly to capitalize on them. A corollary of this is that it is also crucial to exit a "honey pot" before it becomes totally exhausted so as not to get stuck with obsolete resources and the remnants of a depleted opportunity. This is a hard lesson learned by many investors during the Internet boom years. Instead of leaving the market before it reached its saturation point, they re-invested their gains in the hope of making even more. The outcome, with hindsight, was easy to predict, but it is a critical lesson when embarking on exploitive maneuvers.

5.6   Maneuvering and Super-Flexibility

This chapter presents a conceptual framework on how knowledge enterprises can navigate their dynamic trajectory. The objective is to become super-flexible by deploying different types of maneuvers, often in parallel. The concept of a maneuver is a means of aggregating and linking the intent, the capabilities and the opportunities facing a knowledge enterprise. The four types of maneuver we have outlined in this chapter provide conceptual coat-hangers for aggregating strategic initiatives and executive talent across business portfolios in dynamic settings. They provide the granularity to differentiate between diverse capabilities needed to achieve super-flexibility.

The capabilities required for each type of maneuver are demonstrably different. Having the liquidity to exploit an unexpected opportunity, for example, by buying a company, is qualitatively different from possessing a resilient disposition to recover from an accident. Similarly, reliance on insurance, buffers or slack, to protect against potentially damaging situations, is different from being agile or versatile when embarking on a preemptive or an exploitive maneuver. Clearly, these are all in some way related, yet the practicalities of how to act in each situation differ considerably.

Furthermore, in an ever-changing world, the maneuvers framework can be used not only to allocate resources and prioritize strategic initiatives, but to assign executive talent to different types of initiatives. Just as sports teams have different capabilities in defenders versus strikers, businesses also have talent pools that may be better suited to one form of maneuvering, rather than another. It takes a very different person to be a good scanner, quickly recognizing nascent opportunities, compared to a skeptic, who may be ideal at anticipating and thinking through worst case scenarios and preparing for protective maneuvers. Similarly, a turnaround expert, who is good at instilling a sense of urgency and focusing on corrective maneuvers, is quite different to someone who is prospecting or thinking about pre-emptive initiatives for the future.

In embarking on maneuvers, executive teams must also think in terms of deploying parallel maneuvers and considering the right combination of actions, depending on circumstances. Business leaders expect tomorrow to be different from today. However, it is rare for a firm to be prepared to change course mid-stream, even when it knows it should, because of the emotional and psychological momentum that may have been already generated in a particular direction. As Bourcet (1888) observed, strategy should be like the branches of a tree, each one leading to the desired outcome.

The center of gravity of a strategic problem shifts continuously in knowledge enterprises. What might be right one day, may not make sense on another. A dynamic combination of different maneuvers is needed to achieve the appropriate type of flexibility in any given situation. This chapter outlined various forms that these maneuvers might take, although these categories are by no means exhaustive. As illustrated by the examples, the critical point is that maneuvering for super-flexibility requires the conjunction of different capabilities and the deployment of several actions.

Compared to approaches that assume a situation has no antecedents, we recognize the influence of past time periods. Previous actions constrain the freedom to maneuver. This is why the temporal dimension of maneuvering is important. While developing the capacity for achieving a super-flexible response is ideally undertaken before its deployment, its actual value is largely realized from maneuvers executed at a point of engagement. As we discussed in chapter 2, being super-flexible is as much about being spontaneous, as it is about developing the capability to address contingencies ahead of time. Spontaneity requires revising previous positions, as well as developing new ones "on the spot".

The term "potential surprise"(Shackle 1953) encompasses the dramatic as well as the ordinary events that cause future states of the world, as well as stakeholders' values and preferences, to be at variance, or to deviate, from prior expectations. Many firms have adopted a multi-scenario approach as a means of predicting possible future states of the world. Clearly, this circumvents some of the pitfalls associated with uni-dimensional extrapolations. However, since only one future state actually comes into being, it may be expensive to prepare for every imaginable contingency and probably impossible to prepare for the unimaginable. It is, however, precisely because of this paradox that super-flexibility has intuitive value.

In this chapter, we suggested that knowledge firms in dynamic settings have to maneuver in order to navigate their dynamic trajectory. Effective maneuvering requires the conjunction of various actions to provide the capability to do things differently. The maneuvering framework, presented in this chapter, incorporated the time and the intent dimensions and proposed four operational maneuvers as a means of achieving different forms of super-flexibility.

Super-flexibility is at a premium when the rules by which a game gets played are being perpetually redefined, or when the nature of the game itself changes. Experience has shown that it is critical for high technology firms to develop this capability. While the need for such maneuvers, deployed individually or collectively, is almost self-evident in Silicon Valley, its value in other knowledge-based settings should not be underestimated.

6 Recalibrating:
Learning by Exploring and Revising

How do high technology firms embark on major strategic initiatives when most of the relevant information, like a moving target, is shrouded in the mist of uncertainty? How can they be systematic and consistent, when ambiguity is a fact of daily life in their ecosystem? How do their strategic processes embrace deliberate intentions, conscious choices, unexpected developments, and emergent learning? These were some of the questions we explored in order to understand how high technology firms embark on critical moves in dynamic environments.

This chapter is about how technology companies strive for super-flexibility in their decision processes. We present the "recalibration" framework in order to explain how many enterprises engage in action when they have limited information and face moving targets. The recalibration process is about exploring by probing, experimenting, generating factual feedback, and revising plans accordingly. The emphasis is on empirical pragmatism rather than on theoretical consistency. Analogous to the scientific model of discovery, we describe the inter-linked stages of experimentation, escalation, and integration, as a phased approach for exploration in dynamic settings. We conclude the chapter by putting forward a few practical guidelines for implementing the recalibration framework.

6.1 Conceptual Underpinnings

The literature on innovative and decision-making is extensive and spans several disciplines. For our purposes, the dominant themes can be clustered into two broad categories: those that emphasize the deliberate, the intentional, and often the top-down processes that guide action; and those that highlight the emergent, the spontaneous, and the bottom-up initiatives that may coalesce over time and lead to innovative outcomes.[33]

---

[33] This chapter draws on several streams of research. These include models of the innovation process (Utterback 1971, Burgelman 1983, 2002, Chesbrough 2003, Christensen 1997); features of successful innovations (Rothwell *et al.* 1974, Maidique and Zirger 1984, Thomke 2003); factors that impede effective commercialization of innovations (Teece 1987); sources of new innovations (von Hippel, 1986); characteristics of innovative organizations (Kanter 1983, Quinn 1979); organizational arrangements for nurturing innovation (Burgelman and Sayles 1986, Roberts 1980, Romanelli 1987, Tushman and

According to the "deliberate" models, strategies are formulated, on the basis of clear intentions, conscious choices, and careful planning. As depicted in Figure 8, first, objectives are spelled out and preferences clarified. Next, relevant information is collected and analyzed; alternatives are generated and their pros and cons are assessed. Finally, the optimal solution is selected, and the chosen option is implemented. The implicit assumption is that implementation follows planning with a "clean sheet" to work with, and that collecting and analyzing relevant information up front can reduce uncertainties.

Figure 8. The deliberate model

Proponents of the "emergent" model put forward an alternative view. Drawing on studies of "radical innovations" and new ventures in established firms, this school of thought suggests that strategies typically "emerge" spontaneously through actions of autonomous actors.[34] If the appropriate cultural norms and incentive systems are put in place, innovative initiatives will follow. As illustrated in Figure 9, lower-level champions, those closest to action, are empowered to act entrepreneurially and are rewarded accordingly.

O'Reilly 1992); and profiles of high technology enterprises (Cooper and Bruno, 1977, Maidique and Hayes 1984, Meyer and Roberts 1986, Moore 1992).

[34] Classic studies on this perspective include: Allison (1971), Lindblom (1959), March and Olsen (1976).

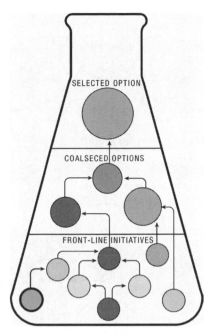

Figure 9. The emergent model

Our observations suggest that neither the emergent nor the deliberate modes portray how successful high technology firms embark on major initiatives; although clearly some elements of both approaches are typically present. In the emergent mode, there is little or no intentional effort to create options. Options may be generated through random events, accidents, luck, or individual initiatives. Sole reliance on purely emergent modes can leave a technology enterprise vulnerable in turbulent settings. It assumes that effective outcomes depend on luck, serendipity, and other forces beyond a firm's control. The purely deliberate mode, on the other hand, does not accommodate spontaneous developments or unique events that may unexpectedly arise. Assumptions embedded in elaborate plans and detailed analyses may become irrelevant or meaningless by surprises, such as the departure of a key executive or the unexpected loss of a critical account.

Embarking on new initiatives in dynamic technology settings is somewhat challenging. Leaders must be decisive and act swiftly since time is limited and opportunities are short-lived. However, decisions have to be taken in the context of incomplete information and fluctuating parameters. Key stakeholders may be reluctant to entertain the risks involved in embarking on a major initiative. So how do executive teams move ahead when faced with such high levels of uncertainty?

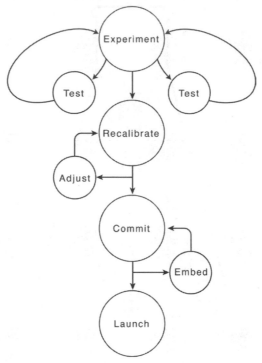

Figure 10. The recalibration model

The realities and complexities may be best illustrated through a case vignette that demonstrates the limitations of traditional approaches in volatile technology settings. Consider the situation facing Shugart Corporation, the disk drive pioneer, discussed in chapters 3 and 4, during the early 1980s. With sales of over $250 million, at the time it was the world's largest supplier of low capacity disk drives. The management team was anxious to extend its leading position. From a competitive standpoint, the company was in a difficult position. It was squeezed in the middle of a pincer movement, between niche start-ups and Japanese electronic manufacturers. In addition, unit prices were falling rapidly in the low capacity floppy end of the market.

This rupturing of the price umbrella had become a major source of pressure on margins. Procurement and manufacturing costs had to be reduced accordingly. Shugart had taken steps to cut costs by setting up a procurement office in Singapore. Attention then shifted to the manufacturing front, on ways that it could provide additional capacity on a fully competitive cost basis. Four options had been seriously considered; creation of a highly automated capability in the U.S.; expansion of the company's existing manufacturing facility in Mexico; partnership with a major manufacturer (such as a Japanese firm); and establishment of a company-owned manufacturing facility in Singapore.

The parent company, Xerox, had insisted that, in accordance with its own planning procedures, all the relevant information about every option should be systematically collected and analyzed, highlighting the costs and the benefits associated with each alternative. This would enable its executives to make an "optimal" decision and provide relevant input.

However, the "relevant" information was in a state of flux. For example, projected sales price and product cost data were revised continuously due to the unexpectedly rapid penetration of low cost Japanese disk drives in the aftermath of the PC explosion in the U.S. market. Component costs (a significant portion of total product cost) were fluctuating. The cost of setting up an offshore facility was increasing because of changing tax laws and rising cost of land and building. Nonetheless, Shugart attempted to convince its parent, through a detailed strategic and financial plan, that the favored option, the Singapore facility, represented the most optimal solution for lowering manufacturing costs.

The process went on for about 18 months as corporate staff requested more detailed information and fine-tuned the financial costs associated with each option. In the meantime, the competitive landscape was being transformed. A number of start-ups at the time had already moved to the Far East, and Japanese manufacturers were making aggressive inroads into the U.S. market.

No tangible action had yet been taken. The search continued for the "perfect information" on which an "optimal" decision could be based. During the intervening time frame, Shugart lost a number of key accounts. This resulted in a significant loss of market share in the low-end floppy disk drive market, where it had traditionally retained a leading position. By 1986, Xerox divested Shugart and the company ceased to exist in its original form. Portions of its business were sold to different investors. While, with the benefit of hindsight, it is easy to speculate, many experts believed that if decisive action had been taken early on to lower its manufacturing costs, the outcome may have been quite different.

6.2   The Framework: Recalibration

While there is extensive managerial literature on how to make "optimal", "best" or "correct" decisions, there is relatively limited attention focused on how to revise a decision if it turns out to be unsatisfactory, or if the assumptions underpinning the original decision change unexpectedly.[35] Many successful innovations or winning business strategies are the result of many revisions made to a product or a service, often driven by the necessity of unfolding circumstances. In technology settings, the challenge is to embark on action, and modify and adjust in evolving circumstances. The imperative is to be decisive, yet surf dynamic waves of market, technological and global uncertainty.

Effective initiatives we have observed in many technology firms over the years share several characteristics: guided intentions, spontaneous developments, tangible feedback, and swift revisions. They can be described as a montage of deliberate intentions, random events, and emergent learning. While they are not entirely chaotic, elements of luck, timing and spontaneity clearly play significant roles. Nor are they purely deliberate and systematically planned *a priori*, although broad intentions circumscribe the boundaries around selected directional pathways. Moreover, experiential learning along the way, coupled with the development of new competencies, underscore their partially emergent character.

The emphasis is on exploring, experimenting, learning, and recalibrating as results become clear, or as new realities unfold.[36] Re-calibration occurs in response to, or in anticipation of, unexpected developments, experiential learning, tangible obstacles, and concrete successes. Following the initial pilots, an idea may be rejected altogether. The deciding criterion is practical "relevance" and factual feedback rather than theoretical elegance and informational consistency. As depicted in Figure 11, the recalibration process blends the most desired features of the deliberate and the emergent approaches, yet it has its own unique characteristics.

The process resembles the scientific method of discovery. Scientists formulate hypotheses and assess their validity by conducting experiments

---

[35] For a practical perspective on making optimal decisions, see Hammond *et al.* (1999).

[36] This emphasis on the importance of learning has been noted by other studies. In describing the birth of the video recorder industry, Rosenbloom and Cusumano (1987) discuss how the development of Betamax and VHS by Sony and Japan Victor Corporation were "the tangible results of fifteen years of learning by trying." (p. 66). Similarly, Maidique and Zirger (1985) characterize the new product development cycle in high technology firms as a learning process in which innovators learn not only by doing, but also by failing. This in turn results in the development of new alternatives and product concepts.

and collecting data. If the initial experiments do not support the original hypotheses, new hypotheses should be framed, and tested yet again. However, scientists are not typically in full control of all the salient parameters. A new discovery, or unexpected results, can change the embedded assumptions and even make the work obsolete.

Similarly, in the recalibration framework, the processes of strategy formation and implementation are closely linked together in an iterative process, especially during the early stage of a new initiative. In unpredictable business settings, it is impossible to iron out all the uncertainties and "derisk" strategies through detailed planning and elaborate analyses. Relevant information is not only limited, but also in flux. It may also be difficult to establish the technical feasibility of a novel idea, or the viability of executing a new initiative, through "theoretical" planning. By engaging in action, new information can be brought to light, and unforeseen limitations, and new possibilities, identified.

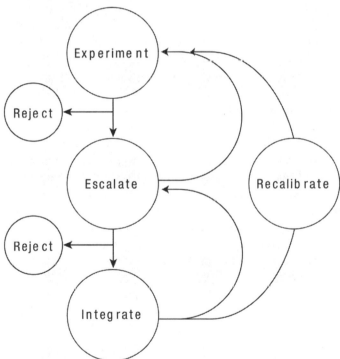

Figure 11. The recalibration process

The recalibration process starts with forging a broad strategic vision, analogous to a scientific hypothesis, testing its feasibility through experimentation and prototyping, and retaining the flexibility to modify plans as new developments unfold. The emphasis is on continuous re-calibration through guided experimentation. The challenge for entrepreneurs and executives is threefold:

- To ensure that time triggers are built into the process,
- To ensure that selected actions lead to effective outcomes,
- To ensure that sufficient flexibility is built in, so the process can adapt over time

6.3   Case History: The Recalibration Process

The recalibration framework can be best illustrated by drawing on the strategic evolution of ROLM Corporation, a Silicon Valley pioneer in the telecommunications industry during the 1970s and early 1980s. ROLM was acquired by IBM in 1984 and has since become part of Siemens, the global electronics giant. ROLM was a pioneering Silicon Valley company, blazing the trail in un-chartered territories. It was the first firm to introduce the concept of off-the-shelf commercial computing to the military market during the early 1970s, an early challenger to AT&T's dominance in the telecommunications equipment field, and a pioneer of "integrated office of the future" during the early 1980s.

ROLM was founded in 1969. Its four founders had known one another first at Rice University, and later at the Stanford Engineering School. The founding team's first business venture was to pioneer a unique commercial approach in selling minicomputers to the tradition-bound military establishment. Although the team established a viable business base in this niche market, their overriding goal was to build a sizeable "commercial" concern. Minicomputers had been a timely opportunity to get the business off the ground. However, after 3 years, the founders became concerned about the limited size of that market and its long-term potential for building a sizeable commercial enterprise.

In the early 1970s, the founding team embarked on a pre-emptive search for a new business opportunity and decided to enter the telecommunications business. The 1968 Carterfone decision of the Federal Communications Commission had partially deregulated the US telecommunications industry, opening up the vast telephone equipment market to a host of new companies. The intention was to leverage ROLM's core skills by developing a computer-controlled telephone switching system, with enhanced capabilities, compared with the traditional electromechanical units.

ROLM had to be navigated through the uncertain and stormy seas of the industry. Computing technology was changing the nature of telephones and telecommunications. There was considerable debate about the eventual de-regulation of the industry, despite AT&T's concerted efforts to retain its long-standing position as a regulated monopoly. The interconnect distribution channel was just beginning to get off the ground, and competition had intensified with the entry of Japanese and European giants in the field. In short, the industry was in a state of chaos and confusion.

At the time, many expert observers questioned the ability of a young, unknown player, like ROLM, to survive, let alone prosper. in a different arena. Despite the initial, often grave, misgivings of many expert observers, ROLM managed to become a leading telecommunications firm during the next 5 years. By the late 1970s, telecommunications products accounted for almost 70% of its total revenues.

ROLM consolidated its strategic position during the early 1980s by making selected forays into the "office of the future", focusing on integrated voice/data terminals, and computerized voice messaging systems. IBM acquired ROLM in the aftermath of AT&T's divestiture in 1984. At the time of the acquisition, ROLM was called "the ship that is creating the wave of innovation in the field" and a "forerunner in the fast-paced (telecommunications) market."[37] These tributes were clearly reflected in its impressive market performance. After only 10 years in the business, ROLM had managed to capture 15% of the market for office telephone switches, only 9% behind AT&T. Another measure of its remarkable success was the dramatic increase in its stock price. Compared with the 1,920 companies that had gone public since 1975, ROLM's stock produced the largest long-term relative gain over its initial offering price.

ROLM's pioneering moves were not based on detailed analyses and elaborate plans, but on a few fundamental principles, many informal discussions, and a series of experiments, designed to test the validity of their business propositions. These were initially tested on a small scale. After producing concrete feedback, they were re-calibrated, and either executed on a large scale, with resource commitment and organizational momentum, or discontinued altogether. This posture is reflected in the way that ROLM evolved its business strategy over a 16 year time frame, moving from military computers, to telecommunications, to energy management, and finally to office systems:

"In building ROLM as a company, we experimented in a number of different areas, people, technology, markets, organization, products and cultural policies... we gave a chance to those whose experience and tangible

---

[37] San Francisco Chronicle, September 26, 1984; For additional perspectives on the ROLM/IBM merger see the Economist, September 29, 1984 and the Wall Street Journal, September 27, 1984.

expertise did not, at least on paper, qualify them to take on certain assignments. For example,... our first CFO, took on the assignment to build our direct sales organization during the late 1970s. We were also constantly experimenting with new organizational arrangements. Some worked and some didn't. For example, in 1980 we set up a 3-person top management team to run the company, and before entrepreneurship became popular, we set up a self-contained autonomous division to build and develop our family of digital telephones. But perhaps the biggest experiments involved our strategic diversification, from Mil-Spec computers, to PBXs, to energy management, and finally office systems. "[38]

The approach that ROLM and many other technology pioneers typically follow can be characterized as a continuous process of engaging, probing, testing, prototyping, and recalibrating. The initial "experimentation" stage clarifies intentions, generates options, assesses feasibility, and tests the stakeholders' reaction to a particular initiative. The initiative is speeded up and brought into a sharper focus during the crucial "escalation" phase, with greater visibility, concentration of effort, and concerted use of resources. During the final "integration" phase, attempts are made to blend the initiative into the broader strategic and organizational context, and to ensure cohesion of thrust across interdependent units.

6.3.1 Experimentation

The desire to embark on a major strategic initiative may be triggered by a number of factors. These may include market trends, competitive moves, technical breakthroughs, management choices, or random events. ROLM's move into telecommunications, for instance, was initially triggered by the top team's concern over the limited size of the military computer market and its long-term viability for a commercial entity.

"ROLM's objective is to grow to be a large profitable company, in an atmosphere where everyone contributing to that growth, learns, grows and is financially rewarded...The military computer business is currently a good, stable base ... however, it has not satisfied our objective of broad customer appeal ... our freedom to develop products on our own funds is severely limited ... stability and growth are essentially dependent on one ... customer ... worst of all is our limited flexibility ... we should (therefore) not sacrifice strategy and principles just for short term growth in the

---

[38] Personal communication with ROLM's co-founder & CEO.

military market ... let's realize that that business is good, but limited, and accept it for what it is."[39]

In general, the experimentation phase enables a leadership team to formulate tentative propositions, test them on a small scale, and generate rapid "factual" feedback. Early experimentation and prototyping also has other advantages. It inculcates an organizational mindset willing to embrace new information. It fleshes out viable options about which there may be limited experience. Moreover, it provides a vehicle for recursive learning. For example, ROLM's early experiments in office systems during the 1980s developed its capability base in terminals and information systems, areas in which it had limited prior experience.

Many of the technology firms we have observed initiate new moves by forming exploratory propositions. These may be based on long-term intentions, opportunities in emerging markets, competitive dynamics, and the perceived capabilities of the organization. The overarching objective during this phase is to clarify intentions, develop capability, and create viable options.

Just as scientists use experiments to check the validity of scientific hypotheses, pilots and prototypes can be used to assess the validity of a business idea. Initiated as deliberate, pre-emptive initiatives, pilots are especially valuable when there are no existing blueprints or proven methods. Experiments can be set up in parallel in order to speed up the learning process. Effective experimentation provides a basis for selecting viable pathways, testing the feasibility of proposed ideas, managing the stakeholders' expectations, and recasting the forged vision.

For example, technical and marketing experiments were the prelude to ROLM's entry into the telecommunications business during the early 1970s. During this time, there was considerable uncertainty about the eventual de-regulation of the industry, the future role of computer technology in telecommunications, and the viability of the emerging interconnect industry as a distribution channel. The ROLM team hired a technical consultant to put together an initial prototype, and recruited a product manager to lead the new PBX initiative. Both had worked for HP for some time and knew one another.

One of the product manager's first initiatives was to interview a number of potential customers about their telecommunications needs and their willingness to buy a PBX system from a young upstart, like ROLM. It was these lead user interviews that convinced the team that the opportunity was

---

[39] Internal memorandum, ROLM Corporation, May 1971.

worth pursuing. This was not just another unique idea, but had traction with the lead users. The PBX team could envision the enhanced capabilities that a computer could bring to the plain old telephone:

"Clearly we had the capability, the computer technology, to solve meaningful customer problems, and save them a lot of money ... we could optimize call routings, or handle toll restrictions ... and handling moves and changes would simply be a matter of re-programming the computer ... no one would have to visit the customer's site."[40]

Various organizational arrangements can be used during this phase. These include use of contractors and consultants, as was the situation in ROLM's PBX case, small internal project teams, and even spin-off units. A financial software company, for example, used an external contractor and temporary consultants, to staff an aggressive development project for a new product. The entire process, from initial pilot to full launch, was completed in 100 days. Use of external contractors was viewed as a flexible, fast, and de-politicized approach to a project that was perceived to be critical to its future success.

In summary, the experimentation stage augments and refines the initial vision. The process enhances learning, develops organizational momentum for a new initiative, reduces uncertainty, and provides a basis for assessing the feasibility of various options. Moreover, speed of feedback in crucial during this phase since time is limited and resources are scarce. Effective experimentation requires a small, dedicated, team of thinkers and doers, who can act and engage cohesively, and who do not have to co-ordinate their actions with a broad range of stakeholders:

"... we can try out 10 different approaches to solving a problem ... we may fail at eight of them, but we still have succeeded at 2 of them. We don't know if something will work ... we can either analyze it to death or we can try it out in a controlled fashion."[41]

6.3.2 Escalation

An experimental attitude and a flexible posture cannot be maintained indefinitely. Once the level of market uncertainty is reduced and the techni-

---

[40] Personal communication with ROLM's Vice President of Marketing and its first PBX Product Manager.

[41] Comment by Hatim Tyabji, CEO of VeriFone, HBS case study on Verifone, #N9-195-088, July 1994.

cal feasibility of a new idea is partly verified, a team must move beyond experimentation and focus on ramping-up promising options. Whereas option generation, action-based exploration, and recursive learning are critical during experimentation, the escalation stage should enhance focus and speed up execution by concentrating resources on selected options.

This stage represents concerted efforts to select and refine the most promising options. It also signals senior management's commitment and their willingness to allocate resources and attention to a promising initiative. The primary objective is to build momentum, "to put the foot on the gas pedal" and to ramp-up a project that may have a short life cycle.

In the many cases we have observed, the decision to escalate, to discontinue, or to revise a project beyond experimentation is based on several factors. These include evolving industry dynamics, experiential learning, and organizational expediency. For example, ROLM's initial "grand" strategy in office automation during the early 1980s embraced several products. These included an application processor, a common engine for the telephone switching equipment and the office products, a proprietary, intelligent workstation to integrate voice and data, and various software modules to provide voice messaging, text messaging, and word processing capabilities. In time, these building blocks were to be integrated and were expected to work with the proprietary workstation. The total package was perceived to provide a comprehensive office automation capability for the end-user.

However, after the initial pilots, it became clear that the strategy was far too complex to execute in its original form. As ROLM's co-founder and the senior executive in charge of the program commented:

"Every time we reviewed the projects, they had slipped another 3 months ... we realized that we weren't getting very far with implementing the grand strategy ... and had underestimated the magnitude of what we had taken on ... if (the strategy) was going to happen, it would have to happen in bits and pieces ... so we had to change our approach, prioritize, and focus on those projects that were feasible to implement and were most critical for our competitive positioning." [42]

The original strategic assumptions had also changed during the intervening period with the introduction of the first generation of IBM Personal Computers. This development had radically changed the word processing business and undermined the rationale behind developing a proprietary workstation. The "grand strategy" was modified to take account of evolv-

---

[42] Personal communication with ROLM's co-founder and Executive Vice President.

ing market dynamics and the experience gained during the early explora-tory moves. The concept of a proprietary workstation was modified into an IBM-PC compatible integrated voice and data terminal, and the word processing project was discontinued. Resources were re-focused instead on the voice-messaging project, and the modified version of the voice/data terminal.

Escalation beyond initial experimentation often results in new organiza-tional arrangements. The intention is to deal with two critical challenges; first, to buffer the new initiative from existing activities, and to minimize distractions; second, to accommodate the growing scope and complexity of a new program. For example, escalation of ROLM's office systems project led to the formation of a separate division with an exclusive focus on new product development initiatives.

Developing effective project management capability is especially criti-cal during this phase. By this stage the initiative has become visible and consumes organizational resources and executive attention. Typically, re-view triggers are built in to assess and monitor progress made in imple-menting pre-defined milestones. These may result in minor revisions or major modifications of the action plan.

Project leadership may also evolve during this phase. Since the initiative is no longer a simple pilot, it may need to be guided through the maze of organizational and political dynamics. A project leader who may have been effective during the experimentation phase, may not have the skills, the experience, or the network to be an effective co-ordinator and bridge-builder during escalation. Even in a young start-up, the guru scientist who may be the early visionary behind a technical prototype, may have to give way to an experienced project manager who is used to tight deadlines and who can manage various stakeholders, including lead users and alliance partners.

6.3.3 Integration

Once an initiative has been successfully launched, it must be blended into the mainstream organizational and business context. The objectives during this "integration" phase are to ensure cohesion of strategic thrust across the business portfolio, and to leverage the existing resource infrastructure. A critical task is to devise organizational arrangements that can integrate the new activity into the mainstream organization.

The choice of integration mechanisms depends on two critical factors: first, the expected growth rate of a new initiative; second, the degree of in-terdependence between the new initiative and existing activities. If, the new business grows rapidly, a separate unit should be set up to focus on its ramp-up, or the unit may even be spun off. Well-known examples include Apple's Claris and Sun's Java Divisions. Similarly, if there is limited interdependence between new and existing activities, an autonomous unit may be appropriate. However, if interdependence is high, or if the new business does not grow rapidly, it can be integrated into the mainstream organization so as to leverage existing infrastructure and resource base.

For example, ROLM formed an autonomous division to consolidate its PBX business when it had generated enough revenues to warrant the formation of a separate unit. A self-contained unit was appropriate because there was limited interdependence between the minicomputer and the telecommunications businesses. The office systems initiative, on the other hand, was closely linked to the telecommunications business. The two sets of products had to work together and were sold through similar distribution channels to the same customer base. The need for extensive co-ordination prompted a company-wide re-organization and led to the formation of a hybrid structure.

After a new initiative "goes live", symbolic changes are also needed to signal the fact that it is no longer "in progress". These may include a change of name, location, logo, leadership, or a broader re-organization. The objective is to emphasize the inflection point and the need for transition and new arrangements.

In summary, deploying the recalibration approach enables executive teams to be decisive and move forward, while keeping their options open. Additionally, this approach minimizes pre-mature psychological and emotional commitment to a high-risk course of action. Critical challenges include customized and variable staffing for each phase, and the timing of the different stages. For example, who should lead the project during experimentation, escalation, and integration? When should a project be initiated and when should it be discontinued? When should a project move on to escalation, with higher levels of investment and commitment? How much time should be allocated to initial experimentation? Under what circumstances should an initiative be put on a "back-burner", and be reconsidered at a later stage?

6.4 Guidelines for Action

Implementing the recalibration framework is challenging. Many companies are used to the top-down, deliberate, approach, with emphasis on planning, data gathering and information analysis. Alternatively, some executives favor the bottom-up or "emergent" approach, assuming that breakthrough initiatives will bubble up, if the culture and the incentives encourage individual champions to kick-start new initiatives.

In a technology setting, resources are typically scarce; time frames are compressed; yet action has to be taken even when there is limited information. Deploying the recalibration framework generates factual feedback from concrete action, and enables teams to revise plans and intentions as new realities unfold. A major trade-off is how to be consistent, yet remain flexible and responsive to emerging realities.

Consider the use of the recalibration approach by a computer peripherals company during the late 1990s. The setting was the annual leadership conference, bringing together the executive team and its top 100 executives. The objective was to reflect on industry changes and to consider future strategic moves. The explosion of the Internet had opened up new growth opportunities for the company. The leadership conference was focused on how best these opportunities could be leveraged. After a series of heated discussions, where contrasting views were presented and debated, the CEO decided to set up two parallel teams, in order to explore two different product/ service possibilities.

Each team, comprising a cross-section of top performers from across the Group, was given eight weeks and a small budget to conduct research, listen to experts, interview potential lead users, and brainstorm alternatives. Two presentations were later made to the executive team, laying out options that could be further explored. After a few hours of debate and discussion, it was decided to set up two pilot projects to explore the feasibility of the proposed options.

The experimentation phase lasted for ten weeks. During this time, each team talked to potential customers and developed technical prototypes. After communicating their findings to the executive team, it was decided to blend "the best of both efforts" since neither pilot had generated conclusive results. The recalibrated project later led to the launch of a major new service business for the company and has since become a significant revenue and profit generator.

Several guidelines should be considered in implementing the recalibration process:

Keep the big picture in mind, but implement in small, bite-sized steps:

Many new initiatives start off as a broad idea, initially triggered by customers' needs, competitive dynamics, lead user feedback, performance crises, and the arrival and departure of key executives. In the absence of a major crisis or a market imperative, new initiatives can get stuck in endless internal debates and discussions, with various factions jockeying for their favorite idea.

Effective approaches we have observed tend to follow a common path. There is intense discussion early on, but these conversations quickly move on to the testing phase. The emphasis is on generating factual feedback that can be used to assess the go/no-go decision and to revise the original idea.

Two sets of activities are crucial during this process: first, identifying and mapping the tough challenges and the easy tasks, characterized as the "low and high hanging fruit". This mapping process gives different stakeholders a common perception of reality and "keeps them on the same page". However, effective use of the recalibration framework starts with the relatively simple tasks, or the "low hanging fruit", that have a quick payoff. This is similar to the findings of other studies that have examined successful change initiatives (Kotter 1996). Quick wins build the core team's confidence, generate credibility among the critical stakeholders, and provide the foundation for taking on the tougher challenges.

Develop focused pilots/test a single or limited hypotheses:

New initiatives can become political battlefields. Each faction seeks to stamp its own agenda on the blueprint. The typical outcome of this factional politics is that the initial pilot is doomed to fail because it is designed to "build consensus", appeal to the lowest common denominator, and ward off potential criticism from vocal cynics and skeptics. In other words, it gets diluted and loses its focus. While this approach may be politically expedient, it is ineffective in terms of generating timely, relevant, fact-based, feedback that can be used to escalate, curtail or recalibrate the initiative.

To avoid this problem, it is important to initially focus on testing only one or just a few propositions, so the pilot does not get "muddied" by too many considerations. When the ROLM team first considered entering the digital PBX business, their main objective was to find out whether telecommunications managers of large companies, their target customers, would forego the relative safety of buying an analog system from the dominant provider, AT&T, instead of taking a chance by buying the latest digital technology from an unknown player. The deciding factor would be the trade-off between the superior technological features of the ROLM product, versus the relative safety of buying an older technology from AT&T.

This idea was tested early on by a number of lead user interviews. The PBX product manager talked to 50 telecom managers in Fortune 500 companies. Their response was overwhelming. If the digital PBX could help account for each department's telephone usage, so they could be billed directly, they would buy the new system. By testing a single hypothesis that was critical to the plan's success, the ROLM team was able to get factual feedback about a subject that would impact the viability of the entire initiative.

Keep a low profile early on and express intentions in general terms:

There is a trade-off between being "consistent" and having the flexibility to modify decisions as new realities unfold. This can pose a problem during the early phases of a new initiative. Leadership teams can limit their flexibility to recalibrate, or to discontinue a project, by committing to a specific course of action early on and by raising their profiles,

It is easier to implement the recalibration framework if leaders keep a low profile, and express their intentions in broad, general terms, especially during the early phases, This enables them to manage stakeholders' expectations, pursue several options within the broader frame of reference, and give the initiators the opportunity to recalibrate at a later date. The original idea can even be dismissed, if the expected benefits do not materialize.

This trade-off is reflected in the approach of a new generation of entrepreneurs whose ventures are known as "stealth start-ups". They prefer to "boot-strap" their ventures, maintain a low profile and keep their options open during the crucial early stages, They are also more reticent to use venture capital early on, believing that money is an insufficient contribution to counterbalance the risks of disclosing the intent of a new venture to a broader community.

Similarly, serial entrepreneurs often stay with their original investors as a way of maintaining "stealth" because they don't have to shop around their business plan to a larger group of investors. Timing plays a critical role here, too. During the boom years, entrepreneurs can ratchet up their valuations by going from one venture firm to another,

Stealth start-ups increase their chances of being first to market by not alerting potential competitors to their business proposition. Another benefit is that they have the flexibility to recalibrate and change tack, without appearing "inconsistent". Investors are not easily convinced that change is a good idea, when it was the original idea that appealed to their judgment. Adopting a stealth posture provides two benefits for entrepreneurial teams; first, it shades their activity from public view and keeps their options open; second, it allows the necessary revisions to be made, without having to justify these to a broader group of stakeholders.

Set up parallel pilots and rapid feedback loops:

Real-time information processing is critical when operating in dynamic environments. It links stimulus, thought and action as one movement. It is no good marching down a path that has become irrelevant or obsolete. Initial pilots should be set up so they can generate factual feedback quickly, before the original assumptions underlying the initiative become obsolete. The most successful pilots we have observed tend to have a 30-60 day time frame. If they linger for much longer, the feedback generated may be interesting, but irrelevant. In the process the initiative can lose momentum and credibility.

Setting up parallel pilots, to test different hypotheses or to address various stakeholders' viewpoints, can speed up the learning cycle. It is also one way to accommodate different internal factions. If implemented effectively, the approach can be used to learn from diverse experiences in compressed time frames.

This is how ROLM orchestrated the implementation of its direct sales and service strategy during the late 1970s. At the time there was no "ideal" approach in terms of how this should be done. Some favored the acquisition route; others preferred building the sales team from the ground up. After some initial discussions, the ROLM team adopted a three-pronged approach. They acquired some of their existing distributors; they set up joint ventures with a few distributors; and they formed their own direct sales force in major metropolitan areas from scratch: *"There was no magic answer ... it had to happen based on given options in each territory ... we tried all three and learned a lot in the process."*[43]

Darwinism is OK — anticipate "worst case" scenarios early and swiftly prune out ineffective initiatives:

A challenging dilemma is how to balance the emotional and the factual elements involved in launching a new initiative. On the one hand, factual feedback should be used to assess the feasibility of a particular idea. On the other hand, people have rationalizing tendencies and become emotionally committed to a given course of action, even when there is factual evidence to the contrary (Staw 1983).

In order to minimize potential problems associated with escalation of commitment to a failing course of action, it is important to anticipate worse case scenarios ahead of time, develop a bandwidth of expectations, and plan contingencies, just in case. What if the technical prototype does not perform according to specification? What if the target market evolves

---

[43] Personal communication with ROLM's CFO and the senior executive responsible for setting up the sales and service organization.

much more slowly than expected? What if we lose some of the key technical talent critical to this project?

These questions should be addressed early on, before stakeholders become committed to a given trajectory. The process enables core teams to consider back-up plans in case they face major setbacks. Additionally, by pruning failed initiatives, recycling them into other activities, or simply putting the initiative on hold for some time, business leaders can redeploy the talent pool as well as the resources and focus on the most promising options.

6.5 Recalibrating and Super-Flexibility

The recalibration framework is predicated on a core assumption. Project management capabilities as well as stakeholder buy-in and commitment, are equally crucial in launching new initiatives. The framework seeks to blend both dimensions and can provide super-flexibility by building resilience, enhancing agility, and developing versatile capabilities.

6.5.1 Building Resilience by Managing Expectations

Deploying the recalibration approach does not guarantee success. However, it does provide an opportunity to test the feasibility of an idea before escalating financial and psychological commitment. If the experiment proves to be infeasible or unsuccessful, losses can be cut quickly, without branding it as a failure, or investing additional resources. An experimental approach can therefore build resilience by managing stakeholder expectations.

For example, the more established venture capital firms often deliberately invest in more than one start-up in a "new category". This is done with the wisdom gained from prior experience. Even with the most sophisticated forecasting, it is difficult to predict in advance, which firm, if any, will evolve to dominate the new arena. By seeding and investing in several start-ups in the same category at the same time, they can increase the odds of succeeding in a low probability game, where the chances of success for a new start-up are around 1 in 30.

This approach has additional benefits. It can increase the breadth of experimentation and the generation of alternative approaches. It can be useful for training a large number of executives and scientists. It can encourage variation in product features, and the ability to meet diverse customer needs. It can expand the lead-user base whose feedback is crucial for revising the product or the service. It can also manage their limited partners' expectations in terms of the winning proposition or the successful business model. As indicated in chapter 4, some ventures are discontinued, and the most promising elements of others are fused together. This is the "recycling" process at work.

6.5.2 Becoming Agile by Speeding Up Implementation

As indicated in the ROLM example, the recalibration approach speeds up implementation and provides agility by focusing on multiple tactical options. This enables an organization to take account of diverse situational needs, and speeds up the learning cycle. By having the ability to jump into several different areas as a "new category" evolves, or by embracing different standards in a device, start-ups develop the agility to quickly regroup behind evolving dominant standard.

6.5.3 Developing Versatile Capabilities

It is crucial to become versatile in dynamic settings by developing new capabilities, especially in areas where there is no previous experience or demonstrable competence. Exploratory experiments can help develop versatile capabilities by enabling learning through trying, failing and retrying from disparate vantage points. This benefit is clearly illustrated by ROLM's exploratory experiments in office systems during the early 1980s, or the way in which Yahoo's co-founders experimented with the Internet during its early days, by keeping track of their favorite television programs.

6.5.4 Summary

The recalibration approach allows deliberate intentions to be tested against emerging realities. It can provide a certain measure of super-flexibility, especially when embarking on new initiatives in unchartered domains. Actions can be framed in the context of a broad vision, yet, decisions evolve as the organization learns new skills and develops capabilities through experimentation and prototyping. The approach is based on generating alternatives, experimenting, and producing factual feedback. Its effectiveness is based on the premise that in fast-moving knowledge-based arenas, feasibility and relevance are critical for success.

It is in this context that super-flexibility is crucial. Recalibration contributes to super-flexibility in several ways:

- It creates versatility by broadening the range of options up front. This expands the scope of qualified information on feasible options. It also enhances knowledge workers' capabilities by exposing them to a wider range of alternatives.
- It instills resilience by removing the stigma of failure and by encouraging recycling and recalibrating, instead of being totally right or exactly wrong.
- It provides liquidity and mobility by recycling failed experiments and releasing knowledge workers so they can be re-deployed and focus on promising options
- It facilitates agility by harnessing alternatives up front, any one of which can be switched into if they become viable at a later stage

There are clear parallels between the recalibration approach and the process of scientific discovery. Scientists update assumptions and hypotheses by taking account of new discoveries and related breakthroughs (Popper 1972, Feyerabend, 1968). Executives of high technology firms have to ensure that their intended plan of action fits with emerging technological, competitive and market realities. Scientific hypotheses have to be corroborated by experimental data. Forged visions of technology entrepreneurs have to be corroborated by market feedback:

"... It is better to loosen things because nobody knows the answer ... give people more space to experiment ... then after you figure it out, we pull in the reins and march in a particular direction." (Interview with Andrew Grove, Outlook magazine, 1997).

7 Orgitechting: Balancing Hard Wire and Soft Glue

How do you create an organizational system that can expand and contract, yet retain its sense of cohesion, purpose and identity? How can technology enhance organizational flexibility without diluting its social fabric? With geo-dispersed virtual teams, how is a sense of cohesion, identity and community achieved? How can an organization be both, robust and resilient, yet agile and versatile?

This chapter describes organizational architectures of technology companies in the context of super-flexibility. We present the "nodal architecture" as a framework that seeks to balance cohesion and stability, together with agility and versatility. We describe the framework's three core building blocks: the clustering, the connective, and the cohesive dimensions. We synthesize the components of each building block, and present a few illustrative examples. We conclude the chapter by putting forward practical suggestions for the effective deployment of nodal architectures.

7.1 Conceptual Underpinnings

The subject of organizational design is often the focus of considerable debate, with wide-ranging pragmatic implications. Flexible architectures have occupied center-stage in recent years because organizational design impacts the execution capability of an enterprise. It determines departmental groupings, accountability patterns, and linking processes. Fundamentally, it determines the alignment between strategy, structure, culture and human resource practices.

The overall objective is to strike a balance between targeted focus through segmentation and modularization on the one hand, and selective co-ordination through synchronization on the other hand. In the classic organizational literature, these twin imperatives are termed "differentiation" and "integration" (Lawrence and Lorsch 1967). A related challenge is to continuously fine-tune and adapt the organizational framework, without reorganizing too frequently so as to cause constant disruption to knowledge workers' productivity.

Flexible architectures are especially critical for execution when there is little time lag between decisions, actions, and consequences. Thinking and doing have to be fused together (Bahrami and Evans 1987). Moreover, in recent years extensive deployment of IT tools has enabled business leaders to experiment with new organizational arrangements (Malone 2004).

The dominant organizational design paradigm of the 1960s and the 1970s, known as the "contingency" perspective, suggested that there is no one ideal configuration suitable for all types of organizations. The thesis is that the appropriate design depends on the organization's age, size, societal conditions during the time of its initial founding, growth trajectory and business diversity. A key contribution of this stream of research is the classification of the dominant organizational archetypes that address various situational contingencies. These range from the "simple", entrepreneurial form to the complex multinational corporation (Miller 1987, Mintzberg 1979). However, contingency factors alone do not explain the adoption of different structural configurations. Notions of strategic "choice" (Child 1972) and "fit" (Miles and Snow 1984) shed additional light on the diffusion of various organizational forms in different contexts. They explain why some organizational forms are more popular and more-widely diffused than others.

Organizational scholars and practitioners have recently turned their attention to the transformational impact of new technologies on organizational design principles and practices. Challenges, such as interdependence, speed and velocity, dis-intermediation, knowledge sharing, paradox and ambiguity, and re-definition of organizational boundaries have taken center stage (Organization Science 1999, Child and McGrath 2001). In general, these studies highlight an overarching theme *"... the traditional function of organizational form, namely to buffer the organization from external uncertainties, is no longer the primary task...as buffering becomes less feasible, we need to offer theories that can help organizations cope with, even embrace, uncertainties."* (Child, personal communication, 2001).

Several recent contributions have focused on emerging organizational architectures and implementation processes that thrive on change and uncertainty. This stream of work is reflected in notions such as the "horizontal" organization, modular structures, business process re-engineering, and knowledge management. The emphasis is on organizational variables that can be leveraged to harness uncertainty, and capitalize on the benefits of technology (Galbraith et al 1994, Galunic and Eisenhardt 2001, Hammer and Champy 1993, Handy 1992, Nonaka and Takeuchi 1995, Quinn 1992, Volberda 1998). Critical areas of research include: How to achieve flexibility as well as efficiency; What is the impact of modularization and standardization; How can charters be changed with speed and efficiency (Child, personal communication, 2001) We hope that our findings on the organizational architectures of high technology companies provide additional insights and offer practical suggestions for addressing a few of the organizational design challenges of the post-digital age.

7.2 Organizational Challenges of Knowledge Enterprises

Creating super-flexible organizational architectures in knowledge-based arenas presents major challenges. Business leaders have to consider several factors concurrently. These include the "people" as well as the business components. Critical "people" challenges include:

- Assembling and grouping talented experts from different disciplines.
- Enabling these experts to deliver results under severe time and resource constraints.
- Accommodating the diverse approaches of multi-cultural employees with complex inter-personal chemistry.
- Co-ordinating different priorities, multi-functional inputs, and geo-dispersed teams.
- Blending together knowledge workers from different generations and industry backgrounds.

There are also significant challenges on the business side. Consider the following complex balancing acts that pre-occupy the leaders of many technology companies:

- Creating an organizational system that can sell and service existing products, services and solutions, while simultaneously nurturing the capacity to design and develop new ones.
- Remaining disciplined, focused, and frugal, while enabling learning, experimenting and re-calibrating.
- Connecting the dispersed organization through the hard wire of IT while ensuring the development of a community-based culture that provides emotional connectivity.
- Developing simple and standard templates and metrics, whilst ensuring the capability for customized approaches that cater for unique, one-off, situations.
- Balancing the need for local accountability and responsiveness, in the context of a well-coordinated global approach.
- Fine-tuning the organizational system to address emerging realities, in the context of a few stable anchors that don't change as frequently:

    "We want an environment that enhances individual creativity but we do not want chaos ... we want people involved in decisions that affect their work and we want teamwork, yet we want our employees to have a bias toward action ... we want small groups of dedicated workers but such groups may feel aimless or may be charging in the

> *wrong direction with hidden agendas ... we want people to stretch to reach tough goals, so our real emphasis is on easily-measured short-term growth and profits, but we should also have time to develop our employees for the longer haul, to promote from within, to monitor the atmosphere for creativity."[44]*

In view of such complex balancing acts, it is not surprising to find that there is no one approach that can address these multi-faceted requirements and constraints. Indeed, during the course of our field research, we have not come across a single entity that has managed to address all these challenges comprehensively. Instead of searching for the ideal recipe or the perfect example, we have found it helpful to distill and synthesize the critical dimensions of organizational architectures that we have observed, and to assess their effectiveness in providing some measure of super-flexibility. By focusing on common, critical levers and by drawing on a few illustrative examples, we hope to propose a framework that can help business leaders diagnose their organizational pain points, and to devise practical solutions. This is a complex and customized task and does not lend itself to standard solutions.

Critical organizational levers are described in terms of the anatomy, or the "clustering" dimension, the circulation or the "connective" dimension, and the personality, or the "cohesive" dimension. While some business leaders favor the clustering dimension as a critical design tool, others focus more on the connective or the cohesive components. The point to note is that when architecting an enterprise for super-flexibility, executive teams have to consider all three dimensions, their mix and match, the required trade-offs, and their fine-tuning over time. The three levers coalesce into a conceptual framework that we label the "nodal architecture".

7.3 The Framework: Nodal Organizational Architectures

Traditional approaches to organizational design emphasize standardization and promote the idea that one approach may fit all. This is clearly evident, for example, in the way that popular organizational designs, such as the multi-divisional form, have cascaded in different industrial enterprises around the world (Chandler 1962). In the organizational hierarchies of the industrial age, the premise was mechanistic: first determine what needs to

---

[44] Internal memorandum from the Executive Vice President and co-founder of ROLM on its business philosophy, May 26, 1981.

be done, and then slot the qualified people into pre-determined roles and prescribed positions.

Knowledge enterprises in Silicon Valley resemble "organic" (Burns and Stalker 1961) sports teams, rock bands, and film studios. Each has a unique and discernable "personality", reflecting the founders' values and its success recipes in the industry. These norms guide their human resource practices and action recipes for attracting and retaining talent (Baron and Hannan 2002). HP and Intel are both respected and established companies in Silicon Valley. HP's culture has been historically anchored around "consensus and collaboration", Intel's has evolved on the premise of "constructive confrontation". Some companies emphasize egalitarian norms; others reinforce the value of elitism. Diversity abounds and there are alternative organizational personalities and talent recruitment and retention strategies.

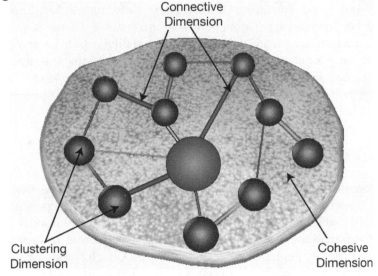

Figure 12. The nodal architecture: An overview

Despite their unique personalities, however, there are also many similarities, especially when assessing their organizational anatomies. For example, technology companies rely on focused teams, project groups, and targeted nodes to address the needs for innovation and speed. Roles and assignments change frequently and individuals perform multiple tasks. They leverage the virtual, IT infrastructure to tie together geo-dispersed teams with common processes. Their organizational structures are simultaneously centralized and decentralized. Hierarchical positions reflect an individual's accountability, not just their authority and status. Staff roles are minimized and line units are critical drivers of business decisions (Bahrami and Evans 1987, Bahrami 1992).

As depicted in Figure 12 the clustering, the connective, and the cohesive dimensions coalesce to form what we term "the nodal architecture". The clustering dimension describes the anatomy of the enterprise. It addresses the traditional challenges of differentiation: how to partition and segment an entity into manageable work nodes, silos, projects and teams, aggregate the nodes into functions, business units, and regions, and focus the talent pool on targeted assignments. This task requires balancing the needs for speed and agility on the one hand, with stability and cohesion on the other.

The connective dimension is about the enterprise's "circulation". The focus is on harnessing synergies and creating linkages. Linkages are largely about integration: how to co-ordinate distributed work nodes by sharing codified knowledge through core processes and an efficient information and communications infrastructure, and uncodified knowledge through key interfaces, personal networks and cross-silo forums.

The cohesive dimension reflects the "personality" of the enterprise. It is about binding together the various components, providing emotional connectivity, and creating a unique identity. A blend of the "hard" and the "soft", it is the physical, the intellectual, the financial, and the emotional glue that keeps the enterprise together.

7.3.1 The Clustering Dimension

The clustering dimension represents the anatomy of the enterprise. It describes reporting relationships, grouping of skills, and assignment of responsibility, authority and accountability. It reflects the traditional component of differentiation and can be most readily observed in organization charts and the segmentation of vertical silos. A key clustering challenge is to strike a dynamic balance between stability on the one hand, and flexibility on the other.

In contrast to the uni-polar and integrated hierarchies of the industrial age, the anatomy of technology enterprises consists of distributed nodes, each focused on a specific task and a targeted assignment. The term "nodal architecture" is used here to depict this notion of "multi-polarity". and distributed authority. "Nodes" refer to work units, departments, or project teams with focused deliverables and targeted accountabilities. This is where work is done and talent is deployed.

Several approaches are used to segment and cluster the nodes. The most common segmentation criteria include product, market, location, and function. Depending on the nature of the business and its stage of growth, some nodes are segmented on the basis of concrete output, such as product type or service category. Many R&D nodes are typically segmented based on time lines; whether their focus is on current or future product development initiatives. Sales nodes are typically segmented on the basis of location and geography. In view of our focus on super-flexibility, we have found it helpful to categorize the nodes based on two critical elements: the frequency of change they might experience; and whether they are focused on an on-going assignment or whether they have a temporary focus, in other words the frequency with which they need to be re-organized. This approach leads us to categorize the nodes into base units and overlay teams.

Base units are the relatively stable component. They are the formal mechanism for grouping skills, clustering talent, and assigning reporting relationships. They refer to functional departments, product divisions, sales offices, manufacturing sites, and research centers. They focus on delivering targeted output and tangible expertise. They are used to compartmentalize work, provide focus, assign accountabilities, and generate a sense of shared identity. Base units "morph" over time, depending on an organization's stage of growth, business imperatives, and preferences of executive teams.

As depicted in Figure 13, start-ups initially organize their base units around the core contributing functions. These include engineering and product development during the early "seed" stage, augmented by other functions, including sales, marketing, (and, at times, manufacturing) when the first prototype has been developed. More complex functional units are formed as a firm grows and diversifies its product portfolio and market coverage. Sales units, for example, are often segmented into domestic and international sales, or departmentalized on the basis of different customer segments, vertical industries or regional groupings. R&D units are typically segmented into core technologies and platforms versus application areas, or different product-related units.

Successful firms rapidly outgrow functional base units. Twin pressures of headcount growth and the introduction of new products and services make it necessary to divide the organization into smaller, more focused units. The adopted "divisional" form largely depends on the interdependencies between different product families and market segments. In view of the close inter-dependencies that exist between product families in technology industries, many companies use centralized R&D and manufacturing, and segment the sales function into geographies or industry groups. Control and support units, including finance, HR, IT and marketing communications, are typically consolidated to minimize duplication; although specialized support-staff are deployed in the divisions as key "liaisons" and interfaces. As a firm evolves and matures, "groups" and "sectors" evolve based on aggregated clusters of product lines, market segments, technologies, or geographies. These groups are the focal points for co-ordination, while operating units within the group umbrella focus on managing day-to-day activities. The morphing patterns of the base units are not always sequential. Some may evolve from functional to group forms; others may revert back to functional units after a financial crisis, a change of senior management, or a dramatic re-structuring of the business portfolio.

The choice of an appropriate segmentation and aggregation strategy depends on several factors: growth potential of a specific product line, business interdependencies, critical pain points, political dynamics, leadership preferences, and industry success recipes. The key point to note is that base units are typically a blend of functional and product clusters, market segments and geographic units, Typically, there are multiple reporting lines and intricate complexities in juggling trade-offs within a "matrix" organization. A key challenge for senior executives is to figure out how to cluster and segment the nodes to implement the targeted strategy, and when to re-structure the base units to address critical triggers in the business model and strategic trajectory. This delicate balancing act is difficult to achieve. On the one hand, business leaders rely on organizational levers in order to execute the business strategy. On the other hand, frequent re-organizations of base units can be highly disruptive to knowledge workers' morale and productivity.

One option is to view the base units as a foundational platform that can provide stability and resilience. Other mechanisms can be used to address the challenge of speed, innovation, and responsiveness. This is where overlay teams are leveraged. They represent the flexible arm or the rapid deployment capability. Their effective deployment enables a firm to rapidly focus on critical assignments without causing major disruptions to the base units. Overlay teams are especially significant when dealing with challenges, transcending functional silos or business units. A complementary blend of knowledge-workers can be pooled together at short notice, put to work on new assignments, and disbanded once their task has been accomplished. In some cases project teams may evolve and eventually become the foundation for a new base unit, depending on critical mass and business scope. Consider the reflections of a senior executive of a $1 billion net storage company:

"We have a functional organization ... it is the most simple from a line of sight perspective ... as your products become more complex and you become geographically dispersed, it starts to fall apart ... so we started what we call virtual business units...they don't own any people ... there'll be a virtual CEO who's responsible for bringing together cross-functional

teams ... let's take the example of our CDBU (content delivery business unit) ... it actually has three people and drives fairly significant revenue...the various functional teams participate as members of both, the functional unit as well as the CDBU."

A complicating factor is that in most technology companies, base units and overlay teams are geo-dispersed, posing additional co-ordination challenges. There are two major reasons for this dispersion. First, technology companies have to take advantage of competitive resources and specialized talent pools scattered around the world. Additionally, the nodes have to be "forward deployed" so they can be close to their customers for speed of response and product/ service customization. For example, a financial software company set up two nodes, comprising technical domain experts and local banking experts, to address the complex needs of its European customers; As its founder and CEO observed:

"... we wanted our global nodes of competence in close proximity to one another ... so in Europe, we had teams of technical and domain experts in London ... (augmented by) financial and market experts in various local offices ..., so we could leverage our technical experts on an as-needed basis, and customize solutions for our banking clients out of our local offices in Paris, Milan and Frankfurt ... after all these people knew about the French, the Italian or the German banking conventions."

A pioneering company in transaction automation systems based its global R&D centers in Bangalore and Paris during the 1980s because of their respective expertise in Unix programming and smart card technology. The rationale was to benefit from the regions' accumulated experience in two critical and relevant domains. Many disk drive companies have set up their procurement and sourcing units in Singapore due to the country's crossroads location and proximity to many sub-system providers. In terms of inculcating super-flexibility, a major challenge is related to timing: when to use short-term measures, such as project teams, task forces, or virtual business units, and when to embark on a major re-organization of the base units. The goal is to minimize organizational disruption and to reduce the de-stabilizing impact of re-organizations on knowledge workers' productivity and business continuity. However, overlay teams need clear charters, focused accountabilities, and specific operational time frames. Otherwise, their efforts may be in conflict, or inconsistent, with the base units. Ambiguous charters and accountability "grey zones" often generate considerable friction, infighting, and overlap.

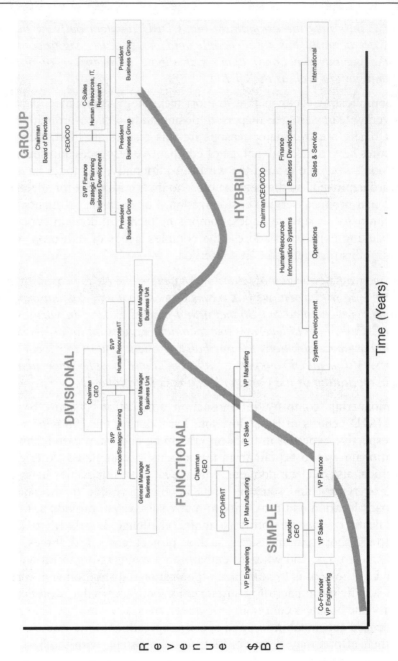

Figure 13. Structural migration pathways

7.3.2 The Connective Dimension

Work has to be somehow co-ordinated amongst the distributed nodes in order to avoid each node marching according to its own tune. Indeed, managing reciprocal interdependencies between the various nodes, is a major determinant of, and a potential barrier to, organizational effectiveness. While the nodes may be focused and semi-autonomous, they have to co-ordinate critical interdependencies with other nodes and rely on them for specialized expertise and know-how. For example, a product node needs the capabilities of group R&D; a regional sales node requires regular input from product development nodes. Even in start-ups, there are clear interdependencies between engineering and marketing, or manufacturing and sales. While these interdependencies are a source of leverage and synergy, they also generate "traffic jams" and friction points, especially at critical intersection points where many interdependencies come together.

In essence the "horizontal" connective dimension complements the vertical anatomy. We suggest that it is analogous to enterprise "circulation". Various linkage tools are used to facilitate communication, co-ordination and knowledge sharing amongst dispersed work nodes and project teams. The challenge is succinctly summed up in the comments of the co-founder and executive vice president of a telecommunications company:

"We like the idea of small, decentralized units with focused accountability ... but our products have to play together ... our customers buy an integrated system ... there is a major element of success that depends on co-ordination and close co-operation between the units."

These linkages are typically a mixture of the virtual, the organizational, and the personal, spanning

- IT Tools
- Core Business Processes
- Cross-Silo Forums
- C-Suite Executives & Operational Hubs

Subsequently, we elaborate on each linkage category.

- **IT Tools**

During the past decade, IT systems have transformed the administrative backbone and communication infrastructure of business enterprises. In the process, they have also created a new form of organizational dynamics. IT's major contribution to organizational effectiveness is the codification, aggregation and diffusion of information. IT infrastructures can also facilitate the design of distributed organizational architectures, and the deployment of virtual teams that operate across time zones, geographies, hierarchical levels, and enterprise boundaries.

Innovative software tools and Internet-based products have made it feasible for nomadic knowledge workers to work at any time, from any location. They have made it possible to create an inter-connected global entity, where like a relay team, tasks are passed on from location to location over different time zones. By means of knowledge management, CRM and other tools, brainpower and critical information is distributed throughout the organization, reducing the size of the physical center. It has given real-time broadcast capability, and access to "unfiltered" information to the dispersed knowledge workers. In the process, proliferation of IT has also led to information overload and information "toxicity".[45] Consider the following comments on the contribution and the impact of IT from three different perspectives:

"... (The real value of IT) is to get information to those doing the work ... information that used to filter only through the hierarchy ... that only managers used to have."[46]

"... Two thirds of our (knowledge workers) are nomadic ... able to work any place, any time ... they can choose when, where, and how they work ... many of our meetings are assigned phone numbers, where people from different locations call in."[47]

"... I feel very confused even when I have access to a lot of information (on our Intranet) ... I have no time to reflect and digest ... I feel overloaded and over-burdened."[48]

A critical challenge in harnessing IT is to configure the right balance between its "push" and "pull" capabilities; for example, when should information be "pushed" to relevant stakeholders? When should it be available to be "pulled" on demand? A large networking company, for example, used its own Intranet for posting updated information about the impact of a major acquisition. At the time, employees were concerned about their jobs,

---

[45] High technology firms are typically early adopters of new technologies. Many firms are the primary sites for testing their own products, and often serve as beta-test sites for other technology firms. Their knowledge workers are well trained, have an ideological commitment to new technologies, and are willing to invest the time and the energy during the initial period of learning. Moreover, due to their recent origin and the disposition of their entrepreneurial founders, many firms are not subjected to problems of structural inertia and institutionalized norms.

[46] Personal communication with the founder & CEO of an ERP software company.

[47] Personal communication with the IT manager of a data networking company.

[48] Personal communication with a project manager in a semiconductor company.

benefits, and overlapping projects. The "merger news" was updated daily and could be accessed by all employees. This minimized the impact of the rumor mill and inconsistent intermediaries. It also saved time and resources since the information did not have to be cascaded through managers and department heads.

Despite its innovative possibilities, there are limits to how IT can provide a bridge across nodes and create effective linkages. For example, the experience of many firms indicates that e-mail is a poor communication tool for building trust, keeping focused accountability, communicating emotionally-charged material, brain-storming new ideas, disciplining non-performers, and orienting new employees into the culture. On the other hand, if used effectively, it can be efficient, inexpensive, and help keep "everyone on the same page". The real challenge is to devise customized protocols that encourage the use of IT for communicating "codified" information, while freeing up "face time" for creative dialogue, conflict resolution, and nurturing trust relationships.[49]

- **Core Business Processes**

One of the biggest impacts of IT systems in recent years has been to add a horizontal dimension to the traditional vertical hierarchy and the silo-based organizational structure. From a business standpoint, this impact has been especially apparent in the design, configuration and use of core business processes that transcend functional and product silos (Hammer and Champy 1993, Hammer 2004). These processes span various activities. The most common we have observed include four categories of business processes:

- ◆ Processes that impact the design, development, production and delivery of products and services, including interaction with critical vendors and partners. Examples include product development, project management, order entry, product manufacturing, order delivery, and supply chain management.

- ◆ Processes that impact the search for, transactions with, and follow-up interactions with customers; examples, include lead generation, lead screening and monitoring, transaction processing, helpdesk, and customer service.

- ◆ Processes that impact the measurement and monitoring of financial performance and the allocation of resources, including planning and budgeting processes, tracking financial results, and aggregating and consolidating financial information.

---

[49] Examples of codified information include electronic routing of forms, purchasing and ordering supplies, tracking sales proposals and leads, communicating job postings, project status updates, budget templates, and purchase requisition systems.

♦ Processes used to manage and compensate knowledge workers during various stages of the employment life cycle. Related sub-processes include talent recruiting (including interview notes and offer letters) talent deployment (such as job postings), training and e-learning (including course catalogues, registration and administration, and content modules), performance and compensation management (such as performance rating, assessing fixed and variable compensation ratios, and external benchmarking) and workforce planning (such as "what if" scenarios).

Another set of processes impact business development, including the search for alliances, partnerships, and acquisition candidates, and in particular, processes used to integrate newly-acquired/ merged companies into the organizational infrastructure. This category is not as prevalent as the other four, since it is directly linked to a growth by acquisition/partnership enterprise strategy. However, as discussed in chapter 5, companies, such as Cisco, that are well-known for their growth by acquisition strategy, have popularized the use of acquisition integration processes.

The effective design and deployment of business processes enables an enterprise to link together its vertical silos around a core activity and keep "everyone on the same page". As depicted in Figure 14, over time, these horizontal linkages can help break down the vertical silo mentality, facilitate cross-pollination of talent and ideas, and provide operational focus. The challenge is two-fold: first, to ensure that core processes are continuously updated and fine-tuned so they remain relevant and ever-green; second, to ensure that they are configured around simple templates that can be easily understood, internalized and accessed by multi-cultural and multi-functional stakeholders.

Connectivity is not only about IT-enabled communication and business processes. These tools, while useful from the standpoint of capturing codified know-how and providing task-related connectivity, do not address the spontaneous and the emotional dimensions of human interaction. This is where networking and communication forums can be leveraged. By bringing together the leaders, the peers, the front-liners, and at times, the external stakeholders, they can facilitate spontaneous exchanges, provide opportunities for creative conversations, and foster informal experience sharing. They can keep senior executives updated on dynamic competitive and market conditions. They can give line managers opportunities to share their views, and receive regular feedback. They can also help break down the silo mentality by providing regular opportunities for cross-pollination and peer group interaction.

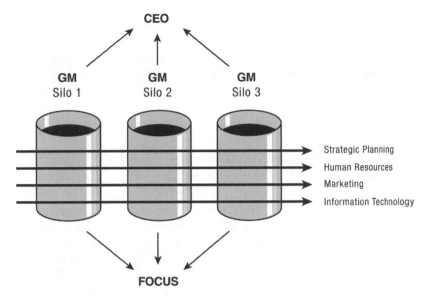

Figure 14. Connecting silos: Horizontal linkages

• Cross-Silo Forums

Many technology companies use periodic review meetings to provide cross-silo updates on products, customers and competitors. Many rely on strategy offsites to reflect on broad trends impacting the business trajectory. They use planning forums to synchronize actions, to update business assumptions, and to co-coordinate inter-silo concerns. They leverage orientation and on-boarding programs to set clear expectations at the outset of the employment relationship. Many senior executives take active roles in teaching new employees, providing role modeling and interaction opportunities in informal settings.

The challenge is to ensure that there is a clear purpose behind the targeted interaction, and to invite the appropriate stakeholders to the right forum. Recently, for example, we attended the annual "strategic planning" meeting of a global medical diagnostics company. The meeting was intended to achieve a number of objectives; to provide an update on the business, to discuss priorities going forward, and to get the participants' input on critical challenges. The audience included the "top 100" executives in this global organization of more than 3000 people. The meeting was held over 1.5 days and included a "state of the firm" address by the CEO and the CFO, several "update" presentations by the business unit heads, and brain-storming discussions and report-backs by break-out teams on four designated priority areas.

- **C-Suite Executives & Operational Hubs at Key Intersections**

Nodal architectures have many intersection points that link together the distributed nodes. Intersection points refer to zones of interdependence where stakeholder interests converge. A "connective" challenge is to ensure that critical intersections and handoffs are managed in order to ensure a smooth "traffic flow". This can be a major pain point for many technology companies that operate within overlapping, matrix structures. R&D hands off to marketing; marketing and manufacturing have to be aligned and both need to ensure that they can be synchronized with the sales organization. In multi-product, or multi-business companies, the challenge is even greater since there are many intersections, entailing different silos.

To complicate matters further, critical handoffs have to be swiftly handled. There is no time for finger-pointing or abdicating responsibility to others. Words, such as "accountability" and "deliverable" are important in the business vocabulary. The deliverable may have to be produced as the result of extensive co-ordination with multiple stakeholders, many of whom may work outside the authority zone of the individual or the team that is ultimately accountable. The challenge is to exercise influence with or without formal authority, and to pull together and synthesize the contributions of various stakeholders, in a way that can lead to measurable action.

This task is generally the role of a "C-Suite Executive", at the strategic level, or an "operational hub", at the execution level. For example, a number of software companies have set up the position of "chief solutions officer" in order to offer integrated, customized solutions, rather than standardized, modular products to their customers. These executives are the focal point for strategizing an overall approach, seeking and integrating different functional inputs, and monitoring the progress made towards its implementation.

Similarly, at an operational level, an account manager's task is to pull together various internal resources and capabilities that may be required to address a key customer's needs. Product managers sit at the intersection point between marketing and engineering. Their role is to ensure that both sets of requirements are considered in designing and delivering a product or a service. As operational hubs, account managers and product managers are single points of contact and the focal points for delivering the customer solution or the product configuration. Both tasks transcend organizational silos, represent critical intersection points, and can be viewed as important sources of horizontal connectivity.

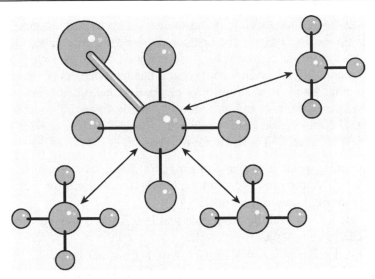

Figure 15. Intersectional hubs

The challenge is to ensure that those assigned to hub roles have both, the competence to do the job, and the inter-personal and communication skills to interact with various stakeholders. This is succinctly summed up in the reflections of the CEO of an enterprise software company:

> *"An interesting note is the way that we selected our CIO (Chief Information Officer) ... who did not grow up through the classic IT organization ... her skill-set was in customer service ... so we chose the diplomatic elements ... to help our various functional organizations come together ... over deep technical experience ... and it has worked very well in our case."*

Depending on their effectiveness, hub roles can be either critical catalysts, or major bottlenecks. Sitting at major intersections, they provide the connectivity between diverse sources of expertise, manage communication links to various stakeholders, and are tangible sources of real-time information. The on-going challenge is to monitor organizational "hot spots" proactively, before they turn into chaotic traffic jams, and to assign credible individuals to hub roles in order to minimize "traffic congestion".

7.3.3 The Cohesive Dimension

Nodal architectures require fusing mechanisms to bind together the distributed nodes. The goal is to provide organizational cohesion and to portray a distinctive identity. Otherwise the organization becomes like a bazaar, with each node driving autonomously in its own direction. This "cohesive" dimension reflects the "personality" of the enterprise. On the one hand, it is about linking the values and expectations of knowledge workers to the broader organizational context and business drivers (O'Reilly 1989). On the other hand, it is about how external stakeholders view the enterprise and perceive its brand and identity. While financial controls provide the "hard" control glue, core values and people policies, provide the motivational "soft glue".[50] These are viewed as:

- Guiding principles that can project a distinctive organizational personality, and promote a unique employment brand for recruiting and retaining knowledge workers.
- Anchors of stability that can instill resilience during difficult and challenging times.
- Leadership pillars that impact daily actions and individual behaviors and that can be reinforced through effective role-modeling and congruent incentive systems.

Consider the comments of the CEO of an enterprise application software company on the importance of clear cultural principles:

"... One of our unwritten cultural tenets is that everyone's a sales and support person ... and that we should use our own products ... in putting our value tenets together, we wanted to think about "what kind of a company do we want to work for" ... the emphasis is on the company, not the management - we even do report cards on how the whole company is living up to its cultural tenets."

Clear core values also give a distributed global entity a sense of corporate identity and tie together its multi-cultural workforce. This attribute is important since many technology firms generate a significant portion of their sales outside their home base, and have a large population of cosmopolitan employees:

"... When you open an office several thousand miles away, it is difficult to export the culture ... (so) we make sure that our new employees spend a

---

[50] Successful technology firms develop cultural mindsets that incorporate diverse assumptions and premises. This means balancing core values, reflecting the "home" culture, while accommodating the multi-cultural viewpoints of global customers, employees, and competitors. Several mechanisms are used to blend the two together; These include composition of employees and senior executive teams, short-term sabbaticals to projects outside the "home" base, re-deployment opportunities, real time global communication forums, and global account management systems.

large part of their time, early on, here at the home base, so they can really experience, feel, and live our culture, and not just read about it." [51]

The CEO and executive team of a young semiconductor company, for example, use the theme of "intellectual honesty" as the company's bedrock corporate value. All employees, regardless of their position, are expected to be honest in communicating business realities, as they see and experience them. The broader implication is that there are no "sacred cows"; you can raise contrarian points of view, as long as you have the factual evidence to support the assertion:

"... we are an intellectually honest company and share facts across the board ... our team is not insecure or arrogant ... so we can talk about facts ... those we like and those that we don't." [52]

The company operates in the US, Germany, Korea, and Japan. The theme of "intellectual honesty" gives its knowledge workers a common communication protocol, regardless of their functional expertise, hierarchical position, or cultural background. This behavioral norm clarifies the "rules of the game" and makes it easier to re-deploy talent in different nodes. Global cultural differences impact the implementation of this principle and flexibility is built into the process. In the US context, for example, it means open debate and frank discussion of issues. In the Japanese context, it is used in one/one conversations rather than in group discussions.

As previous studies have shown, founders can play a decisive role in shaping the core values of an organization during its early formative years. Often, they even provide the DNA or the cultural imprint of an enterprise. This is a deciding factor in shaping the HR policies that reinforce the core values (Baron and Hannan 2002). While behavioral norms can be a powerful engagement, socialization and control mechanism, they can also become a major source of inflexibility, especially if they are not re-assessed at critical inflection points. The pulse has to be taken on a regular basis to ensure that the enterprise "personality" is in synch with emerging business realities and market dynamics.

Our observations point to four sets of people practices that are at the heart of the "cohesive" dimension:

---

[51] Personal communication with the vice president of worldwide sales of an application software company.

[52] Personal communication with the founder and CEO of a semiconductor company.

- **Screening & recruiting for "fit":**

The productivity of knowledge workers depends on the appropriate fit between personal values, expectations, and competencies and the organization's context, values, and business focus. A knowledge worker who values consensus, for example, may not fit into a confrontational environment. Someone who is interested in work/life balance may not be the right fit for a hard-driving company. An expert specialist, who may be uncomfortable taking on assignments outside the core expertise, may not fit into an environment where employees are expected to wear different hats and switch between assignments at short notice.

The appropriate "fit" between the individual and the organization's core values can be best assessed during the initial recruiting and screening phase, when expectations on both sides have yet to be set (Chatman and Cha 2003). Popular approaches include employee referral programs, extensive interviews with a board range of stakeholders over extended time frames, internships, contractor and consulting assignments, and targeted recruiting from selected universities and companies.

- **Performance management and compensation systems**

A related challenge is to ensure that the desired cultural norms and behavioral values can be reinforced through the appropriate compensation and performance management systems. If "intellectual honesty" is the desired norm, it has to be reinforced through the feedback process, and reflected in the incentive and compensation system. Those who can effectively communicate "bad news" should be encouraged to do so in the future. If customer orientation is the norm, it has to be reflected in the reward system and the promotion criteria in a way that can be individually reinforced and assessed.

We have seen a lot of variation in the way that Silicon Valley companies use performance management and compensation systems to reinforce the desired behaviors. Some assume that effective screening during the early recruiting cycle, or referrals from "reliable sources who know us", or alignment through the ownership structure and the granting of stock options, provide sufficient reinforcement. Others use rigorous performance management systems, linked to the congruent reward criteria.

The selected approach largely depends on the size of the organization, the attitude of its leaders, and its stage of development. Start ups, for example, tend to rely on informal screening and the ownership structure to promote alignment. Larger, more diverse organizations, at a later stage of development, tend to favor formal compensation and performance management tools. Whatever the selected approach, the challenge is to ensure that there is a clear "line of sight" between an individual's performance and the core values that are promulgated.

- **Visible signals**

In fast-moving domains, people pay attention to signals they can quickly scan and readily observe. Visible signals can be a powerful tool for reinforcing desired behavioral norms. Many companies use symbols and signals, intentionally and unintentionally, to convey their "personality".

For example, several companies in Silicon Valley value egalitarian norms. These are reflected in two visible areas. First, office cubicles are the same size, irrespective of the person's rank, position, and title. Second, senior executives have the same travel privileges as other employees in that they travel coach, although they can use their own resources to upgrade to the next class of service.

Visible signals apply to other daily artifacts as well. For example, the founder of a network server company wanted to promote the critical importance of customer responsiveness to their technically-sophisticated knowledge workers. They used the top executives' business cards as one visible signal. Every executive officer had his/her home phone number printed on their business cards. The rationale was that they could be contacted at any time since their product was "mission-critical" for their customers. In addition, the CEO set up a red phone as the "hotline" in his office, and gave the number to all their customers. The idea was that he could be contacted personally in case of need. The employee surveys indicated that the "golden rule" of customer responsiveness, symbolized by the "red phone", was not just a platitude. The fact that the CEO and the top team were willing to "walk the talk" was a critical re-inforcer of this desired norm.

- **Campus design**

In addition to people practices and cultural anchors, symbolic norms can also be conveyed through workplace design. Facilities' layout can either convey egalitarian sentiments or it can reinforce hierarchical segmentation. It can emphasize the importance of group interaction instead of individual contribution. It can signal the role of transparency rather than secrecy. If aligned with behavioral norms, and business success factors, workplace design can create a sense of community, and facilitate the development of trust and personal relationships. Recently, attention has also focused on how physical and virtual spaces should be aligned to bring about "convergent" architecture (Huang 2001).

During a recent encounter between senior executives from a European multinational and a young knowledge worker from a large Silicon Valley company, the conversation turned to whether cultural norms had a real impact on employees' daily behaviors and perceptions. The knowledge worker was asked whether the stated culture of "fairness and egalitarianism", promoted by her company, was actually reinforced in the leaders' daily actions. The response was immediate: *"when you come and visit our offices ... the CEO's cubicle is exactly the same size as mine and he doesn't have any windows either."*

Consider the campus layout of an established technology company in Menlo Park, California. Like many others in Silicon Valley, it was designed to facilitate group collaboration and informal interaction amongst multi-functional knowledge workers. A key feature is a central thoroughfare, analogous to downtown or "Main Street", with office complexes built around it. This acts as a central artery and facilitates informal interaction. Knowledge workers from different silos "bump" into each other as a matter of daily routine. The staircases are wider than normal to allow for continuity of dialogue amongst teams. White boards are placed along the corridors to enable people to spontaneously reflect on their creative thoughts. Shared common rooms take center-stage, as they provide group space, while individual cubicles and offices are of secondary importance.

In summary, the cohesive dimension is critical in nodal architectures. It can instill bedrock values, provide "sameness", and give emotional cohesion to a distributed knowledge enterprise. It can help articulate and disseminate the critical ingredients of the genetic code and the desired behaviors. It can be used as an employee selection and screening tool and project a distinctive employment brand for recruiting and retaining knowledge workers. The key challenge is "figuring out what has to be the same across all nodes so that everything else can be different." In other words, it is important to clarify and communicate the non-negotiable behavioral norms that every organizational citizen is expected to live by, and to reinforce these through the appropriate HR policies and symbolic norms.

7.4 Illustrative Case Study

It may be helpful to illustrate the three dimensions of the nodal architecture through an illustrative case study. While the company in question is very successful, the vignette should be viewed as "food for thought", rather than as "best practice". It shows the clustering, the connective, and the cohesive dimensions at work. It also indicates how different companies may put the emphasis on one dimension, rather than another. In this case, the connective dimension is at the heart of this company's approach to organizational design.

ABC is a $1Billion, public company in the network storage business. Founded in 1991, it has 2400 employees, 4 remote development centers, and operates in 60 countries. It was spun off from another Silicon Valley company that was a pioneer in the file-server business.

The clustering dimension: From an organizational standpoint, it continues to rely on a classic functional organization and makes extensive use of temporary teams, projects, and task forces to focus on new opportunities and assignments. The functional structure is the core foundation, although other tools have been developed to address co-ordination bottlenecks These include reliance on virtual business units (that don't own many people, but address new opportunities, and typically drive significant revenue), various types of meetings, including monthly cross-functional meetings of every team, cross-functional product reviews, and annual thematic meeting of the senior leaders. Senior executives characterize their organization as "networked silos" and use the term in their internal communication and orientation programs.

The connective dimension: In addition to the more conventional co-ordination meetings, the company has introduced a quarterly "all hands" meetings with the entire employee base around the world. The objective is to keep "everyone on the same page" and update them on the most significant trends impacting the business. This is an innovative departure from conventional practice and demonstrates how new technology, if used appropriately, can be a powerful tool to link up distributed nodes and provide flexibility in real-time communication.

The program entails live quarterly broadcasts by the senior executive team, spelling out emerging priorities and key accomplishments in order to "inform, align, and focus employees". Using its own technology and "content delivery network", the goal is to "strengthen communication and build bridges." The broadcast connects the corporate HQ, four remote development sites, and 33 sales and customer service offices around the world. Live broadcasts are also recorded for those who are unable to join in. They are divided into bite-sized segments, each lasting less than 2 minutes, Remote locations also hold their own meetings, before and after the live broadcast, in order to reflect on its implications for their function and geography.

ABC's VP of Product Development and East Coast Operations reflected on the value of live broadcasts: *"we have acquired a number of companies here and you want these new employees to be successful, to feel connected, and to be fully integrated ... I wasn't always effective when I tried to explain our culture to them. But after watching a few streamed "all hands" meetings, they started to get it. Our culture became real and understandable to them."*

The point of this case is that ABC leveraged the potential of new technology to create a novel form of connectivity; one that creates a neighborhood feel in a distributed entity; one that can convey a key message on a regular basis and keep everyone moving in broadly the same direction, one that can be used offensively, to launch new products, and defensively, to emphasize the need for expense cuts:

In March 2001, in response to the general economic downturn, the company called on its employees to exercise restraint in discretionary spending *"... we launched the campaign by sending an e-mail, with links to a VOD (video on demand-modular segments of a live broadcast linked to specific topics and themes) by our CEO, which enabled us to come together quickly as a company. It was as though someone had turned off a faucet. Discretionary spending simply stopped."* The money saved contributed significantly to the company's financial health. *"To reinforce the message, we followed up with monthly VODs from other executives. As companies grow, they tend to lose agility, but this kind of communication can restore it."*[53]

The cohesive dimension: Like many start-ups, the founding team had set out to codify their core values early on, depicting its desired "personality" and the kind of entity we wanted to build. *"... Our culture can be summed up as flexible and light on its feet. Our original tagline was "fast, simple, and reliable". We keep repeating these words all the time and judge everything we do based on them ... these are more than just aspirations written on a piece of paper ... we actually use them to structure the organization and to measure our performance ... so, for example, fast is measured in terms of how quickly we close our books, get the product out, and get the stock options out to our employees."*[54]

7.5 Implementation Guidelines

What are the critical action steps needed to create a nodal organizational architecture? Where is the appropriate starting point? How can a leadership team keep the big picture in mind, but implement in manageable bite-sized steps? Our observations point to a number of pragmatic steps that may be critical during the prioritization process. These include:

- Clear, well-communicated, and actionable "federal" mandates.
- Effective hubs placed at critical organizational intersections.

---

[53] Personal communication with ABC's Vice President of People and Places.
[54] Personal communication with ABC's Vice President of People and Places.

- Emphasis on creating horizontal linkages to augment the vertical silos.

A major difference between distributed, nodal architectures and traditional hierarchical structures is the importance of thinking in terms of "trade-offs" rather than "either/or" binary choices. For example, traditional structures have been viewed as either centralized, with tight central control exerted by the HQ, or decentralized, leaving country managers a great deal of discretion.

Designing a nodal architecture is less about centralization/ decentralization and more about clarifying "federal/state" tensions (see Handy 1992 for a discussion of the federalist" approach) . Federal mandates are non-negotiable ground rules that apply to every citizen and every node. However, there is a need for built-in flexibility to make it easier for front-line "states" and work units to take the initiative and customize their actions, Federal mandates may be about financial targets, business processes, strategic trajectory, brand image, or people practices. In the organizational context, they are about clarifying the "go/no go" areas and setting clear expectations.

A case in point is the positioning of IT groups. In many larger companies in Silicon Valley, "Corporate or Group IT" is responsible for providing the standard IT infrastructure and communication services used by all the nodes, irrespective of their "special needs". These services are funded through a "tax", as part of corporate overhead allocation. However, business units are able to take the lead in identifying their own "customized application needs". They may use the "corporate IT function" as an "internal vendor", or go outside for sourcing the required services. In addition, these "state" services are initiated and funded by the business units. The critical task is to isolate the commonalities across the various zones of "federal/state" tensions, what has to be the same across all nodes, so that everything else can be locally customized."[55]

Second, while IT tools provide connectivity in the context of "codified" knowledge, individual initiative is needed to share and cross-pollinate uncodified and spontaneous know-how. This is where "hubs" come into play. As discussed earlier, hubs are knowledge workers who pull together the dispersed nodes and sit at the intersections of key constituencies. They may include product managers, project leaders, account representatives,

---

[55] This is one of Jack Welch's accomplishments at GE. He clarified the federal mandate for all the GE business units (in being #1 or #2 in their markets). He also clarified and reinforced the federal cultural glue, around the themes of speed, simplicity and self-confidence.

and critical interface functions like marketing, IT, HR. and business development. If deployed effectively, hubs can minimize filtering, synthesize input, and provide real-time connectivity. This capability allows the rapid routing of danger and opportunity signals from the front-liners to the leaders. The challenge is to identify key intersections and to assign credible individuals to hub positions.

Third, given our traditional emphasis on the vertical hierarchy, emphasis has to shift to the horizontal dimension. The typical breakdowns we observe have little to do with elegant structures; they have a lot to do with inter-silo communications, keeping everyone on the same page, and minimizing duplication of effort. There is a need to identify critical horizontal bottlenecks that impede action and use the appropriate tools to address the specific pain points. The solution may entail a core business process (such as how to set business priorities during the planning and budgeting process, or the portfolio alignment process), regular thematic updates on business direction and challenges (as is the case with the quarterly all hands meetings at ABC), and ensuring informal interaction between various silos by providing focused opportunities for cross-pollination.

7.6 Orgitechting and Super-Flexibility

In this chapter, we described the clustering, the connective, and the cohesive dimensions of nodal architectures. This framework is proposed as a tool for diagnosing and organizing knowledge-based enterprises. A mixture of the vertical and the horizontal, geo-dispersed nodes are welded together with the "hard wire" of IT and communication systems and the soft glue of behavioral norms, HR practices, and visible symbols.[56]

Nodal architectures can provide super-flexibility in several ways. Their modular, multi-polar, nature is amenable to adaptation and evolution. Nodes can be added, spun off, dissolved, or enlarged. They can be dissected, segmented, and re-positioned. They can be kept small and focused in order to provide speed. They can also be enlarged to minimize duplication. They can be semi-permanent, in order to deliver standard transactions and execute routine activities. They can be set up as temporary nodes, focusing on assignments that have a limited life cycle. They can be used as templates for integrating acquired companies. Their critical attribute is their ability to be modular, focused, targeted and accountable, while link-

---

[56] There are parallels between the nodal architecture and the notion of a "heterarchy" observed in Swedish multinationals. See Hedlund (1986).

ing and interacting with peer nodes for acquiring relevant know-how and competence.

Developing the core building blocks is the first step towards creating a super-flexible organization. It is a necessary but not a sufficient condition. While many firms have the right foundation, they do not behave in a manner that results in a super-flexible posture. This may be due to several factors: over-emphasis on one building block (such as technology) at the expense of others; relying on "old rules" while playing a new game, passive leadership, cosmetic gestures, or lack of accountability. Those that strive to be super-flexible are proactive, work hard at being flexible, reinforce its importance through concrete initiatives and tangible deliverables, and are vigilant at taking the pulse and recalibrating their orientation at critical junctures.

The critical differentiator is how these three building blocks are leveraged and deployed; how they impact enterprise attitude and disposition, and its ability to tune in to reality in a timely manner. It is no good having the organizational architecture, but not the desire or the mindset to deploy it. Similarly, having the right mindset cannot go far in the absence of core capabilities that can be dynamically deployed. The test of super-flexibility largely depends on the ability to modify the organizational framework over time. In this context, a critical variable is the attitude, intentions and disposition of the leadership team in terms of their collective desire to take the pulse, recalibrate at critical junctures, and explain the rationale to knowledge workers.

The challenge is further exacerbated in knowledge-based enterprises due to many ambiguities and paradoxes. The art of organizational design in dynamic settings is not about being either totally chaotic or tightly synchronized. Effective utilization of IT and remote work protocols does not reduce the importance of behavioral norms, personal networks, and face-to-face interaction. The focus must be on generating short-term results while not losing sight of the long-term direction. Front line workers should be listened to and regularly surveyed, but there also needs to be clear mandates and directional guidelines from the top.

Nodal organizational frameworks do not fit into the "either/or" premises of the traditional mechanistic structures. They need to accommodate opposing needs and yet have a shared mission and climate. They have to embrace diversity and yet have a clear purpose and identity. From time to time, they should deviate from their trajectory, yet provide a few anchors of stability and cohesion. Nodes should be focused with clear accountabilities, yet they should interact with peer units to leverage horizontal synergies.

The plethora of emerging, knowledge-based enterprises that we have observed, underscores the need for versatile capabilities to address, on the one hand, technological sophistication, complex innovation, short-lived opportunities, and competitive intensity, and on the other hand, effective ways to assemble, engage, guide and motivate expectant knowledge workers. We need to think more in terms of "shades of gray", establishing "trade-offs", and continuous "fine-tuning" of the organizational architecture, and less in terms of ideal configurations and perfect solutions.

This chapter has focused on organizational building blocks that enable an enterprise to maneuver and shift its trajectory, while providing a few anchors of stability and cohesion. This is not a simple task and does not lend itself to "cure all" or "one size fits all" solutions. Every company is unique and faces different challenges. Entrepreneurs and executives have divergent values and contrasting points of view in terms of how these challenges should be addressed. The three dimensions of the nodal framework should be viewed as elements of a diagnostic tool-kit. They provide a checklist of options that can be considered during the design and the redesign processes over time.

Creating super-flexible organizational architectures poses a pragmatic challenge because our existing organizational systems, managerial vocabularies, and professional mindsets have evolved to address the challenges of the industrial era, and its inherent focus on standardization, binary thinking, and uni-dimensional recipes. While the current turbulence in the business environment offers exciting opportunities for experimentation, innovative thinking, and diversity in organizational designs, we have to be willing to lift our blindfolds and move away from standard solutions.

8 Aligning: Placing an Iron Hand into a Velvet Glove

How do high technology companies get the most out of their knowledge workers? How do they keep them intellectually and emotionally engaged in the face of considerable uncertainty? How do they set clear guidelines and mandates, yet allow sufficient elbow room for individual and team initiatives? How do they guide nomadic teams of multi-cultural knowledge workers and provide a sense of community and identity?

Silicon Valley is an entrepreneurial ecosystem built on knowledge-based assets. Indeed, the critical challenge is staffing, motivating, guiding, and retaining knowledge workers. It would be inappropriate to use "managing" or "supervising" to describe these practices. However, knowledge workers have to be cajoled, led, coached, directed, motivated and guided. Otherwise, collective efforts may be dispersed, fragmented, and ultimately ineffective.

This chapter discusses the concept of "aligning", a term we use to describe how knowledge workers are motivated, engaged and guided in dynamic settings. Aligning is about "peer-to-peer" leadership practices, viewing bosses, subordinates, and colleagues as "peers", or as adults, rather than as parents or as children. It is about "keeping everyone on the same page", moving broadly in a similar direction. It seeks to blend together leadership practices that have historically been viewed as paradoxes: for example, exercising tight control, while enabling decentralized initiatives; balancing fact-based assessments together with intuitive judgments; acknowledging the importance of emotional as well as financial drivers for motivating knowledge workers; recognizing that tasks have to be accomplished, results delivered and output generated, typically under tight deadlines and with limited resources; at the same time, knowledge enterprises have to provide opportunities for intellectual engagement, emotional connectivity, and learning and development for their expectant knowledge workers. In essence, peer-to-peer approaches are analogous to the old expression, "placing an iron hand into a velvet glove".

8.1 Knowledge Workers: Motivational Patterns and Work Challenges

The term "knowledge worker" is used here to refer to employees with unique, and often intangible, intellectual capital or what is sometimes perceived as "magical" expertise. This know-how has to be captured, leveraged, transformed, and packaged into marketable products, services, and solutions. Moreover, knowledge workers do not operate as autonomous islands of expertise. Their efforts have to be synchronized with the work of other specialists, under time and resource constraints, in order to lead to tangible outcomes.

We define knowledge workers as professionals who cannot be easily replaced, and whose contribution is critical to the enterprise success. This expertise is difficult to emulate and hard to capture. Engaging and motivating these core contributors is a critical priority since it can have a direct impact on the profitability and growth of a knowledge-based entity.

Knowledge workers take on various guises. We have found it helpful to segment them based on the type of know-how they have and how their expertise is deployed. As depicted in Figure 16, some may be engaged in creative processes, such as R&D, product design and business development. Others may be engaged in the application of knowledge, with a primary focus on real-time delivery and execution; examples include sales people and customer service professionals. Others may sit at the intersection between the two, such as product managers, account managers, marketing professionals, and quality experts.

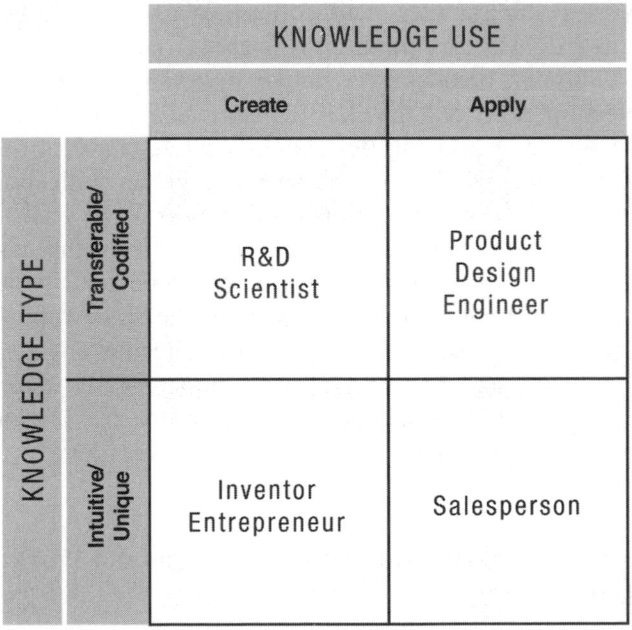

		KNOWLEDGE USE	
		Create	Apply
KNOWLEDGE TYPE	Transferable/ Codified	R&D Scientist	Product Design Engineer
	Intuitive/ Unique	Inventor Entrepreneur	Salesperson

Figure 16. Categories of knowledge workers

The challenge is to devise policies, actions and tools intended to motivate, engage, and create an environment that enables different categories of knowledge workers to pool together their collective talents in realizing common goals. These embrace motivation and engagement, as well as project management and collaborative teamwork.

Knowledge workers have diverse and complex motivational patterns. They expect to have a "good chemistry" with their peer group, want intellectually challenging assignments, and desire recognition and feedback. Work is intense, and thanks to modern technology, they are always accessible and reachable. As a result, professional and personal lives are often intertwined. It is difficult to disentangle knowledge workers' careers from their "life styles". Typically, these are bundled together:

"... Our people want honesty and openness, expect challenging work, support for learning, respect and recognition, and control over how work gets done ... they basically want to make a difference. "[57]

Our observations point to three broad categories of motivators that impact knowledge workers' hearts and minds. These include:

- "Fair" compensation, (in this context fairness is defined in terms of how the total compensation package compares to similar jobs in the same company and industry)
- Intellectual stimulation, including opportunities for personal growth, learning, and future employability
- "Emotional" connectivity, reflecting the relationship and the chemistry between the knowledge worker, the boss, and the peer group, as well as the fit between personal and organizational goals and values.

Clearly, the mix between the three components varies significantly. Some knowledge workers put more emphasis on financial rewards; others are motivated more directly by intellectual or emotional drivers. While all three categories are important in understanding the motivational profiles of knowledge workers, our observations indicate that "psychic income" and emotional engagement are especially significant in the context of super-flexibility.

Work is intense and all consuming. Many projects are pioneering, address short windows of market opportunity, and entail collaborative teamwork. Commitment and focus are related to how a knowledge worker is touched in the heart, not only the head. It is the critical motivator that gen-

---

[57] Personal communication with the Senior Vice President of HR in a networking company.

erates commitment, enhances trust, and provides anchors of stability around which knowledge workers can function flexibly and move between assignments. These emotional bonds give teams the capacity to do that little bit extra when resources are constrained, or provide the resilience to face difficult times.

Creating emotional connectivity presents major challenges for many technology companies. Reliance on virtual work means that there is limited face time and minimal opportunities to build relationships of trust. Many knowledge workers have to function in collaborative, multi-cultural contexts, where they are dependent on the contribution of others, including contractors, vendors, and partners from different parts of the world. The idea of "psychic income" typically gets traction during boom years when talent is in short supply, not in difficult economic times when it is urgently needed. There is the real danger of information "overload" and information "toxicity". Knowledge workers are always on, accessible and reachable; they can be contacted at any time in any location. Burnout and lack of work/life balance are realities that have to be confronted, not ignored.

These challenges are not easy to address. Business leaders have to accommodate diverse styles, motivational traits, and lifestyle expectations. They have to retain mobile knowledge workers with different career options. They need to exercise "influence" not just exert their formal authority. Oftentimes, they have to deal with big egos and *"prima donna"* attitudes. A critical imperative is to turn potential arrogance into commitment and creative work, and to provide "guidance" without "supervision":

"... Our knowledge workers are typically individual contributors who have healthy egos ... want to build their skill sets, have to make a difference in our industry, and are motivated by a spirit of discovery."[58]

Since everyone has to be a doer in some capacity and be willing to be deployed on a variable basis, initiative-seeking behavior, versatile capabilities, and the capacity for self-management are critical for success. There is little time for micro management, handholding, detailed supervision, and checking the "rule book". The modern knowledge worker is analogous to a "digital artisan", having to create tangible value out of intangible know-how, under tight deadlines, competitive pressures, limited resources, and incomplete, yet overloaded, information.

---

[58] Personal communication with the CEO and founder of a financial software company.

8.2 Aligning through Peer-to-Peer Leadership

The biggest challenge is to develop a leadership style that keeps the knowledge workers aligned, keeping them on the "same page, and moving in a similar direction. The most effective approaches we have observed are a mixture of soft influence and hard authority. That is why we characterize it in terms of "placing an iron hand in a velvet glove". On the one hand, leaders have to be decisive, set clear direction, and make the tough calls. They have to confront non-performers, and resolve conflict on a daily basis. On the other hand, they have to exercise influence without authority, be a team player, listen carefully, and empathize with different points of view. Effective leadership in a knowledge-based entity is about integrating both dimensions and switching gears between the two modes, without being perceived as inconsistent or as schizophrenic. The process entails aligning knowledge workers behind a common goal, and re-aligning them as new realities unfold. It seeks to acknowledge the emotional as well as the intellectual components of the leadership challenge. This is easier said than done, especially in view of knowledge workers' complex motivational profiles, the pioneering nature of knowledge-based work, and the volatility, speed, and competitive intensity of knowledge-based businesses.

At an operational level, we use the term "peer-to-peer" to describe daily practices of effective leaders. As depicted in Figure 17, differences between "parent-child" and "peer-to-peer" approaches are deceptively simple to understand but challenging to put into practice. In a peer-to-peer regime:

- The "boss" is the fulcrum of accountability, not just authority. Authority has to be earned through tangible expertise and concrete contributions. It is not a "given" due to rank, seniority, position, and title.
- The relationship between superior and subordinate is multi-faceted, not binary. The boss may be the source of authority in one context, and the follower and the doer in another. The challenge is to recognize when to take off one hat and put on another.
- One size does not fit all. Every knowledge worker is unique, in terms of achieving style, cultural orientation, and personality profile. Some may need detailed guidance; others are self-directed. Some expect constant recognition and feedback; others are self-directed and self-motivated. Some are proactive in taking the initiative and making things happen; others are passive reactors, waiting to be told what to do. Leaders have to customize their approach and accommodate the unique requirements of different knowledge workers.

Parent/Child	**Peer-to-Peer**
Standard Approach	Customized Approach
Focus on Procedures	Focus on Outcomes
Binary Thinking	Multi-faceted Approach
Monologue Oriented	Dialogue Oriented
Generates Compliance	Generates Commitment

Figure 17. A comparison between "parent/child" and peer-to-peer" leadership practices

- The focus is on the "what" and the "why" rather than the "how". Leaders' most critical task in knowledge-intensive settings, we argue, is to clarify the desired outcomes and the process ground rules, not to specify the methods and the procedures for getting the job done. There is no time to micro-manage and provide detailed supervision in rapidly changing environments.
- Effective relationships are based on conversations and dialogue, not orders and monologue. The goal is to arrive at mutually agreed options and decisions to which knowledge workers can commit, and to take the pulse at critical junctions.

Peer-to-peer practices have a direct impact on daily activities. They influence hiring and firing practices, conflict resolution and communication styles, and attitudes towards authority, loyalty, and career development. Bosses are challenged and questioned rather than obeyed. Conflict resolution is typically viewed in terms of brainstorming, rapid problem solving, factual assessment and getting to the core of an issue. Promotion practices are based on reputations and merit, rather than seniority or patronage.

Communication is grounded in facts and "brutal honesty", rather than a sanitized version of reality. Authority is another word for accountability, being responsible for critical outcomes, rather than having the formal power to tell others what to do. Loyalty is analogous to an intense, often fleeting, friendship, which may or may not last, rather than the traditional obligations of a binding marriage. Employees are in the driving seat of their own careers, whilst employers provide the tools and the opportunities. As the CFO of a software company commented:

"Career development in our company is about competency development and is learner-oriented ... our employees are responsible to learn ... it is not the company's responsibility to train them."

Peer-to-peer thinking is also reflected in how knowledge workers' expectations are managed. In the parental paradigm, "employees" have certain expectations from their "employer". These may include benefits and perks, educational opportunities and career advancement. The basis for reciprocity is unquestioned loyalty. In knowledge-based entities, employers do provide many opportunities, but these have to be "earned" and paid for.

A case in point is how a global networking company funded a range of "life services" on its Silicon Valley campus for its knowledge workers. The feedback from internal employee surveys suggested that many wanted to simplify their hectic lives by having access to "life services", such as dry cleaning, grocery store and other everyday amenities, on their campus. It was hoped that access to these facilities would improve their work-life balance. They could do their routine chores during the normal working week, freeing up the weekend for family, leisure and recreation activities. The company's response was clear: *"We'll introduce life efficiency services as long as it is self-funding."* The employees understood the rationale behind this argument and agreed to fund the project through their own financial contributions.

Peer-to-peer thinking puts the emphasis on meritocracy and egalitarian norms. For example, employees of many firms in Silicon Valley, regardless of rank and position, fly economy or coach, and have similar-sized offices or cubicles. Power is based on one's reputation and value-added contributions. "Political" rumors can be quickly exposed by rapid diffusion of information, and quick market feedback.

The "peer" mentality is also reflected in employees' access to, and control of, personal information. Due to the diffusion of B2E software and employee self-service capabilities, in many companies knowledge workers have access to their confidential personal records and can update these on a regular basis. The underlying thought process is that "I am responsible for the information". As one executive observed:

"In traditional companies, we tend to build our systems for the 1% (of employees) who might abuse the opportunity ... not the 99% who do it right."

Knowledge workers resemble nomadic tribes. They move across projects, teams and companies to where new challenges and opportunities may be found, and where their shifting preferences and life style expectations can be accommodated. As depicted in Figure 18, it is not sufficient to consider how to lead knowledge workers in a generic mode. In order to figure out how to guide them and leverage their capabilities, business leaders have to understand the dynamics of knowledge worker employment life cycle, and the leadership practices that are critical during each phase:

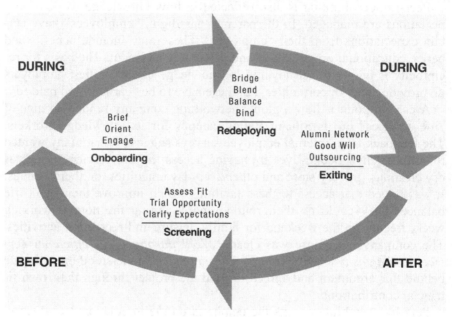

Figure 18. Knowledge worker employment life cycle

Consider the following vignette, illustrating the employment life cycle in action:

"Meeta is in her late 30s. An Indian by birth, she completed her engineering degree in India and came to Silicon Valley during the early 1990s to attend Stanford University as a Masters student in Computer Science. After graduation, she worked for a large software company, as a member of the product management team. She left 2.5 years later and joined a start-up, founded by a former Stanford colleague. She left the start-up a year later when they failed to secure the financing needed to expand the business. She joined the product management team of a mid-sized software company, and enrolled in Berkeley's Executive MBA program. She left her employer when the technology industry faced a major downturn in

2000, and her company made drastic cutbacks. Through her Berkeley and Stanford network, she came across an opportunity in a venture-backed start-up, focusing on the security software market. She joined the company as their first marketing professional and has since expanded her scope of responsibilities to include product management."

During her 13 years of work and study in Silicon Valley, Meeta has worked for four different companies, attended two major universities, but has lived in the same area and the same ecosystem. A potential employer has to recognize that career mobility and inter-company movement is a critical feature of a knowledge-based ecosystem. Leadership strategies and people practices have to evolve within the dynamic context of the employment life cycle.

The challenge is to clarify critical actions that should be taken before a knowledge worker joins a company, those that are critical during the actual employment phase, and important actions that should be considered after they have left for another opportunity.

8.3 Front-Line Practices

A number of leadership practices have evolved on the front-line to operationalize the peer/peer approach. Some of these address "emotional" drivers, such as the need to feel "connected" or to be "recognized". Others are focused on task-related challenges, such as delivering results under tight deadlines. As depicted in figure 20, we have synthesized these practices into four inter-related themes:

- Bridging or interactive communication of context.
- Blending different knowledge workers into complementary teams.
- Balancing directed guidance and empowered delegation.
- Binding knowledge workers to the organizational community.

While some are more critical before a knowledge worker joins a company, others are important during their time of actual employment; and a few are relevant after they have left for another opportunity.

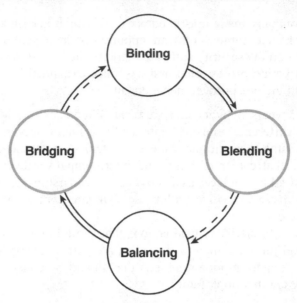

Figure 19. A framework for guiding knowledge workers

Binding: Although we have observed common motivational patterns, it is important to recognize that every knowledge worker is unique. The environment, incentives, and practices that motivate one knowledge worker may be quite different to those influencing another. This is why it is important to bind the knowledge worker to the enterprise community by ensuring an effective fit between personal goals, values, and expectations, and the enterprise's desired behavioral norms. This "binding" element is especially significant before a knowledge worker joins a company, and after they leave for another opportunity.

Blending: No one knowledge worker has all the expertise and know-how needed for the completion of an urgent and complex assignment. Since work is typically done in distributed, collaborative projects, knowledge workers have to be selected, "fused" and blended together for virtual teamwork.

Balancing: Knowledge workers want to be guided, not managed. Effective guidance implies that limits have to be set. They need strategic, behavioral, and task boundaries within which they can autonomously operate. Broad boundaries, rather than detailed rules and procedures, can be used to strike a balance between guided direction on the one hand, and individual empowerment on the other. Effective goal setting and performance management are critical enablers in this context.

Bridging: As the realities continuously evolve, knowledge workers have to understand how the business setting and the work "context" change, and how their individual contributions fit into the bigger picture. The business "story" has to be told and re-told as new realities unfold. This requires bridging the work of individual contributors and project teams to the broader objectives of the enterprise by communicating the context within which work is embedded. As the founder of a software company observed: *"my real job is to try and keep everyone, inside and outside, on the same page"*.

8.3.1 Binding

Traditional bureaucracies staff their organizations on the basis of "person-job" fit. The main concern during the initial recruiting process is to ensure a fit between the requirements of the job and the experience and qualifications of the individual. Historically, this approach made sense since people were recruited to fill pre-determined roles in hierarchical settings. Moreover, human resource and personnel practices were designed to enforce this fit in the context of administrative rules and legal constraints.

The challenge in a knowledge-driven enterprise is somewhat different. The organization is in a constant state of flux; tasks change continuously; and roles are forged around the capabilities and reputations of individuals. It is impractical to recruit someone for a given task, when the assignment is likely to evolve and morph rather quickly. In these settings, it is important to ensure that there is a fit between the person's values, motivations, and expectations, and the organization's norms, opportunities, and context (Chatman and Cha 2003, O'Reilly and Chatman 1996). As a founder of a high tech company commented:

"When I recruit, I try to understand the person's motivation and attitude first, because even if they don't have a particular skill, they can learn on the job ... if they have the wrong motivation and attitude, no amount of skill and experience can help fill the gap."

- **Screening for fit**
Various approaches are used to ensure person-organization fit. These range from employee referral programs, extensive interviewing and peer screening, internship opportunities, probation periods, and consulting/contractor assignments. A number of firms rely on behavioral interviewing, and look for certain competencies and personality traits that are consistent with their organizational norms. Others focus on testing the fit in a tangible work context, where the prospective employee may work on an assignment as a

contractor, an intern, or a consultant. The overall intention is to give both sides concrete opportunities to test the values "fit".

A good example is the case of a global company whose culture is based on the theme of "constructive confrontation". To be successful, employees have to address conflict in a de-personalized and fact-based manner. The recruiter on a university campus wanted to simulate the realities of operating in a confrontational environment. The goal was to convey the importance of this value to potential applicants. He minimized the time spent on the initial warm-up conversation and went on to ask a detailed technical question. Putting a stopwatch on the table, he asked the interviewees to draw a particular chip design within a specified time frame. The students had different reactions to this "no-nonsense" experience. Some thought that it was an honest and direct way to assess their technical competence. A few felt humiliated and patronized. Clearly, a simple interview helped both parties assess, to a limited extent, how they may fit into a confrontational culture.

- **Performance assessment and feedback**

Apart from recruiting practices, behavioral fit is further reinforced through performance assessment, regular feedback, and individual coaching. The objective is to evaluate performance based on task contribution as well as observable behavior. This is easier said than done. There are challenges involved in making "objective" evaluations of behavioral characteristics, especially in global companies that have large numbers of multi-cultural knowledge workers. Nonetheless, many technology companies strive to create "total performance management systems" in order to define and operationalize behaviors that exemplify their bedrock value systems, with coaching and feedback built into the cycle. Many processes incorporate software tools and specific criteria on how to assess behaviors and performance. In many cases, equal weight is given to the behaviors, not just the business results.

Consider the experience of a semiconductor equipment company. Its performance management template describes desired managerial behaviors, based on its eight bedrock "core values". These include "achievement", "honesty and integrity", "innovation and continuous improvement", "mutual trust and respect", "open communication", "ownership and accountability", "teamwork", and "think: customer, company, individual".

For example, "ownership and accountability" is specifically described as follows: "takes responsibility for one's own actions or the actions of one's group, whether successful or unsuccessful. Takes initiative for problem solving, both within and outside the scope of their responsibility, and stays with the issue until it is successfully resolved. Delivers on commitments." Teamwork is described as *"Proactively identifies cross-organi-*

zational issues where partnering leads to resolution. Works with others co-operatively to achieve a common goal. Focuses on company priorities. Represents his/her interests and yet is fair to other groups. Actions taken are in support of the common good. Ensures all team members are clear on their objectives, roles and responsibilities." A 360 degree feedback process is used to gauge how effectively the individual, whose performance is under review, has demonstrated these values in undertaking daily tasks.

- **Alumni relationships**

Binding the person to the organization is not confined to the duration of a knowledge worker's employment with the company. Since turnover rates are relatively high in knowledge-based entities, many firms strive to forge effective "alumni" relationships with their former employees, after they leave for other opportunities. These post-employment connections may evolve into different types of relationships. For example, the employee may become a future contractor, partner, vendor, or customer.

Alumni relationships do not have to be forged on a formal basis or in an institutional context. Typically, they are forged organically through established friendships and working networks among former colleagues. For example, during the past decade, many former employees of HP have moved on to different companies around the Valley. While HP may not hold re-union meetings for its alumni, informal networks thrive and flourish. Some alumni gatherings serve a social and emotional purpose; others may have a business focus. For example, one of the early groups of seed investors in new start-ups, known as the "Band of Angels", was originally started by a group of former HP employees. Over time, it expanded to include others. However, the initial alumni group was critical in creating its core foundation. The challenge is not to force the alumni opportunity into an induced institutional mode, but to be aware of its power in extending emotional connectivity beyond the formal employment contract.

8.3.2 Blending

Work in knowledge-based companies is typically done in complementary teams of specialists, focusing on dynamic projects. Additionally, knowledge workers often work in virtual, distributed teams with multi-cultural colleagues. Many operate inter-dependently over different time zones. Some teams may work on on-going assignments, for example in account management or in customer service. Others may work on projects that have a limited life cycle and a distinct deliverable, as is the case with new product development initiatives.

This is where "blending" comes in. It refers to work practices intended to create complementary and focused teams that can deliver tangible results under tight deadlines and resource constraints[59]. Blending is about balancing variety, spontaneity, and complementarity on the one hand, with uniformity, predictability, and consistency on the other. This is why it is critical to address the subjective dimensions of teamwork, such as interpersonal chemistry, as well as the more objective dimensions, for example, in setting clear ground rules for conflict resolution. Our observations point to a few characteristics that effective teams we have observed have in common.

- **Team complementarity and chemistry**

Effective teams blend together diverse skills and perspectives, with a unified mission and purpose. Much like sports teams, they strive for common goals and shared outcomes. At the same time, they represent different functions, complementary capabilities, and cross-cultural perspectives. They assemble eternal optimists and devil's advocates, thinkers and doers, pragmatists and idealists, talkers and listeners, and "cowboys and suits". In addition, effective team leaders set out to build relationships of trust by exposing their members to an intense process of discussion and socialization at the beginning of an assignment. Face-to-face interactions give team members the opportunity to check their chemistry, get to know one another, present different points of view, and in the process, build relationships of trust. As indicated by other studies (Hinds and Kiesler 2002) virtual interactions are more effective when team members have had the opportunity to interact face-to-face early on and on a regular basis.

- **Critical ground rules**

Effective teams develop clear ground rules for addressing critical challenges, typically at the beginning of the team assignment. These include protocols for resolving conflict, building consensus, and collaborating remotely. Clear ground-rules enable teams to de-personalize problems and resolve conflict on a factual basis, especially when they operate in virtual contexts (Griffith, Mannix and Neale 2003). In addition, they minimize coordination bottlenecks and time constraints involved in resolving one-off problems.

Collaborative work often entails extensive co-ordination through virtual interactions. Effective teams segment their interactions into distinct categories and develop customized ground-rules for information sharing, decision making, or brainstorming purposes. For example, brainstorming inter-

---

[59] See Lipman-Blumen and Leavitt (1999) for a detailed description of "hot groups" what the authors refer to as a "task-obsessed state of mind, an attitude shared by a group's members" (p. xv).

actions need differentiated input from diverse sources, such as customers, peers, vendors or partners. Effective information sharing requires standard templates that provide consistency and uniformity. Decision-making contexts are more complex. They require pre-planning, advanced preparation, and one/one conversations with the key stakeholders. Information sharing meetings can be conducted remotely, using IT tools, whereas brainstorming meetings are more effective when they are "face-to-face".

- **Clear charters and accountabilities**

Effective teams assign clear roles and accountabilities to individual members, in the context of well-defined charters. Role clarity does not have to be limited to knowledge workers' technical or functional contributions. They also address the adoption of varied, yet targeted, stakeholder perspectives. This enables teams to examine a problem from different vantage points. For example, team members may be asked to portray the viewpoint of a "devil's advocate", a potential customer, a future competitor, or a front-liner.

This approach has two benefits. It gives team members an opportunity to make unique contributions to the team effort, over and above their functional expertise. It can also enhance individual competencies and can evolve into a real-time "development" opportunity. For example, a technical engineer, who has to think about product features from the vantage point of a customer, may become more versatile as a result of going through a different thought process.

- **Common understanding of the low/high hanging fruit**

Effective leaders recognize the complexities and challenges involved in undertaking team assignments. They try to boost team members' confidence and enhance the team's credibility by producing tangible deliverables early on. An effective practical approach we have observed is to map out the "high and the low hanging fruit", or the easy and difficult tasks, at the outset of the assignment, Once the mapping process is completed, effective teams initially focus on those tasks that can be completed with relative ease, and that have a quick payoff. This approach can help build team members' confidence and generate credibility amongst the relevant stakeholders.

8.3.3 Balancing

Even volunteers need some rules of conduct and a framework within which to operate. Otherwise, the organization becomes like a dysfunctional orchestra, with each group "playing its own instrument", instead of sounding like a synchronized orchestra. This presents a real dilemma. On the one hand, knowledge workers want to be led, guided, and motivated. On the other hand, they demand the freedom to act independently and the empowerment to use their discretion. A major challenge is to clarify work-related boundaries, so the "what and the why" as well as the "do's and don'ts" can be clearly understood, At the same time, these parameters have to be flexible enough so they can evolve and provide room for front-line initiatives. Three sets of parameters are particularly important for knowledge workers. These include contextual, behavioral, and project parameters:

- Contextual parameters spell out the broader mission and direction, and clarify how the individual or the team assignment fits into the bigger picture of where the unit and the enterprise is heading: *"we want to be in the remote storage business and this project is a key element of making that happen ... we are focusing on the end-users of storage products rather than the intermediary or the distributor ... your team's focus will be on core product design ... we'll subcontract the more peripheral design elements."*
- Behavioral parameters spell out the critical behaviors that are essential for the project's success and that take account of the enterprise's core values. At a micro level, they clarify the basic do's and don'ts of implementation. *"A key element of our core values is collaborative consensus ... as you carry out the assignment, you are expected to keep the key stakeholders in the communications loop and get their input on a regular basis."*
- Project parameters specify the specifics of the task at hand. They clarify the expected deliverables, the time frame, the resources, and the accountabilities. *"... we are looking for a working prototype by the end of the year ... a budget of $500,000 has been allocated for this project ... we want to set up two self-organizing teams in parallel ... each team is directly accountable for the results ... the executive team is not interested in detailed reports, but would like weekly updates on critical milestones, using a standard template ... the team reports to Jane on engineering and technical details and to Joe on budgeting and financial matters."*

Setting a few clear parameters is especially significant when dealing with virtual, nomadic or remote workers. Without the forced discipline and the context cues of physical co-location, telecommuters, contractors, and nomadic workers need clear parameters within which to operate. True empowerment, in other words, goes hand in hand with clear direction. If used effectively, conceptual controls and visible symbols clarify parameters and create a framework so knowledge workers can experience "structured freedom".

A good case in point is the approach used by a mid-sized software company. Their core values emphasize self-initiative and a sense of urgency in making things happen. These are reinforced through pre-determined guidelines that give knowledge workers some level of autonomy in challenging existing processes. Process improvement teams, for example, can be autonomously formed by groups of five employees to challenge a specific process or an operating policy currently in use. However, they can only challenge a process if they fulfill two sets of requirements: first, if they can persuade at least five other colleagues to share their concerns; second, if they can follow clear training guidelines and a pre-determined methodology for generating constructive solutions that can improve the process.

In practice, this approach works in the following way: the company provides a voluntary training and certification program on process improvement. Employees can choose to enroll in the program and devote some of their own time to its completion. If five certified employees agree that a process is dysfunctional and needs to be improved, they can get together, form a team, follow the methodology, and propose changes to management. While there are no absolute guarantees that the recommended changes will be implemented, the system allows employees to take the initiative and challenge working practices.

In summary, setting clear parameters can provide focused opportunities for delegation. As one senior executive commented:

"... we like to treat our people as adults ... instead of micro managing, we expect them to internalize a few key guidelines, like our mission and values, and act within the scope of those guidelines."

8.3.4 Bridging

Knowledge-based companies operate in volatile and dynamic settings. An objective that makes sense today may become irrelevant tomorrow. In order to ensure that knowledge workers are motivated to contribute to their full potential, it is necessary to communicate and re-communicate the unfolding realities. Knowledge workers need context so they can assess how their work fits into the bigger picture, and how the big picture has itself evolved. This is the challenge of bridging - ensuring that every mechanism is used to take the pulse, to recalibrate, and to re-tell the business story based on emerging realities. The leadership challenge is to communicate and re-communicate the context in which the work is embedded. Knowledge workers can decide how best to get the job done in the face of new realities and the unfolding big picture.

"... we let out people know what the vision is or how it is changing, but then let them decide what they are going to do (to make it happen)... "[60]

A key component of bridging is setting up effective communication channels between the leaders and the front liners. This linkage makes it possible to identify opportunities early, devise and implement decisions quickly, and forge a spirit of togetherness, community, and commitment. The analogy with guerrilla warfare may illustrate the point:

"... the principles of guerrilla warfare are useful for managers who find themselves in a constantly changing environment ... in the heat of the battle, a guerrilla commander needs accurate information and the ability to communicate quickly with the troops ... successful guerrilla forces are led by commanders who also are in the thick of the battle ... willing to get in the trenches." (Gibbons 1987, p. 124)

Several approaches can be used to address the "bridging" challenge. Some focus on the message or the content of what is being communicated; others are about tools and processes used to communicate in geo-dispersed settings.

- **Informal, direct access:** Egalitarian communication protocols enable senior executives to frequently interact with front-line knowledge workers. Direct access is enhanced by the open plan physical layout of offices and work settings, limited reliance on corporate staff and intermediaries who act as "gatekeepers and filters", and social and recreational opportunities for informal interaction. Many companies also use their on-boarding, orientation, training and development programs to bring together the leaders and the front-liners in a "risk-free" environment.

- **On-line dialogue:** IT tools provide unprecedented opportunities for communication across hierarchical levels, functional silos, and organizational boundaries. High technology firms are typically early adopters of new technologies. Many firms are the primary sites for testing their own products, and often serve as beta-test sites for other technology firms. As indicated in chapter 7, technology companies make extensive use of IT tools. These range from expert video bytes and daily "state of the union" broadcasts, to pulse employee surveys and customer dialogue sessions. Cited benefits included senior executives' ability to stay in touch with front-line realities, rapid

---

[60] Interview with Tim Koogle, CEO, Yahoo, Stanford Engineering School Video Series, April 1997.

transmission of information across time zones and international boundaries, and information transparency and immediacy.

- **Single points of contact:** There are limits to how IT can capture intangible know-how and facilitate communication. Additionally knowledge workers are typically overloaded with virtual information. They need to interpret and relate the information to their own realities and experiences. They need to go somewhere, an Intranet site, an individual, or a department, to update and make sense of the information. As indicated in chapter 7, a critical bridging tool is to assign credible individuals to hub roles, deployed at critical organizational intersections. They become the neural connectors who fuse and make sense of disparate pieces of information. In short, they connect, integrate, synthesize, and synergize. They put people in touch with one another, become critical points of contact, and bring in various views to bear on a decision.

Hub roles can be categorized under four broad headings. Core hubs refer to critical line activities like research and development, sales, customer service, supply chain management, and product management. Control hubs are the finance, accounting, and treasury functions. Infrastructure hubs, include IT, human resources, and facilities. They shape the work context and provide the foundational backbone of the organization. Finally, strategic hubs provide the linkage between today's business and tomorrow's opportunities. Examples include strategic investments, business development, and learning and development.

Hub roles entail performing multiple tasks in parallel at pivotal junctions. One set of tasks may be operational, another strategic. Consider a mid-sized software company whose product divisions are organized around functional groups. Key hub roles are assigned to group executives who concurrently perform a number of tasks.

Managing vertical linkages: With operational responsibility for the divisions under their control, they spearhead the co-ordination and implementation of divisional strategies, and are the focal point for resolving inter-divisional tensions.

Co-ordinating horizontal inter-dependencies: Group executives are responsible for resolving inter-group concerns and making decisions that transcend group boundaries. For example the executive in charge of system development is responsible for addressing product development issues with his counterparts in sales, operations, international, and finance groups.

Fusing strategic and operational roles: Group executives- as members of the top management team, are collectively responsible for charting the strategic direction.

Hubs can also block, rather than promote, communication, synthesis and dialogue. The critical success factor is their perceived reputation and credibility. They also need the versatility to deal with multiple agendas, the flexibility to "speak the languages" of different stakeholders, and the interpersonal skills to relate to knowledge workers from different cultures and functional backgrounds.

8.4   Aligning and Super-Flexibility

Knowledge-intensive firms are a montage of versatile capabilities, informal networks, and professional relationships, rather than a series of pre-determined roles and positions. Their productivity depends on employees' capabilities, commitments, motivations, and relationships. They cannot be programmed around pre-determined roles and positions in machine-like hierarchies. In a similar vein, a knowledge worker's effectiveness is based on results and credibility, perceived reputation, and network of relationships, rather than on formal authority, job descriptions, and position in the hierarchy. It is in this dynamic context that we need to understand the action principle of "aligning".

The aligning orientation of knowledge-based entities and the supervisory tilt of traditional enterprises differ in three broad areas: exercising control by providing "context", clear parameters and critical ground-rules; treating knowledge workers in a peer-to-peer, rather than a parent-child, framework; and recognizing the importance of emotional, not only financial and intellectual, drivers in motivating knowledge workers.

The ebbs and flows of knowledge-based environments are such that knowledge workers have to be "continuously seconded" to dynamic portfolios of assignments, oftentimes, with little notice and careful planning. Staffing the organization for this level of variability implies that it is more important to match the motivation and values of an individual to the culture and overarching mission of the organization since "jobs" and "positions" evolve quickly and often unexpectedly.

Peer-to-peer leadership re-defines our traditional expectations of the employer-employee relationship. Loyalty is analogous to an intense friendship, rather than a long-lasting marriage. The employer provides training resources, an organizational network, and career opportunities. However, it is up to individual knowledge workers to take advantage of these and manage their own careers:

"... we now say our employees own their own employability ... our responsibility is to give them tools, not make development plans for them ... they need to determine their developmental issues ... they are ultimately accountable for themselves." (Interview with Andy Grove in Outlook Magazine 1997)

9 Transitioning Guidelines: Evolving from Dukedoms to Ecosystems

How can established enterprises learn from the experiences of Silicon Valley and its technology companies when they may not operate in an entrepreneurial milieu? How can they refresh their core practices in order to address the challenge of continuous innovation and perpetual transformation when their organizational DNAs and cultural gene pools were encoded in an earlier historical era? What may be a few useful starting steps? This final chapter focuses on these critical questions.

Our over-arching theme for transitioning is straightforward. Silicon Valley's knowledge enterprises operate in dynamic domains. They strive to become super-flexible by functioning as, and within, a fluid, loosely-coupled, knowledge ecosystem. The ecosystem has specialized, independent, modular building blocks, and a shared, common climate. Its distinctive "macro-climate" is characterized by "meritocratic norms", limited safety nets, transparent *de facto* standards, open feedback loops, inter-dependent relationships, and a dual focus on competition and co-operation. Distinctive "micro-climates" co-exist within the broader "macro-climate", providing additional stimuli to adapt to unique industry and enterprise norms. The ecosystem, we argue, provides the "meta" context within which entrepreneurial firms can deploy the dynamic action principles of recycling, maneuvering, recalibrating, orgitechting and aligning, as described in previous chapters.

Our observations lead us to conclude that a pivotal factor separates the *modus operandi* of Silicon Valley and that of traditional entities. Many established enterprises have historically evolved as hierarchical "dukedoms". While the use of new technologies has brought about cosmetic changes, their foundational building blocks continue to be rigid and traditional. They are segmented, uni-polar, conflict-averse, and rely on the vertical hierarchy. Leadership practices are analogous to "parent-child" relationships. Above all, they view stability and sustainability as the overarching goals. The critical transitioning challenge facing established enterprises, we suggest, is how to shift their cultural mindsets and core practices, and view themselves as dynamic ecosystems, capable of harnessing and surfing successive waves of innovation and change.

The need to view the enterprise as a dynamic construct has been noted by a number of scholars in recent years. Concepts, such as dynamic "capabilities" (Conner and Prahalad 1996, Henderson 1994, Teece *et al.* 1997), dynamic "communities" (Galunic and Eisenhardt 2001), and dynamic "boundaries" (Afuah 2001) are gaining theoretical momentum, extending the pioneering contributions of Hart (1940) and Stigler (1939). From an organizational standpoint, dynamic constructs extend the original notion of "organic" structures (Burns and Stalker 1961), a term used during the early 1960s to depict organizational forms that operate in changing environments.

The pragmatic question facing business leaders is how to transform their enterprises and operate as dynamic, super-flexible "ecosystems". We suggest that, as a conceptual construct, they can set about creating their own ecosystems, using their dukedoms' core building blocks. This approach, we suggest, may provide a framework for speeding up the adaptation process, unleashing the capacity for enterprise renewal and metamorphosis.

Naturally, there are many barriers to achieving this fundamental transformation. Major constraints include institutionalized norms reinforced over long time frames, administrative heritage, organizational inertia, political dynamics, over reliance on conventional recipes within familiar "comfort zones", and the dominance of old success formulas. Many leaders are unwilling to take risks and experiment with new approaches in the absence of a major crisis or dramatic market failure. This is understandable. There is a perception that there is a lot to lose, and little to gain, at least in the short-term. However, in view of the heightened levels of surprise, both internally with respect to corporate governance, and externally due to geo-political and technological factors, doing nothing to bring about a major transformation is hardly an option.

The remainder of this chapter focuses on practical starting points in how to evolve traditional dukedoms into super-flexible ecosystems. First, we reflect on the conceptual differences between "dukedoms" and "ecosystems" in order to provide food for thought, and an opportunity for reflection. Second, we propose a few concrete action steps that may be useful starting points during the transitioning process. Finally, we conclude by reflecting on the broader implications of our findings.

9.1 Contrasting Dukedoms with Ecosystems

During the past ten years, we have hosted several delegations of senior executives, board members, government officials and high potentials from different parts of the world. They have been interested in Silicon Valley for a number of reasons: to get a glimpse into new technologies and process innovations, to learn about the dynamics of entrepreneurship and new venture formation, and to find out about emerging management practices and organizational experiences. We have concluded each visit by debriefing our visitors on their key impressions, overarching lessons, and useful takeaways that have surprised them. Our perspective has been enhanced by teaching the material presented in this book in business seminars and executive programs in various parts of the world, where our impressions were interpreted through the lens of other cultures and diverse business environments.

Drawing on these collective impressions, we have synthesized our perceptions of the key differentiators between dukedoms and ecosystems. These distinctions have implications for leadership practices, organizational design, talent deployment, and ultimately enterprise adaptation. Our hope is that this comparison can highlight the critical levers that business leaders can use in striving for super-flexibility. These are:

- Tightly-coupled integration versus loosely-coupled modularity
- Focus on "consistency" versus emphasis on "relevance".
- Closed, impermeable borders versus porous, multi-tiered boundaries.
- Uni-polar versus multi-polar organizational architecture.
- The leader as the omnipotent ruler versus the leader as the "fair judge".
- Aristocracy versus meritocracy.

Typically, established corporations are highly integrated and operate much like giant "super-tankers". Silicon Valley enterprises are more modular. They are configured more like an armada of boats, of different shapes and sizes, moving at different speeds. However, when the weather changes or the currents shift, their modular nature facilitates rapid adaptation. Since many established corporations are configured more as integrated super-tankers, they tend to change direction, configuration, or crew, only when they face a major crisis. The strategic response is typically to rely on a "big bang" solution, such as an across-the-board re-organization, a major acquisition, or a new CEO. Ecosystems have to continuously adapt to changing climatic conditions, as illustrated by the sailing analogy depicted on the cover of this book. They have to tack back and forth, sideways and, at times, backwards. As described in chapters 5 and 6, continual, stochastic maneuvering and recalibration are features of everyday life.

Traditional dukedoms place a high value on "consistency". This is hardly surprising since maintaining the "*status quo*" is critically important. The focus is on doing "what you said you'd do" and so deviation is discouraged. Things happen because they have "already been announced" or because "they are on the calendar", not because they still make sense. Ecosystems thrive on empirical pragmatism. While a proposed idea may have made sense three months ago, it may have to be modified, or even rejected, in line with the current realities.

Personal exposure to front-line realities makes it easier to recalibrate and develop corrective actions based on real-time feedback. It is common for CEOs and executive teams of even large companies in Silicon Valley to spend a substantial amount of their face time with customers and front-liners. Business leaders can make decisions based on the world "as it is" today, rather than the "way we wish it to be" or the "way it was yesterday". Dukedoms find it harder to recalibrate because many business leaders are cushioned from front-line realities by "courtiers". Positioned between the leaders and the front-liners, they act as filters, and may shield the leaders from "unfavorable" news they may prefer not to hear. By the time the news becomes reality, it may be too late to make the necessary recalibrations or to embark on corrective actions.

Dukedoms typically have closed borders, with an impermeable skin around them. In addition, they are hierarchically segmented and vertically configured. A business ecosystem has multi-tiered, porous boundaries. It is open, modular, and thrives on horizontal, peer relationships. This orientation impacts the mapping of enterprise "boundaries", attitudes towards collaborative partnerships, and scoping of outsourced activities. As indicated in chapter 3, one reason for the success of Silicon Valley is the extensive support infrastructure of specialists that operate independently. They provide variable, just-in-time, complementary expertise, so an entity can get traction by focusing exclusively on its core activities.

Dukedoms are "unipolar" in that typically there is a single center of power, residing at the top. Historically, we have used terms, such as centralization and decentralization, to characterize allocation of power amongst the various stakeholders. Silicon Valley enterprises resemble multi-polar "heterarchies" (Hedlund 1986) and multi-dimensional federations (Handy 1992). They have "federal" rules and climatic conditions that apply uniformly to all their citizens. At the same time, they allow for autonomous "state" initiatives and the creation of "micro-climates" in different business units. The objective is to balance "uniformity" and "diversity" or "standardization" and "customization". The challenge is to figure out what has to be the same across the entire enterprise so that everything else can be flexibly customized. As indicated in chapter 6, setting up modular work nodes with distinctive accountabilities, and clarifying "federal" mandates, are critical in this context.

Dukedoms maintain continuity by ensuring "familial" succession. The leader is the omnipotent ruler, the "final" arbiter on critical issues, and the enterprise's "custodian" before it is passed on to the next generation. The leader's hand-selected protégé, or heir apparent, succeeds to the top leadership position. In the Silicon Valley ecosystem, continuity and change have to co-exist; there is no continuity, if there is no change. Enterprises have to continuously adapt, reconfigure, maneuver, recalibrate and re-align as new realities unfold. In knowledge-intensive and fast-moving enterprises, no single individual has all the scientific expertise and the leadership capabilities to address the multi-faceted and complex decisions that have to be made in real-time contexts. A leader has to rely on the collective wisdom, the specialized expertise, and the complementary capabilities of peers and colleagues. His or her most significant contribution is to be the symbolic focal point, the "fair-minded judge", and the synthesizer of team decisions. The difference between the two is best characterized in the context of "parent-child" versus "peer-to peer" leadership practices described in Chapter 8.

Dukedoms create a strong sense of "security" and "loyalty" amongst their "favorite courtiers". Their power and influence is largely derived from their proximity to, and association with, the leader. This attitude is underscored by the phenomenon of "patronage" and the predominance of parent-child relationships. As described in chapter 8, many enterprises in Silicon Valley operate on the basis of person-culture fit, egalitarian norms, and peer-peer relationships. They thrive on a healthy dose of "paranoia" that keeps their employees "on their toes" (Grove 1996). Knowledge workers are rewarded based on how they contribute to enterprise success in concrete, measurable ways, not by whether they have "paid their dues and been loyal subjects'. Personal reputations, based on tangible contributions, are the ultimate source of authority and credibility. As indicated in chapter 8, "brutal honesty" and "fact-based" performance assessments are the norm, not the exception.[61]

A super-flexible ecosystem operates as a meritocracy, rather than as an aristocracy. The comparison is not meant to suggest that dukedoms have become irrelevant, or that ecosystems provide a simple solution for becoming super-flexible. Indeed, we believe Silicon Valley can learn a great deal from "dukedoms" when it comes to resilience and robustness. Instead, our hope is that such a comparison can help our executive audience achieve two related goals; first, to diagnose enterprise characteristics that constrain adaptation; second, to identify "bedrock" elements that are critical to their identity and that should be kept at any cost. The practical outcome of this assessment would be for business leaders is to clarify "what to keep",

---

[61] We recall the example of a CEO/founder who had to fire his close friend, the vice president of sales, because the facts on the ground gave him no other choice. Two weeks later they went on vacation together with their families. It was not a question of personal loyalty but business realities.

"what to discard", and "what to acquire", in terms of new capabilities, con-figurations, and behavioral norms.

9.2 Execution Guidelines

A dukedom can not evolve into an ecosystem overnight. There are no magic formulas or simplistic solutions. The challenge is to identify critical actions that may be useful starting points, that are actionable, and that provide the momentum to move forward. We have proposed concrete guidelines for implementing the five action principles of super-flexibility. These are described in the concluding parts of chapters 5 to 8. This section focuses on three "meta" themes that augment our action principles.

During the past decade we have discussed critical pain points facing business leaders in a number of established companies around the world. While the flavor of each conversation is somewhat unique, they address similar challenges and concerns. Common themes include: How to amend the role of the center or the HQ in an age of distributed authority and information transparency? How to leverage the wisdom of experienced, seasoned executives and knowledge workers while bringing in "new blood" to refresh the talent pool? How to balance the needs of today's business while vectoring towards tomorrow's opportunities? We propose three pragmatic action steps that may be useful starting points. They include:

- Re-freshing the task portfolio for the center or the headquarters.
- Cascading the enterprise knowledge pool across internal boundaries.
- Vectoring the future by linking today's operations with tomorrow's opportunities.

As discussed earlier, one way to become super-flexible is to re-orient the enterprise away from uni-polarity towards multi-polarity. The goal is to create several centers of gravity by "putting the available eggs in different baskets". This theme is reflected in two of our action principles: maneuvering and orgitechting. Maneuvering emphasizes the deployment of pre-emptive, opportunistic, protective and corrective moves. The objective is to develop a flexible business portfolio, incorporating offensive and defensive components. Orgitechting highlights the inherent flexibility associated with a multi-polar organizational architecture. If designed and deployed effectively, a multi-polar architecture enables business leaders to fine-tune their organization, without causing major disruptions associated with "big bang" re-organizations of an integrated structure.

We propose two practical interventions that may be useful starting points in creating a multi-polar orientation. The first is focused on the role of the headquarters, traditionally viewed as the center of gravity and the custodian of organizational know-how. The second is about cascading tacit organizational knowledge in order to minimize sole reliance on the hierarchical leaders as the keepers of unique business wisdom.

9.2.1 Modifying the Role of Headquarters

Visiting delegations to Silicon Valley often ask two similar questions: Who or what is the main center of power in Silicon Valley today? Who was in charge of creating the "grand-plan" that led to the rise of the "Valley"? They expect the answer to the first question to be the venture capital community. After all, they have the financial resources to make or break a new venture. However, as indicated in chapter 3, this is clearly not the case. While the venture community is an important component of the ecosystem in scaling new ventures, it needs the contribution of others - the universities and research laboratories, the support infrastructure of specialists, and the passion, creativity and dedication of entrepreneurial knowledge workers.

The implication for established enterprises is clear. To create a multipolar organization, they need to modify the role of the headquarters, not just by "edict", but by sending strong symbolic and substantive messages to their front-line communities. HQ units should be re-organized as modular nodes, with differentiated portfolios of tasks, and above all else by visible and measurable accountabilities. This transformation process is already underway in many global companies. It has been largely driven by the need to cut costs, reduce overhead expenses, and create financial transparency and accountability. The pace of change is being further accelerated as many administrative functions, historically undertaken by the headquarters, are now being automated and embedded in IT systems, or outsourced to offshore vendors..

Business entities clearly need some kind of headquarters. However, the HQ nodes have to behave, less as omnipotent rulers, and more as accountable colleagues, with clear roles and responsibilities. Critical success factors include value-added deliverables, targeted accountabilities, clear interaction rules, transparent "taxation" policies, and fact-based performance assessment. The experience of larger technology firms in Silicon Valley indicates that corporate headquarters typically undertake several tasks. As depicted in Figure 20, these include:

- The compliance, or the "controller" role, focusing on activities that are legally-mandated, as is the case with investor relations and corporate audit.
- The business mandated initiatives, or the "director" role, emphasizing activities that are linked to the execution of a chosen business strategy. Examples include business development, mergers and acquisitions, corporate venture capital, performance management, succession planning and IT infrastructure
- The shared services or the "vendor" role, emphasizing activities that can be leveraged by line units across the entire organization. The objective is to minimize duplication, save overhead costs, and provide centers of competence. Examples include elements of HR, IT, finance and marketing functions.
- The "enabler" role, emphasizing horizontal synergies and talent cross-pollination. The objective is to leverage common interests and complementary capabilities of various nodes across the entire organization. Examples include executive and leadership development, workforce mobility, talent deployment, and business development.
- The binding role, emphasizing the creation of an enterprise community and a common "look and feel". Examples include facilities management, internal communication, brand management, and aspects of human resources.

There are several variations on how such a multi-faceted task portfolio can be put into practice. Emphasis placed on different categories depends on the enterprise's genetic encoding, executive pre-dispositions, industry and cultural norms, and administrative heritage. Some companies prefer to emphasize the controller or the vendor roles, while others value the gluing or the enabler roles. In principle, the overarching role of the HQ is to orchestrate the strategic vision, develop the organizational infrastructure, and create the cultural glue that can leverage synergies, and ensure unity of mission and purpose. However, these tasks should be undertaken together with the line nodes, not dictated to them.

Several critical challenges should be considered in moving forward in this area. First, as discussed in chapter 7, there is a need to isolate the commonalities across what may be characterized as "federal/state" tensions; what has to be the same across all nodes, so that everything else can be locally customized." Federal mandates may address broad behavioral norms, such as ethics and integrity. They may focus on financial nonnegotiables, or on strategic imperatives, such as GE's mandate that "every business has to be a #1 or a #2 player in its target market". They may apply to HR policies, including succession planning and leadership development, or the use of a common brand, and a standard look and feel.

The second challenge is to ensure that the HQ is staffed by a combination of experienced line operators, bringing in the front-line perspective, as well as functional "staff" experts, providing specialist know-how. A global engineering company, for example, appoints experienced line manager to head up its corporate HR function for up to three years. Functional HR specialists augment the business perspective by providing expert input on staffing, compensation, succession planning, relocation, and development. While line executives typically move to other assignments after 2-3 years, functional specialists stay on and provide a sense of continuity within the function.

The third challenge is to ensure that regular forums are set up to discuss contentious issues and difficult questions with operating units. Examples include "federal mandates" and "federal tax policies". Sources of corporate taxation and allocation of overhead expenses continue to generate tension in many companies. These topics occupy a great deal of executive time and mindshare. The tension can also be somewhat relieved by clarifying the differentiated roles of the HQ nodes, by clarifying the ground rules that apply to each task portfolio, by setting regular forums to discuss contentious issues openly, and by providing factual transparency in what they deliver and how they use the allocated resources.

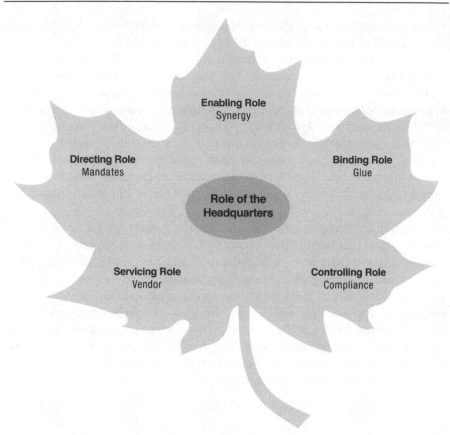

Figure 20. Differentiated task portfolio for HQ functions

9.2.2 Cascading Organizational Knowledge

A major barrier to super-flexibility is sole reliance on a small cadre of top executives who are viewed as the "high priests" or as the "keepers" of organizational wisdom and "savoir faire". This situation can present a dilemma. On the one hand, there is a need to disseminate unique business wisdom, to improve organizational memory, and to minimize reliance on a few key executives and knowledge workers. On the other hand, it is critical to bring on board new talent from time to time. The objective is to provide versatility, develop new competencies, and generate fresh perspectives.

Much has been written in recent years about codifying knowledge by leveraging IT-based "knowledge management" systems. A complementary approach, we suggest, is to turn the "leader into a teacher". The process can help capture, codify and disseminate tacit know-how across organizational silos. This is a common practice in a number of technology companies. A few, such as Intel, have used it for over twenty years. In recent years, GE, under Welch's leadership, further popularized the approach, leveraging it as an enterprise transformation tool. The objective is to spell out "what we do and how we do things around here". In addition, it provides opportunities for interactive dialogue and risk-free discussion on critical business priorities.

A case in point is the use of this approach in an established global, engineering company. It operates in more than 100 countries, and has nine business units, ranging from civil and infrastructure engineering, to pipelines, power plants, aviation, and transportation construction. Historically, the company had relied on its vertical hierarchy for decision-making. Members of its executive committee, the most senior policy-making unit, included seasoned executives who had been in the business for some time. As such, they were viewed as critical sources of authority and wisdom. However, the business center of gravity was in field operations.

In 2000, the company was faced with performance challenges in several business units. The problem was partly due to inconsistent business approaches used by its critical hubs, the regional general managers. Some had been with the company for some time; others were more recent recruits. After extensive discussions, the Executive Committee decided to devise and deliver a "general management" program, in order to address some of the performance challenges among the regional GM population. The goal was to capture the unique know-how and business wisdom of its top executives, and the "lessons learned" from their field successes and setbacks around the world. The objective was to provide a "consistent" set of business ground rules and best practices for 300 regional general managers. The program was to be taught entirely by members of the Executive Committee.

The course focused on subject areas critical for its business success. Drawing on expert staff assistance from "Corporate HR", and external specialists, Executive Committee members developed and delivered various modules related to their core areas of expertise. Since their business model is based on engineering and construction "deals", the course had six core modules:

a. The "strategy" module: An overview of their "unique" business strategy and an assessment of its market and competitive position.

b. The "people" module: Leadership practices and talent strategies critical for the execution of its business strategy.

c. The "financial" module: Unique financing challenges faced in forging partnerships with host governments and other third parties over extended time frames.

d. Three modules on "structuring", "selling" and "executing" a deal.

The program was delivered during the following two years to nearly 300 general managers. It has been very effective in codifying and disseminating its unique business practices. It has also been a significant aligning tool, "getting everyone on the same page", and has provided an engagement and communication opportunity between its business leaders and other significant contributors. The next step is to modularize the program into bite-sized segments, and to cascade it to other target populations across the entire company.

9.2.3 Vectoring Today and Tomorrow

To create an internal ecosystem, an enterprise must reconfigure its talent deployment practices. As indicated in recent studies (O'Reilly and Tushman 2004) a critical goal is to balance the needs of today's cash-generating business, with tomorrow's growth opportunities. However, many enterprises are just focused on the short-term. They deploy their most seasoned executives for running today's businesses, although much lip service is paid to creating tomorrow's growth opportunities.

To further exacerbate the situation, venturing inside established companies has had a poor track record. With the exception of a few publicized cases, skunk works, incubators, and internal venture groups have not been effective in generating significant growth opportunities inside established companies. According to a recent study (Campbell *et al.* 2003), the three major reasons for this failure include: Lack of top management sponsorship and visibility; resentment by the cash-producing parts of the business; and feelings of loneliness, isolation from peer groups, and perceptions of second class citizenship.

In order to create a more effective balance between today and tomorrow, attention should be focused on the allocation of roles and the staffing profiles for new ventures. In chapter 5 we proposed four different maneuvers for dealing with triggers that transform the *status quo*. If we use the maneuvering framework for talent deployment, it becomes clear that some executives have capabilities that are better suited for one type of maneuver versus another. For example, some have dispositions that may be effective in dealing with turnarounds; others may be better-suited to pre-emptively creating new business opportunities.

In order to stimulate pre-emptive maneuvers and the generation of growth opportunities, a knowledge enterprise can learn from the role played by the venture capital community in Silicon Valley. As discussed in chapter 3, venture capitalists play a pivotal role in hatching and scaling new ventures. In dynamic settings, as we suggest in Chapter 6, new ventures need rapid and frequent recalibrations before they become successful. Seasoned venture capitalists do this by bringing an external and "unemotional" perspective to the boardroom.

Our suggestion is easy to understand but challenging to implement. One option may be to carefully select a cadre of seasoned executives to mentor entrepreneurial teams, act as objective sounding boards, connect them with others, and provide an objective basis for rapid recalibration and "pulling the plug", if needed. In the past, this task had generally been assigned to the up and coming "high potentials" as part of the business development function. The logic was that they would bring a fresh perspective, coupled with the motivation and the energy needed to drive new initiatives.

Our belief is that, much like an effective venture capital firm in Silicon Valley, venture management needs a blend of seasoned judgment and youthful energy. Nurturing new ventures may be a valuable role for senior executives who are close to retirement, and an avenue for talented knowledge workers who may not fit into current operations. Both groups may be more willing to experiment with the unconventional and, as such, may be more likely to innovate. Just like venture capitalists in Silicon Valley, venture executives must be held directly accountable for the ventures they nurture and compensated accordingly. Their compensation package, for example, may include carried interest, as a bonus, directly tied to the financial performance of a new venture. Complementary teams of venture executives can partly address the future, freeing up general managers to focus on running today's business.

9.3 Concluding Thoughts

As described in chapter 2, striving for super-flexibility is about developing and leveraging a broad range of capabilities, from agility, versatility and adaptability, to robustness, resilience and hedging. As depicted in Table 1, these multi-faceted capabilities are reflected in, and impact, the anatomy as well as the personality of an enterprise. It is no good being flexible in one dimension but not in another; for example, by having a super-flexible strategy without the supporting organizational architecture and human resources practices. This is why our five action principles for achieving super-flexibility focus on the "total" enterprise, not just its individual components. They address strategic management as well as organizational design. They focus on leadership practices as well as ecosystem dynamics. We set out to adopt a "holistic" perspective in addressing the multi-dimensional capabilities and the varied approaches that are important for achieving super-flexibility.

In conclusion, becoming super-flexible revolves around 3 basic principles that we raised in chapter 2, and elaborated further in chapters 3-8.

- View super-flexibility as a means of being spontaneous, going through "knot holes" and "shedding skin", rather than just expecting pre-programmed actions to lead to forecasted outcomes. Knowledge enterprises should undergo frequent metamorphosis; otherwise they stagnate and die. The challenge is to regularly figure out what to keep, what to acquire and what to discard, based on empirical pragmatism and tangible feedback. As discussed in chapters 4 and 6, systematic "spring cleaning", recycling the best elements of the "old", "recalibrating", and "selectively pulling the plug" are critical actions in this context.

- Deal with "difficult" issues by clarifying potential points of friction and setting up "lubricants" ahead of time. Effective lubrication is needed to generate momentum by removing points of friction. As discussed in chapters 7 and 8, one way to achieve this is to place effective hubs at critical intersections, and to create regular opportunities for risk-free discussion on controversial topics.

- Keep things simple; it is difficult enough to change without the added impediment of gratuitous complexity. Critical actions, as discussed in chapters 5 and 7, include categorizing strategic initiatives as "maneuvers" in terms that can be readily understood, clarifying "federal mandates" and non-negotiables that apply to all the enterprise "citizens", and creating streamlined processes and linkages that foster cross-fertilization. As the Duke of Wellington remarked of Napoleon's Generals:

"They plan their campaigns just as you make a splendid piece of harness. It looks very well; and answers very well; until it gets broken; and then you are done for. Now I made my campaigns of ropes. If anything went wrong, I tied a knot and went on." (Longford 1969, p. 442)

10 References and Additional Readings

Aaker, D.A. and Mascarenhas, B. (1984): The Need for Strategic Flexibility, Journal of Business Strategy, 5, 1984, 74-82.

Ackoff, R.L. (1977): Towards Flexible Organizations: A Multidimensional Approach, Omega 5 (6), 1977, 649-662.

Adler, P.S. (1988): Managing Flexible Automation, California Management Review, 30, 34-56.

Afuah, A. (2001): Dynamic Boundaries of the Firm: Are Firms Better Off Being Vertically Integrated in the Face of a Technological Change?, The Academy of Management Journal, 44, December 2001, 1211-1228.

Albrecht, J.W. and Hart, A.G. (1983): A Putty-Clay Model of Demand Uncertainty and Investment, Scandinavian Journal of Economics, 85, 393-402.

Allison, G.T. (1971): Essence of Decision: Explaining the Cuban Missile Crisis, Little Brown & Co, Boston, MA.

Ansoff, H.I. (1965): Corporate Strategy, Penguin Books, Harmondsworth, U.K.

Ansoff, H.I. (1975): Managing Strategic Surprise by Response to Weak Signals, California Management Review, 8, Winter 1975, 21-33.

Backman, J. (1940): Flexibility of Cheese Prices, Journal of Political Economy, 48, 479.

Bahrami H. and Evans, S. (1989b): Emerging Organizational Regimes of High Technology Firms: The Bi-modal Form, Human Resource Management, 28, Spring 1989b, 25-50.

Bahrami, H. (1992): The Emerging Flexible Organization: Perspectives from Silicon Valley, California Management Review, 34, Summer 1992, 33-52.

Bahrami, H. and Evans, S. (1987): Stratocracy in High Technology Firms, in: G. Carroll and D. Vogel (eds.): Organizational Approaches to Strategy, Ballinger Publishing Company, Cambridge, MA.

Bahrami, H. and Evans, S. (1989a): Strategy Making in High Technology Firms: The Empiricist Mode, California Management Review, 31, Winter 1989a, 107-127.

Bahrami, H. and Evans, S. (1997): Human Resource Leadership in Knowledge-based Entities: Shaping the Context of Work, Human Resource Management, 36, Spring 1997, 23-28.

Bahrami, H. and Evans, S. (2000): Flexible Recycling and High Technology Entrepreneurship, in: M. Kenney (ed.): Understanding Silicon Valley: The Anatomy of an Entrepreneurial Region, Stanford University Press, Stanford, CA.

Bahrami, H. and Evans, S. (2003): Architecting Flexible Enterprises: Organizational Design in the Post-Internet Era, in: H. Österle and R. Winter (eds.): Business Engineering, Springer Verlag, Berlin.

Baron, J. and Hannan, M. (2002): Organizational Blueprints for Success in High-Tech Start-Ups, California Management Review, 44, Spring 2002, 8-36.

Bartlett, C. and Ghoshal, S. (1988): Organizing for Worldwide Effectiveness: The Transnational Solution, California Management Review, 30, Fall 1988, 54-74.

Bastien, D.T. (1988): Jazz as a Process of Organizational Innovation, Communication Studies 15, 582-602

Bonder, S. (1976): Versatility: An Objective for Military Planning, Keynote address presented at the 37th Military Operations Research Symposium, Fort Bliss, Texas, June 1976.

Bourcet, J.P. (1888): "Principles de la Guerre de Montagne", Paris 1766.

Bourgeois, L.J. and Eisenhardt, K.M. (1987): The Anatomy of the Living Dead in the Computer Industry, California Management Review, 30 (1), Fall 1987, 143-159.

Brown, S. and Eisenhardt, K.M. (1998): Competing on the Edge: Strategy as Structured Chaos, Harvard Business School Press, Boston, MA.

Burgelman, R.A. (1983): A Process Model of Internal Corporate Venturing in the Diversified Major Firm, Administrative Science Quarterly, 28, 223-244.

Burgelman, R.A. (2002): Strategy is Destiny, The Free Press, New York.

Burgelman, R.A. and Sayles, L.R. (1986): Inside Corporate Innovation, The Free Press, New York.

Burns, T. and Stalker, G.M. (1961): The Management of Innovation, Tavistock, London.

Buzacott, J.A. (1982): The Fundamental Principles of Flexibility in Manufacturing Systems, Proceedings of the First International Conference on Flexible Manufacturing Systems, Brighton, U.K.

Campbell, A., Birkinshaw, J., Morrison, A., and Van Basten Batenburg, R. (2003): The Future of Corporate Venturing, Sloan Management Review, 45, 30-38.

Carley, D.H. and Cryer, T.L. (1964) Flexibility of Operation in Dairy Manufacturing Plants: Changes 1944-1961, U.S.D.A. Agricultural Economic Report #61, October 1964.

Carpenter, S., Walker, B., Anderies Marty, J., and Abel, N. (2001): From Metaphor to Measurement: Resilience of What to What?, Ecosystems, 4, 765-781.

Carver, C.S. (1998): Resilience and Thriving: Issues, Models, and Linkages, Journal of Social Issues, 54 (2), Summer 1998, 245-266.

Chandler, A.D. (1962): Strategy and Structure, M.I.T. Press, Cambridge, MA.

Chatman, J.A. and Cha, S.E. (2003): Leading by Leveraging Culture, California Management Review, 45, Summer 2003, 20-34.

Chen Wei and Lewis, K. (1999): Robust Design for Achieving Flexibility in Multidisciplinary Design, AIAA Journal, 37 (8), August 1999, 982-989.

Chesbrough, H.W. (2003): Open Innovation: The New Imperative for Creating and Profiting from Innovation, Harvard Business School Press, Boston, MA.

Child, J. (1972): Organization Structure, Environment and Performance: The Role of Strategic Choice, Sociology, 6, 2-22.

Child, J. and McGrath, R.G. (2001): Organizations Unfettered: Organizational Form in an Information-intensive Economy, Academy of Management Journal 44, Special Research Forum on New and Evolving Organizational Forms, December 2001, 1135-1148.

Child, J. and Smith, C. (1987): The Context and Process of Organizational Transformation: Cadbury Limited in its Sector, Journal of Management Studies, 24, 565-593.

Christensen, C., (1997): The Innovator's Dilemma, Harvard Business School Press, Boston, MA.

Clemons, E.K. and Santamaria, J.A. (2002): Maneuver Warfare, Harvard Business Review, 80, April 2002, 56-65.

Coffield, F.J. (1999): Breaking the Consensus, Lifelong Learning as Social Control, European Conference on Lifelong Learning, February 1999, 25-27.

Collingridge, D. (1983): Hedging and Flexing: Two Ways of Choosing under Ignorance, Technological Forecasting and Social Change, 23, 161-172.

Collins, J.C. and Porras, J.I. (2000): Built to Last, Random House Business Books, New York.

Collins, N.R. (1956): Gains in Profits from Flexible as Compared with Inflexible Use of Resources with Reference to the Specialized Grain Producing Firm, unpublished Ph.D. Dissertation, Harvard University, Boston MA.

Conner, K.R. and Prahalad, C.K. (1996): A Resource-based Theory of the Firm: Knowledge versus Opportunism, Organization Science, 7, 477-501.

Cooper, A.C. and Bruno, A. (1977): Success Among High Technology Firms, Business Horizons, 20 (2), 16-22.

Cowden, J.M. and Trelogan, H.C. (1948) Flexibility of Operation in Dairy Manufacturing Plants, U.S.D.A. Circular #799, September 1948.

Cyert, R.M. and March, J.G. (1963): A Behavioral Theory of the Firm, Prentice Hall, Englewood Cliffs, N.J.

D'Aveni, R.M. (1994): Hypercompetition, The Free Press, New York.

Day, R.H. (1969): Flexible Utility and Myopic Expectation in Economics, Oxford Economic Bulletin, 299-311.

De Meyer, A., Nakane, J., Miller, J.G., and Ferdows, K. (1989): Flexibility: The Next Competitive Battle. The Manufacturing Futures Survey, Strategic Management Journal, 10 (5), 135-144.

Del Prete, C., Melenovsky, M., Turner, V., and Waxman, J. (2003): Enabling Business Agility: Hewlett Packard's Adaptive Enterprise Strategy, IDC White Paper, May 2003.

Draaisma, J.J.F. and Mol, A. (1977): Is Steam Cracker Flexibility Economical?, Hydrocarbon Processing, 56 (4), 149-155.

Earle, E.M. (1943): Makers of Modern Strategy, Princeton University Press, Princeton, New Jersey.

Eccles, H.E. (1959): Logistics and the National Defense, Stackpole Company, London.

Ekstrom, M.A. and Bjornsson, H.C. (2003): Evaluating IT Investments in Construction: Accounting for Strategic Flexibility, Center for Integrated Facility Engineering, Stanford University, CFE Technical Report#136, March 2003.

Eppink, D.J. (1978a): Managing the Unforeseen: A Study of Flexibility, Unpublished Ph.D. Dissertation, Vrije Universiteit, Amsterdam.

Eppink, D.J. (1978b): Planning for Strategic Flexibility, Long Range Planning, 11 (4), 9-15.

Evans, J. (1982a): Flexibility in Policy Formation, unpublished Ph.D. Dissertation, Technology Policy Unit, Aston University, U.K.

Evans, J. (1982b): Strategic Flexibility in Business, S.R.I. International, Business Intelligence Program, Research Report #678, Menlo Park, CA, December 1982.

Evans, J. (1991): Strategic Flexibility for High Technology Maneuvers, Journal of Management Studies, 28, 69-89.

Feyerabend, P.K. (1968): How to be a Good Empiricist - a Plea for Tolerance in Matters Epistemological, in: P.H. Nidditch (ed.): The Philosophy of Science, Oxford University Press, U.K.

Fiering, M.B. (1982): A Screening Model to Quantify Resilience, Water Resources Research 18, 27-32.

Foch, F. (1921): The Principles of War, (Third Impression, translated by H. Belloc), Chapman and Hall, London, U.K.

Frazer, R.W. (1985): Demand Fluctuations, Inventory and Flexibility, Australian Economic Papers, June 1985, 105-111.

Freeman, R.C., Horsley, A., Jervis, V.T.P., Robertson, A.B., and Townsend, J. (1974): SAPPHO updated - Project SAPPHO, Research Policy, 3, 258-291.

French, B.C., Sammet, L.L., and Bressler, R.G. (1956): Economic Efficiency in Plant Operations with Special Reference to the Marketing of California Pears, Hilgardia, 24, 577.

Friedman, Y. and Reklaitis, G.V. (1975): Flexible Solutions to Linear Programs Under Uncertainty: Inequality Constraints, AICHE Journal, 21, January 1975.

Fuller, J.F.C. (1946): Armament in History, Eyre and Spottiswood, London.

Fuss, M. (1977): The Demand for Energy in Canadian Manufacturing, Journal of Econometrics, 5, 1977.

Galbraith, J.R., Schein, E.H., and Beckhard, R. (1994): Competing with Flexible Lateral Organizations, Addison-Wesley, Reading, MA.

Galunic, D.C. and Eisenhardt, K.M. (2001): Architectural Innovation and Modular Corporate Forms, The Academy of Management Journal, 44, December 2001, 1229-1249.

Gerwin, D. (1982): Do's and Don'ts of Computerized Manufacturing, Harvard Business Review, 60, March-April 1982, 107-116.

Ghoshal, S. and Bartlett, C.A. (1997): The Individualized Corporation, Harper Collins, New York.

Gibbons, F.M. (1987): The Secrets of Guerrilla Management, Inc. Magazine, February 1987, 124-125.

Goldman, S.M. (1978): Portfolio Choice and Flexibility, Journal of Monetary Economics, 4, 263-279.

Goldman, S.M. (1974): Flexibility and the Demand for Money, Journal of Economic Theory, 9, 203-222.

Griffith, T.L., Mannix, E.A., and Neale, M.A. (2003): Conflict and Virtual Teams, in: C.B. Gibson and S.G. Cohen (eds.): Virtual Teams that Work, Jossey Bass, San Francisco.

Grove, A. (1996): Only the Paranoid Survive, Doubleday, New York.

Grümm, H.R. (1976): Definitions of Resilience, Research Report 76-6, International Institute for Applied Systems Analysis, Vienna.

Grümm, H.R. and Breitenecker, M. (1981): Economic Evolutions and Their Resilience: A Model, Research Report 81-5, International Institute for Applied Systems Analysis, Vienna.

Guerico, V.J. (1981): Feedstock Flexibility, Chemical Engineering, 82, 63-5.

Gunderson L.H. and Holling, C.S. (2001): Panarchy: Understanding Transformations in Human and Natural Systems, Island Press, Washington, D.C.

Gunderson, L. (1999): Resilience, Flexibility and Adaptive Management: Antidotes for Spurious Certitude?, Conservation Ecology, 3, 7.

Hagel, J. (2004): Offshoring Goes on the Offensive, The McKinsey Quarterly, 2, 82-91.

Hahlway, W. (1966): C. von Clausewitz: Schriften, Aufsätze, Studien, Briefe, Göttingen.

Hamblin, D.J. (2002): Re-thinking the Management of Flexibility- A Study of the Aerospace Industry, Journal of the Operational Research Society, 53, 272-282.

Hambrecht, W.R. (1984): Venture Capital and The Growth of Silicon Valley, California Management Review, 26, Winter 1984, 74-82.

Hamel, G. and Valikangas, L. (2003): The Quest for Resilience, Harvard Business Review, September 2003, 52-63.

Hammer, M. (2004): Deep Change: How Operational Innovation Can Transform Your Company, Harvard Business Review, April 2004, 84-95.

Hammer, M. and Champy, J. (1993): Re-engineering the Corporation: A Manifesto for Business Revolution, Harper Business, New York.

Hammond, J.S., Keeney, R.L., and Raiffa, H. (1999): Smart Choices: A Practical Guide to Making Better Decisions, Harvard Business School Press, Boston MA.

Handy, C. (1992): Balancing Corporate Power: A New Federalist Paper, Harvard Business Review, 70, 59-72.

Harker, J.M., Brede, D.W., Pattison, R.E., Santana, G.R., and Taft, L.G. (1981): A Quarter Century of Disk Drive Innovation, IBM Journal of Research and Development, 25, September 1981, 677-689.

Harrigan, K.R. (1980): The Effect of Exit Barriers on Strategic Flexibility, Strategic Management Journal, 1, 165-176.

Harrigan, K.R. (1985): Strategic Flexibility: A Management Guide for Changing Times, D.C. Heath and Company, Lexington, MA.

Hart A.G. (1940): Anticipations, Uncertainty and Dynamic Planning, University of Chicago Press, Chicago.

Hart, A.G. (1937a): Anticipations, Business Planning and the Cycle, Quarterly Journal of Economics, February 1937, 272-293.

Hart, A.G. (1937b): Failure and Fulfillment of Expectations in Business Fluctuations, Review of Economic Statistics, XIX, 69-78.

Hashimoto, T., Stedinger, J.R., and Loucks, D.P. (1982a): Reliability, Resiliency and Vulnerability Criteria for Water Resource System Performance Evaluation, Water Resources Research, 18, February 1982a.

Hashimoto, T., Stedinger, J.R., and Loucks, D.P. (1982b): Robustness of Water Resources System, Water Resources Research, 18, February 1982b.

Hatum, A. and Pettigrew, A.M. (2003): Adaptive Responses under Competitive Pressure: Organizational Flexibility in an Emergent Economy, paper presented at the Strategic Management Society Conference, Buenos Aires, March 2003

Hedlund, G. (1986): The Hypermodern MNC: a Heterarchy?, Human Resource Management, 25, 9-35.

Heidegger, M. (1977): The Question Concerning Technology, Translated by W. Lovitt, Harper & Row, London.

Heimann, S.R. and Lusk, E.J. (1976): Decision Flexibility: An Alternative Evaluation Criterion, The Accounting Review, January 1976, 51-64.

Henderson, R.M. (1994): The Evolution of Integrative Capability: Innovation in Cardiovascular Drug Discovery, Industrial and Corporate Change, 3, 607-630.

Henry, C. (1974): Investment Decisions Under Uncertainty: The Irreversibility Effect, The American Economic Review, 64, December 1974, 1006-1012.

Hinds, P.J. and Kiesler, S. (2002): Distributed Work, M.I.T. Press, Cambridge, MA.

Hittle, J.D. (1947): Jomini's Art of War, The Telegraph Press, Harrisburg, PA.

Holling C.S. (1986): The Resilience of Terrestrial Ecosystems: Local Surprise and Global Change, in: W.C. Clark and R.E. Munn (eds.): Sustainable Development of the Biosphere. Cambridge University Press, Cambridge, U.K.

Holling, C.S. (1973): Resilience and Stability of Ecological Systems, Annual Review of Ecological Systems, 4, 301-321.

Holling, C.S. (1979): Expect the Unexpected: An Adaptive Approach to Environmental Management, International Institute for Applied Systems Analysis ER-79-001, November 1979, Austria.

Holopainen H. (2002): Corporate Governance Structures: How Investment Incentives Interact with Strategic Flexibility, EBHA Annual Conference, Helsinki, August 2002.

Huang, J. (2001): Future Space: A Blueprint for Future Architecture, Harvard Business Review, 79, April 2001, 3-11.

Hutchinson, G.K. (1973): Flexible Manufacturing Systems, Industrial Engineering, 5, December 1973.

Iravani, S.M., Buzacott, J.A., and Posner, M.J.M. (2003): Operations and Shipment Scheduling of Batch on a Flexible Machine, Operations Research, 51, July-August 2003, 585-601.

Johnson, G. (1988): Rethinking Incrementalism, Strategic Management Journal, 9, 75-91.

Jones, R. and Ostroy, J. (1976): Liquidity as Flexibility, Discussion Paper 73, Department of Economics, U.C.L.A.

Jones, R. and Ostroy, J. (1984): Flexibility and Uncertainty, Review of Economic Studies, 51 (1), 13-32.

Kanter, R.M. (1983): The Change Masters, Simon & Schuster, New York.

Keeney, R.L. (1983): Issues in Evaluating Standards, Interfaces, 13, 12-22.

Kenney, M. (2000): Understanding Silicon Valley, Stanford University Press, Stanford, CA.

Kenney, M. and Florida, R. (2000): Venture Capital in Silicon Valley: Fueling New Firm Formation, in: M. Kenney (ed.): Understanding Silicon Valley. Stanford University Press, Stanford, CA, 98-123.

Kerchner, O.G. (1966): Economic Comparisons of Flexible and Specialized Plants in the Minnesota Dairy Manufacturing Industry, unpublished Ph.D. Dissertation, University of Minnesota.

Kindleberger, C.P. (1937): Flexibility in Demand in International Trade Theory, Quarterly Journal of Economics, 51, 352-361.

Klein, B.H. and Meckling, W. (1958): Application of O.R. to Development Decisions, Operations Research, May-June 1958, 352-363.

Knight, F.H. (1921): Risk, Uncertainty and Profit, Houghton Miflin and Company, Boston, MA.

Koopmans, T.C. (1957): The Construction of Economic Knowledge, McGraw Hill, New York.

Koopmans, T.C. (1964): On Flexibility of Future Preferences, in: M.W. Shelly and G.L. Bryan (eds.): Human Judgment and Optimality, Wiley, New York.

Kotkin, J. and Grabowicz, P. (1982): California, Inc., Rawson Wade Publishers, New York.

Kotter, J. (1996): Leading Change, Harvard Business School Press, Boston, MA.

Kreps, D.M. (1979): A Representation Theorem for Preference for Flexibility, Econometrica, 47, 565-577.

Kretchmar, L. (1989): Auspex Serves Notice, Upside Magazine, November-December 1989, 17-18.

Krijnen, H.G. (1979): The Flexible Firm, Long Range Planning, 12, (2) April 1979, 63-75.

Kuhn, T.S. (1962): The Structure of Scientific Revolutions, The University of Chicago Press, Chicago.

Lange, O. (1944): Price Flexibility and Employment, Cowles Commission for Research in Economics, Monograph no. 8, Principia Press, 1944.

Lawrence, P.R. and Lorsch, J.W. (1967): Organizations and Environments: Managing Differentiation and Integration, Graduate School of Business Administration, Harvard University, Boston, MA.

Liddell Hart, B.H. (1929): The Decisive Wars of History, Little Brown & Co., Boston, MA.

Liddell Hart, B.H. (1954): Strategy: The Indirect Approach, Faber and Faber, London.

Lindblom, C.E. (1959): The Science of Muddling Through, Public Administration Review, Spring 1959, 79-88.

Lipman-Blumen, J. and Leavitt, H.J. (1999): Hot Groups, Oxford University Press, New York.

Longford, E. (1969): Wellington, the Years of the Sword, Harper and Row, New York (Wellington's original quote was published in Sir William Fraser, Words on Wellington: The Duke, Waterloo, the Ball, John C. Nimmo, London, 1899, 37).

Lund R. (1998): Organizational and Innovative Flexibility Mechanisms and their Impact on Organizational Effectiveness, Danish Research Unit for Industrial Dynamics, Working Paper #98-23, October 1998.

Maidique, M.A. and Hayes, R.H. (1984): The Art of High Technology Management, Sloan Management Review, Winter 1984, 17-31.

Maidique, M.A. and Zirger, B.J. (1984): A Study of Success and Failure in Product Innovation: The Case of the U.S. Electronics Industry, IEEE Transactions on Engineering Management EM, 31, Nov. 1984, 192-203.

Maidique, M.A. and Zirger, B.J. (1985): The New Product Learning Cycle, Research Policy, December 1985.

Malone, M.S. (2002): Betting It All, Wiley, New York.

Malone, T.W. (2004): Bringing the Market Inside, Harvard Business Review, 82, April 2004, 106-114.

Mandelbaum, M. (1978): Flexibility in Decision Making: An Exploration and Elaboration, unpublished PhD Dissertation, University of Toronto, Canada, 1978.

Mandelbaum, M. and Brill, P.H. (1989): Examples of Measurement of Flexibility and Adaptivity in Manufacturing Systems, Journal of the Operational Research Society, 40, 1989.

Mandelbaum, M. and Cunningham, A.A. (1979): The Use of Flexibility in Decision Making: Hedging against Model Deficiencies, paper presented at ORSA/TIMS Conference, 1979.

March, J.G. (1981): Decisions in Organizations and Theories of Choice, in: A.H. Van de Ven and W.F. Joyce (eds.): Perspectives on Organization Design and Behavior, Wiley, New York.

March, J.G. and Olsen, J.P. (1976): Ambiguity and Choice in Organizations, Universitetsforlaget, Norway.

Marschak, T. and Nelson, R. (1962): Flexibility, Uncertainty and Economic Theory, Metroeconomica, 14, 42-58.

Mason, E.S. (1938): Price Inflexibility, Review of Economic Studies, 20, 53-64.

Mason, S.P. (1986): Valuing Financial Flexibility, in: B.M. Friedman, (ed.), Financing Corporate Capital Formation, University of Chicago Press, Chicago.

Masten, A.S., Best, K.M., and Garmezy, N. (1990): Resilience and Development: Contributions From the Study of Children Who Overcome Adversity, Development and Psychopathology, 2, 425-444.

McKendrick, D.G., Doner, R.F., and Haggard, S. (2000): From Silicon Valley to Singapore: Location and Competitive Advantage in the Hard Disk Drive Industry, Stanford University Press, Stanford, CA.

McKinsey, J.O. (1932): Adjusting Policies to Meet Changing Conditions, American Management Association, General Management Series GM-116, July 1, 1932.

Meffert, H. (1969): Zum Problem der Betriebswirtschaftlichen Flexibilität, Zeitschrift für Betriebswirtschaftslehre, 39, 779-800.

Merkhofer, M.W. (1975): Flexibility and Decision Analysis, unpublished PhD Dissertation, Stanford University, 1975.

Merkhofer, M.W. (1977): The Value of Information Given Decision Flexibility, Management Science, 23, 716-727.

Merkhofer, M.W. and Saade, W.M. (1978): Decision Flexibility in a Learning Environment, unpublished Report, SRI International, Decision Analysis Group, 1978.

Meyer, M.H. and Roberts, E.B. (1986): New Product Strategy in Small Technology-Based Firms: A Pilot Study, Management Science, 32, 806-821.

Miles, R.E. and Snow, C.C. (1984): Fit, Failure and the Hall of Fame, California Management Review, 27, 1-19.

Miller, D. (1987): The Genesis of Configuration, Academy of Management Review, 12, 686-701.

Mintzberg, H. (1979): The Structuring of Organizations, Prentice-Hall, Englewood Cliffs, New Jersey.

Moore, G.A. (1992): Crossing the Chasm, Harper Business, New York.

Mulvany, R.B., Thompson, L.H., and Haughten, K.E. (1975): Innovations in Disk File Manufacturing, in: An Overview of Disk Storage Systems, Proceedings IEEE, 63, 1148-1152.

Nicholls, W.H. (1940): Price Flexibility and Concentration in the Agricultural Processing Industry, Journal of Political Economy, 48, 883.

Nonaka, I. and Takeuchi, H. (1995): The Knowledge-Creating Company, Oxford University Press, New York.

O'Reilly, C.A. (1989): Corporation, Culture and Commitment: Motivation and Social Control in Organizations, California Management Review, 31, 9-25.

O'Reilly, C.A. and Chatman, J. (1996): Cultures as Social Control: Corporations, Cult, and Commitment, in: L. Cummings and B. Staw (eds.): Research in Organizational Behavior, JAI Press, Greenwich, CT.

O'Reilly, C.A. and Tushman, M.L. (2004): The Ambidextrous Organization, Harvard Business Review, 82, April 2004, 74-83.

Organization Science (1999): Focused issue on "Coevolution of Strategy and New Organizational Forms", 10 (5).

Paret, P. (1976): Clausewitz and the State, Princeton University Press, Princeton, New Jersey.

Paret, P. (1986): Makers of Modern Strategy, Princeton University Press, Princeton, New Jersey.

Perrow, C. (1970): Organizational Analysis: A Sociological View, Tavistock, London.

Piore, M. and Sabel, C. (1984): The Second Industrial Divide, Basic Books, New York.

Popper, K.R. (1972): Conjectures and Refutations: The Growth of Scientific Knowledge, Fourth Edition, Routledge & Kagan Paul, London.

Porter, M.E. (1980): Competitive Strategy, The Free Press, New York.

Porter, M.E. (1990): The Competitive Advantage of Nations, The Free Press, New York.

Pye, R. (1978): A Formal Decision Theoretic Approach to Flexibility and Robustness, Operational Research Quarterly, 29, 1978.

Quinn, J.B. (1979): Technological Innovation, Entrepreneurship, and Strategy, Sloan Management Review, Spring 1979, 19-30.

Quinn, J.B. (1992): Intelligent Enterprise: A Knowledge and Service-based Paradigm for Industry, The Free Press, New York.

Raynor, M.E. (2001): Strategic Flexibility in the Financial Services Industry, Deloitte Research.

Raynor, M.E. and Bower, J.L. (2001): Lead From the Center: How to Manage Divisions Dynamically, Harvard Business Review, 79, September-October 2001, 92-100.

Roberts, E.B. (1980): New Ventures for Corporate Growth, Harvard Business Review, 58, July-August 1980, 134-142.

Rock, A. (1987): Strategy versus Tactics from a Venture Capitalist, Harvard Business Review, November-December 1987, 63-67.

Rogers, E. and Larsen, J. (1984): "Silicon Valley Fever", Basic Books, New York.

Romanelli, E. (1987): New Venture Strategies in the Minicomputer Industry, California Management Review, Special issue, Fall 1987, 160-175.

Rosenbloom, R.S. and Cusumano, M.A. (1987): Technological Pioneering: The Birth of the VCR Industry, California Management Review, (4), Summer 1987, 51-76.

Rosenhead, J. (1980): Planning Under Uncertainty: I & II, Journal of the Operational Research Society, 31, a. 209-215, b. 331-341.

Rosenhead, J., Best, G., and Parston, G. (1986): Robustness in Practice, Journal of the Operational Research Society, 37, 463-478.

Rosenhead, J., Elton, M., and Gupta, S.K. (1972): Robustness and Optimality as Criteria for Strategic Decisions, Operational Research Quarterly, 23, 413-428.

Rothwell, R., Freeman, C., Horsley, A., Jervis, V.T.P., Robertson, A.B., and Townsend, J. (1974): SAPPHO Updated: Project SAPPHO, Research Policy, 3, 258-291.

Saleh, J.H., Hastings, D.E., and Newman, D.J. (2001): Extracting the Essence of Flexibility in Systems Design, M.I.T. Engineering Systems Division, Working Paper ESD-WP-2001-04, August 2001.

Saxenian, A. (1994): Regional Advantage: Culture and Competition in Silicon Valley and Route 128, Harvard University Press, Cambridge, MA.

Schroeder, D.H., Wiggins, L.L., and Wormhoudt, D.T. (1981): Flexibility of Scale in Large Conventional Coal-Fired Power Plants, Energy Policy, June 1981, 127-135.

Schumpeter, J.A. (1934): The Theory of Economic Development, Harvard University Press, Cambridge, MA.

Schwartz, P. (1991): The Art of the Long Run, Currency Doubleday, New York.

Shackle, G.L.S. (1938): Expectations, Investment and Income, Oxford University Press, Oxford, U.K.

Shackle, G.L.S. (1953): The Logic of Surprises, Economica, 20, 112-117.

Sherman, W.T. (1875): Memoirs of General W.T. Sherman, D. Appleton & Company, New York.

Shi, D. and Daniels, R.L. (2003): A Survey of Manufacturing Flexibility: Implications for E-business Flexibility, IBM Systems Journal, 42, 414-427.

Spur, G., Mattle, H.P., and Rittinghausen, H. (1976): Flexible Manufacturing Cells in Multiple Station Production, Annals of the C.I.R., 329-334.

Staw, B.M. (1983): The Escalation of Commitment: A Review and Analysis, in: B.M. Staw (ed.): Psychological Foundations of Organizational Behavior. Second Edition, Scott, Foresman and Company, Glenview, Illinois, 329-333.

Stevens, L.D. (1981): The Evolution of Magnetic Storage, IBM Journal of Research and Development, 25, September 1981, 663-675.

Stigler, G.J. (1939): Production and Distribution in the Short Run, Journal of Political Economy, 47, June 1939, 305-327.

Strotz, R. (1955): Myopia and Inconsistency in Dynamic Utility Maximization, Review of Economic Studies, 23, 165-180.

Suchman, M. (2000): Dealmakers and Counselors: Law firms as Intermediaries in the Development of Silicon Valley, in: M. Kenney (ed.): Understanding Silicon Valley, Stanford University Press, Stanford, CA, 71-97.

Taylor, M.B. (1959): The Uncertain Trumpet, Harper, New York.

Teece, D.J. (1987): Profiting from Technological Innovation: Implications for Integration, Collaboration, Licensing and Public Policy, in: D.J. Teece (ed.): The Competitive Challenge: Strategies for Industrial Innovation and Renewal, Ballinger Publishing Company, Cambridge, MA.

Teece, D.J., Pisano, G., and Shuen, A. (1997): Dynamic Capabilities and Strategic Management, Strategic Management Journal, 18, 509-533.

Thomke, S.H. (2003): Experimentation Matters: Unlocking the Potential of New Technologies for Innovation, Harvard Business School Press, Boston, MA.

Thompson, J.D. (1967): Organizations in Action, McGraw-Hill, New York.

Tilak, A.G. (1978): Job Shop Scheduling with Routing and Resource Flexibility, unpublished Ph.D. Dissertation, Texas Tech University.

Timoshenko, V. (1930): The Role of Agricultural Fluctuations in the Business Cycle, Michigan Business Studies, 11.

Tinbergen, J. (1932): Notions of Horizon and Expectancy in Dynamic Economics, Econometrica, 1, July 1932, 247-264.

Tomlinson, R.C. (1976): Operational Research, Organizational Design and Adaptivity, Omega, 4 (5), 527-537.

Triantis, A.J, and Hodder, J.E. (1990): Valuing Flexibility as a Complex Option. Journal of Finance XLV, June 1990.

Trigeorgis, L. (1996): Real Options: Managerial Flexibility and Strategy in Resource Allocation, M.I.T. Press, Cambridge, MA.

Trigeorgis, L. and Schwartz, E. (2001): Real Options and Investment under Uncertainty: Classical Readings and Recent Contributions, M.I.T. Press, Cambridge, MA.

Tushman, M.L. and O'Reilly, C.A. (1992): Winning Through Innovation, Harvard Business School Press, Boston, MA.

Upside (1991): Back to Basics at Hewlett-Packard, June 1991, 38.

Upside (1991): Now Comes the Real Battle at Oracle, May 91, 32.

Utterback, J.M. (1971): The Process of Technological Innovation within the Firm, Academy of Management Journal, March 1971, 75-88.

Van der Vet, R.P. (1977): Flexible Solutions to Systems of Linear Inequalities, European Journal of Operational Research, 1, 247-254.

Volberda, H.W. (1998): Building the Flexible Firm, Oxford University Press, Oxford, England.

von Ghyczy, T., Bassford, C., and von Oetinger, B. (2003): Clausewitz on Strategy, Wiley, New York.

von Hippel, E. (1976): Users as Innovators, Technology Review, 5, 212-239.

von Hippel, E. (1986): Lead Users: A Source of Novel Product Concepts, Management Science, 32, 791-805.

Wadhwa S. and Rao, K.S. (2003a): Flexibility and Agility for Enterprise Synchronization: Knowledge and Innovation Management Towards Flexagility, Studies in Informatics and Control, 12, 111-128.

Wadhwa, S. and Rao, K.S. (2003b): Enterprise Modelling of Supply Chains Involving Multiple Entity Flows: Role of Flexibility in Enhancing Lead Time Performance, Studies in Informatics and Control, 12, 1-16.

Watson, T. (1963): A Business and Its Beliefs, McGraw Hill, New York.

Wegener, H. (2002): Agility in Model-Driven Software Development? Implications for Organization, Process and Architecture, OOPSLA 2002 Workshop "Generative Techniques in the Context of Model-Driven Architecture", Seattle, WA, November 5, 2002.

Weick, K.E. (1982): Management of Organizational Change among Loosely-Coupled Elements, in S. Paul and Associates (eds.): New Perspectives in Theory, Research and Practice, Jossey Bass, San Francisco.

Werner, E.E. (1993): Risk, Resilience and Recovery: Perspectives from the Kauai Longitudinal Study, Development Psychopathology, 5, 503-515.

Young-Ybarra, C. and Wiersema, M. (1999): Strategic Flexibility in Information Technology Alliances: The Influence of Transaction Cost Economics and Social Exchange Theory, Organization Science, 10, 625-636.

Zhang, J. (2003): High Tech Start-Ups and Industry Dynamics in Silicon Valley, Public Policy Institute of California, San Francisco, CA.

11 Index

12 Biographies

Dr. Homa Bahrami is an international educator, speaker, and author, specializing in global knowledge workers and knowledge-based enterprises. She is a Senior Lecturer at the Haas School of Business, University of California, Berkeley, where she has been on the faculty since 1986. She was a research associate at the Graduate School of Business, Stanford University, from 1982-86, and completed her PhD in organizational behavior at Aston University, U.K. in 1982. She is the co-author (with Harold Leavitt) of "Managerial Psychology: Managing Behavior in Organizations", published by the University of Chicago Press in 1988. Homa serves on several advisory boards in Silicon Valley, is active in executive education in the US and Europe, and is an executive coach to senior executives of technology companies. She can be reached at homa@pdgy.com.

Dr. Stuart Evans is the Chairman of Pedagogy, Inc. in Menlo Park, California, a Senior Associate at the Judge Institute of Management, University of Cambridge, U.K., and a Senior Research Fellow at the University of Birmingham, U.K. He specializes in high tech entrepreneurship and technology venturing. He completed his PhD at Technology Policy Unit, Aston University, U.K., in 1982 and started his career in the Decision Analysis Group at SRI International (formerly Stanford Research Institute) in Menlo Park, California. He has since worked at Bain and Company (Menlo Park, California), Shugart Corporation (Sunnyvale, California), and Sand Hill Venture Group (Menlo Park, California). He was a Visiting Scholar at the Graduate School of Business, Stanford University, from 1987-89. He can be reached at stuart@pdgy.com.